The Trickster

A STUDY IN
AMERICAN INDIAN MYTHOLOGY

by

PAUL RADIN

With commentaries by
KARL KERÉNYI
and
C. G. JUNG

GREENWOOD PRESS, PUBLISHERS
NEW YORK

The Library of Congress cataloged this book as follows:

Radin, Paul, 1883–1959.
    The trickster; a study in American Indian mythology, by
Paul Radin. With commentaries by Karl Kerényi and
C. G. Jung. New York, Greenwood Press [1969, °1956]
    xi, 211 p. 23 cm.

    1. Winnebago Indians — Religion and mythology.   I. Kerényi,
Károly, 1897–   II. Jung, Carl Gustav, 1875–1961. III. Title.

E99.W7R142   1969   299′.7   74–88986
SBN 8371–2112–4   MARC
Library of Congress   70 [4]

To

John S. Martin

and

William E. Martin

CONTENTS

page

PREFATORY NOTE BY PAUL RADIN   ix

Part One

THE TRICKSTER MYTH
OF THE WINNEBAGO INDIANS

  I. The Winnebago Trickster Cycle   3
  II. Notes to Pages 3–53   54

Part Two

SUPPLEMENTARY TRICKSTER MYTHS

    I. The Winnebago Hare Cycle   63
   II. Notes to Pages 63–91   92
 III. Summary of the Assiniboine Trickster Myth   97
 IV. Summary of the Tlingit Trickster Myth   104

Part Three

THE NATURE AND MEANING OF THE MYTH
BY PAUL RADIN

      I. The Text   111
     II. Winnebago History and Culture   112
   III. Winnebago Mythology and Literary Tradition   118
   IV. The Winnebago Hare Cycle and its Cognates   124
    V. The Winnebago Trickster Figure   132
   VI. The Attitude of the Winnebago toward Wakdjunkaga   147
 VII. The Wakdjunkaga Cycle as a Satire   151
VIII. The Wakdjunkaga Cycle and its Relation to other North
      American Indian Trickster Cycles   155

Part Four *page*

THE TRICKSTER IN RELATION TO GREEK MYTHOLOGY
BY KARL KERÉNYI, TRANSLATED BY R. F. C. HULL

    I. First Impressions   173
   II. Style   177
  III. Parallels   180
   IV. Nature of the Trickster   184
    V. His Difference from Hermes   188

Part Five

ON THE PSYCHOLOGY OF THE TRICKSTER
FIGURE BY C. G. JUNG, TRANSLATED BY
R. F. C. HULL 195

PREFATORY NOTE

Few myths have so wide a distribution as the one, known by the name of *The Trickster*, which we are presenting here. For few can we so confidently assert that they belong to the oldest expressions of mankind. Few other myths have persisted with their fundamental content unchanged. The Trickster myth is found in clearly recognizable form among the simplest aboriginal tribes and among the complex. We encounter it among the ancient Greeks, the Chinese, the Japanese and in the Semitic world. Many of the Trickster's traits were perpetuated in the figure of the mediaeval jester, and have survived right up to the present day in the Punch-and-Judy plays and in the clown. Although repeatedly combined with other myths and frequently drastically reorganized and reinterpreted, its basic plot seems always to have succeeded in reasserting itself.

Manifestly we are here in the presence of a figure and a theme or themes which have had a special and permanent appeal and an unusual attraction for mankind from the very beginnings of civilization. In what must be regarded as its earliest and most archaic form, as found among the North American Indians, Trickster is at one and the same time creator and destroyer, giver and negator, he who dupes others and who is always duped himself. He wills nothing consciously. At all times he is constrained to behave as he does from impulses over which he has no control. He knows neither good nor evil yet he is responsible for both. He possesses no values, moral or social, is at the mercy of his passions and appetites, yet through his actions all values come into being. But not only he, so our myth tells us, possesses these traits. So, likewise, do the other figures of the plot connected with him: the animals, the various supernatural beings and monsters, and man.

Trickster himself is, not infrequently, identified with specific animals, such as raven, coyote, hare, spider, but these animals are only secondarily to be equated with concrete animals. Basically he possesses no well-defined and fixed form. As he is represented in the version of the Trickster myth we are publishing here, he is primarily an inchoate being of undetermined proportions, a figure foreshadowing the shape of man. In this version he possesses intestines wrapped around his body, and an equally long penis, likewise wrapped around his body with his scrotum on top of it. Yet regarding his specific features we are, significantly enough, told nothing.

Laughter, humour and irony permeate everything Trickster does. The reaction of the audience in aboriginal societies to both him and his exploits is prevailingly one of laughter tempered by awe. There is no reason for believing this is secondary or a late development. Yet it is difficult to say whether the audience is laughing at him, at the tricks he plays on others, or at the implications his behaviour and activities have for them.

How shall we interpret this amazing figure? Are we dealing here with the workings of the mythopoeic imagination, common to all mankind, which, at a certain period in man's history, gives us his picture of the world and of himself? Is this a *speculum mentis* wherein is depicted man's struggle with himself and with a world into which he had been thrust without his volition and consent? Is this the answer, or the adumbration of an answer, to questions forced upon him, consciously or unconsciously, since his appearance on earth?

On the basis of the very extensive data which we have today from aboriginal tribes it is not only a reasonable but, indeed, almost a verifiable hypothesis that we are here actually in the presence of such an archaic *speculum mentis*.

Our problem is thus basically a psychological one. In fact, only if we view it as primarily such, as an attempt by man to solve his problems inward and outward, does the figure of Trickster become intelligible and meaningful. But we cannot properly and fully understand the nature of these problems or the manner in which they have been formulated in the various Trickster myths unless we study these myths in their specific cultural environments and in their historical settings.

The following paper is the presentation of one such Trickster myth, that found among the Siouan-speaking Winnebago of central Wisconsin and eastern Nebraska. To see it in its proper perspective I have added, in Part Two, the Winnebago Hare myth in full and summaries of the Assiniboine and Tlingit Trickster myths.

PAUL RADIN

Lugano, 1956

Part One

THE TRICKSTER MYTH
OF THE
WINNEBAGO INDIANS

I

THE WINNEBAGO TRICKSTER CYCLE

1. Trickster cohabits with woman before war party.
2. Trickster wishes to go on warpath alone.
3. Trickster discourages his followers from accompanying him on warpath.
4. Trickster kills buffalo.
5. Trickster makes his right arm fight his left.
6. Trickster borrows two children from his younger brother.
7. Children die because Trickster breaks rules.
8. Father of children pursues Trickster.
9. Trickster swims in ocean inquiring where shore is.
10. Trickster chases fish.
11. Trickster mimics man pointing.
12. Dancing ducks and talking anus.
13. Foxes eat roasted ducks.
14. Trickster burns anus and eats his own intestines.
15. Penis placed in box.
16. Penis sent across water.
17. Trickster carried by giant bird.
18. Women rescue Trickster.
19. Trickster and companions decide where to live.
20. Changed into woman, Trickster marries chief's son.
21. Last child of union cries and is pacified.
22. Trickster visits wife and son.
23. Trickster and the laxative bulb.
24. Trickster falls in his own excrement.
25. Trees mislead Trickster in finding water.
26. Trickster mistakes plums reflected in water for plums on tree.
27. Mothers seek plums while Trickster eats children.
28. Skunk persuaded by Trickster to dig hole through hill.
29. Mothers lured in hole by Trickster and eaten.

30. Tree teases Trickster, who gets held fast in fork.
31. Wolves come and eat Trickster's food under tree.
32. Flies in elk's skull lure Trickster, who gets caught in elk's skull.
33. People split elk's skull off.
34. Trickster changes self into deer to take revenge on hawk.
35. Bear lured to his death by Trickster.
36. Mink outwits Trickster and gets bear meat.
37. Trickster pursues mink in vain.
38. Chipmunk causes Trickster to lose part of his penis.
39. Discarded pieces of penis thrown into lake and turn into plants.
40. Coyote leads Trickster to village.
41. Trickster imitates muskrat who turns ice into lily-of-the-valley roots.
42. Trickster imitates snipe's method of fishing.
43. Trickster imitates woodpecker's way of getting bear.
44. Trickster imitates pole-cat in getting deer.
45. Mink soils chief's daughter as Trickster planned.
46. Coyote is duped into being tied to horse's tail.
47. Trickster removes obstacles on the Mississippi.
48. Waterfall is forced to fall on land by Trickster.
49. Trickster eats final meal on earth and retires to heaven.

I

Once upon a time there was a village in which lived a chief who was just preparing to go on the warpath.[1] The men who were to obtain the material with which to build the fire, that is, to prepare for the feast, were summoned. To them the chief said, 'You who are to obtain the wherewithal for the fire, bring me four large deer.' These were soon secured and brought to him and then those who had brought them, his nephews,[2] immediately put them on the fire.

The people who had been invited to the feast now began to arrive. Was not the chief, himself, going on the warpath? And so, as many as were capable of fighting decided to join him.

When they had finished their feast, the chief suddenly arose and left them and proceeded towards his own lodge. The guests remained there waiting for him to return. When, after a while, he did not reappear, some of them went over to his lodge to see what had happened. There, to their chagrin and horror, they found him cohabiting with a woman.[3] So they returned to the feasting-place and informed the others, whereupon everyone dispersed.

Shortly afterward it was again rumoured that the chief was going on the warpath. Again, someone was dispatched to find the fire-builders. When they were brought to the chief, he told them to bring him two large deer and two large bears. Soon his nephews came back bringing these animals with them. They killed the precise animals he had asked for, two large deer and two large bears. Then the nephews immediately put them on the fire. However, as the animals were being eaten, the chief, the one for whom the feast was being prepared, left them. Even as the guests were eating, indeed before those honoured with invitations to the feast had finished, the chief left them.[4] They waited for some time but he did not return. Since, however, he had not said anything about dispersing, one of the guests went to look for him while the others waited. As before, so again, he found him at home cohabiting with a woman. 'All the people are waiting for you,' the messenger said, addressing him. 'Is that so? Why, what else is there to be done? When the food has been consumed, one is done,' he replied.[5] Thereupon the messenger returned and reported to those waiting what he had witnessed, and all the guests went to their separate homes for, truly, there was nothing further to be accomplished.

After a while it was again rumoured that the chief wished a feast to be prepared for him because he was going on the warpath. When he was asked what kind of animals he wanted, he said, 'Four of the largest kind of male bears.' Only such, he commanded, were to be obtained. As on the former occasions, the nephews went out to hunt them. Soon, they brought the animals that had been asked for and then put them on the fire to cook. Those invited to take part in the feast now began to arrive. Then the feast started. Shortly after it had been designated what people were to be given heads to eat,[6] the leader arose and went out. He did not return. So, after a while, those he had invited to the feast sent one of their number to look for him. There, in his home, they found him again cohabiting with a woman. When this was

5

reported, all the guests departed. They had expected to go on the warpath!

Shortly after, for the fourth time, it was rumoured that the chief was going on the warpath. By this time, because of what had happened before, all those invited realized that this was all mere talk. There would be a feast to which they would all go. But they also knew that the chief had no intention of going on the warpath. As on the three former occasions, so now, the chief commanded his nephews to bring four animals, this time four large female bears.[7] Soon they returned with them and, immediately, the kettles were put on to cook. They all sat down for the feast. There, among them, sat the chief with those who had been invited and, surprisingly enough, he was still there when the feast was over.[8]

2

Now just as the feast was over, the chief arose and, taking his warbundle and his arrowbundle,[9] exclaimed, 'It is I, I, who am going on the warpath!'[10] Then he descended until he came to where there was a boat. Into this boat he stepped immediately. All those who had been at the feast accompanied him and all those capable of fighting[11] got into their boats also. As a matter of fact all the able-bodied men went along because it was the chief who was going on the warpath.[12] Then they pushed out from the shore. It was a large body of water they were descending. As they paddled along the leader unexpectedly turned the boat back toward the shore again. As he landed, he exclaimed loudly, 'It is I who am going on the warpath to fight, I!' Turning to his boat, he shouted, 'You cannot fight! Why should you come along?' Thereupon he pulled it up on land and smashed it to pieces.[13]

Then those who had before thought he was a wicked person were convinced and returned home. Some, however, remained and accompanied him on foot.

3

After a while they crossed a swamp where they saw masses of grass protruding above the ground. There he stopped and exclaimed again, 'It is I who am going on the warpath, I! I am capable of fighting, that is why I am going. I can move about easily. But you, warbundle, cannot do this, you can do nothing of value. It is only when I carry you on my back that you can move. You, cannot, of yourself, move about, nor can you move anything. How, therefore, can you go on the warpath? You are simply a nuisance; that's all.' Thus he shouted. Thereupon he stamped his warbundle into the ground.[14] A part of those still accompanying him turned back at this point.

Again he started out. Suddenly he threw his arrowbundle[15] away exclaiming, 'You are unable to go on the warpath! It is only I who can do that. It is I who can fight, not you, and that is why I am going on the warpath!' Now, the last few people who still remained with him turned back because they saw that he was indeed a wicked person.

From there on he continued alone. He ambled along calling all the objects in the world younger brothers when speaking to them. He and all objects in the world understood one another, understood, indeed, one another's language.[16]

4

As he, Trickster, walked along, suddenly, he came in sight of a knoll. As he approached it, he saw, to his surprise, an old buffalo near it. 'My, my, what a pity! If I only hadn't thrown away that arrowbundle, I would now be able to kill and eat this animal,' he exclaimed. Thereupon he took a knife, cut down the hay and fashioned it into figures of men. These he placed in a circle, leaving an opening at one end. The place was very muddy.[17] Having constructed this enclosure, he went back to where he had seen the buffalo and shouted, 'Oho! My younger brother, here he is! Here he is indeed eating without having anything to worry about. Indeed let nothing prey on his mind! I will keep watch for him against intruders.' Thus he spoke to the buffalo who was feeding to his heart's content. Then he continued, 'Listen, younger brother, this place is completely surrounded by people! Over there, however, is an opening through which you might escape.' Just then the buffalo raised his head unsuspiciously and, to his surprise, he seemed really to be completely surrounded by

people. Only at the place Trickster had designated did an opening appear. In that direction, therefore, the buffalo ran. Soon he
sank in the mire and Trickster was immediately upon him with
his knife and killed him. Then he dragged him over to a cluster
of wood and skinned him. Throughout all these operations he
used his right arm only.

5

In the midst of these operations suddenly his left arm grabbed
the buffalo. 'Give that back to me, it is mine! Stop that or I will
use my knife on you!' So spoke the right arm. 'I will cut you to
pieces, that is what I will do to you,' continued the right arm.
Thereupon the left arm released its hold. But, shortly after, the
left arm again grabbed hold of the right arm. This time it
grabbed hold of his wrist just at the moment that the right arm
had commenced to skin the buffalo. Again and again this was
repeated. In this manner did Trickster make both his arms
quarrel. That quarrel soon turned into a vicious fight and the left
arm was badly cut up. 'Oh, oh! Why did I do this? Why have I
done this? I have made myself suffer!' The left arm was indeed
bleeding profusely.

Then he dressed the buffalo. When he was finished he started
off again. As he walked along the birds would exclaim, 'Look,
look! There is Trickster!' Thus they would cry and fly away. 'Ah,
you naughty little birds! I wonder what they are saying?'[18] This
continued right along. Every bird he met would call out, 'Look,
look! There is Trickster! There he is walking about!'

6

As he walked along, he came unexpectedly to a place where he
saw a man with a club. 'Hoho!' said Trickster, 'my younger
brother, he, too, is walking about! Younger brother, what are you
doing?' But he received no answer. Suddenly this man spoke, 'O,
my poor children! They must be very hungry.' Trickster plied
him with many questions. Indeed he made quite a nuisance of
himself with his questions. Yet not once did he receive an answer.
Trickster now saw the man do as follows. It so happened that he
was near a knoll. He took his club, struck the knoll and, to

Trickster's surprise, killed a large, old bear. After this he built a fire and singed the hair off the bear's body. Then he took a pail which he was carrying along with him and boiled the bear in it. As soon as it was cooked he served the meat and spoke again, 'Hurry, children, hurry for you must indeed be very hungry!' Thereupon he took a wooden bowl, put some soup in it and cooled it. Finally he untied a bladder which he had attached to his belt. In it there were four tiny little children. To these it was that he had been speaking so lovingly.

Then Trickster said, 'My, my, younger brother, what fine little children you have!' Thus spoke Trickster. The father of the children let them eat but he was careful not to let them eat very much. When they finished, he put them back again into the bladder and attached it to his belt. After this he broke off some branches, dished out the remaining contents of the kettle and, sitting down, began to eat himself. He ate all in the bowl. Then he drank all the soup that he had cooled in the pail.

Finally, when he was all through, and only then, did he speak to Trickster, 'I was busy before, that is why I did not speak to you.'[19] Thereupon Trickster replied, 'Truly, you have beautiful children, younger brother. Would you not care to entrust two of them to me?' 'No, indeed, you would certainly kill them.' 'No, indeed, younger brother, that is not so,' said Trickster, 'you exaggerate. I wish merely to have the children as companions. That is why I am asking you to let me have them. I will take care of them in the same manner you have been doing.' Thus he continued and finally persuaded the man to let him have two of the children. The father gave him a club, a pail, a bowl and the bear he had killed. Then he took the bladder that was suspended from his belt and put two of the little children in it. 'Now, Trickster, remember, if you kill any of these children you will die. Remember if you kill these little children, no matter where you may be, I will pursue and kill you. Keep what I am giving you and feed these children once a month. Do not change this rule. If you change it in any respect, you will kill them. You have seen what I have done and do you do the same.' Thus he spoke and Trickster replied, 'My younger brother, you have spoken and I have heard. Just as you have ordered so I will do.' Then they separated, each one having a bladder suspended from his belt.

7

Not long after they had separated, as Trickster was walking along, he suddenly exclaimed to himself, 'My, my! My dear little children must be hungry by now. But why waste time talking about it? I will let them have something to eat immediately.'[20] He was quite near a knoll, so he took his club, struck it and in this manner killed a large old bear. Then he hurriedly built a fire and singed the hair off the bear. The body he cut up and boiled. As soon as it had begun to boil a little, he dished the meat out, cooled it and when it was cool opened the bladder and said, 'My dear little children, I miss them a great deal!'[21] Then he uncovered them and fed them. He filled the wooden bowl high and gave it to them. In spite of all that the man had told him he did many things strictly forbidden to him. After he had done all these prohibited things, he put the children back in the bladder and attached it dangling to his belt.

He had been gathering together pieces of broken wood as he walked along and now he was ready to sit down for his meal. He ate up everything that remained and drank all the soup that was in the pail. Then he proceeded on his journey. All the animals in the world mocked him and called out, 'Trickster!'[22]

After a little while he himself got hungry. 'The little children were to eat once a month I was told,' he thought to himself. But now he himself was hungry. So again he said, 'My, my! It is about time for my dear little children to be hungry again. I must get something for them to eat,' He immediately searched for a knoll, struck it and killed a bear of enormous[23] size. He then built a fire, singed the hairs off the bear; cut it up and put it on to boil. As soon as it was boiled he dished it out and cooled it quickly. When it was cooled off he took the bladder attached to his belt and opened it. To his surprise the children were dead. 'The dear little children! How unfortunate that they have died!'

8

Just as he said this the father of the children appeared and said, 'Well, Trickster, you will die for this! I will kill you, as I said I would if you killed my children.' As he approached him, Trickster exclaimed appealingly, 'O my younger brother!' However the man rushed at him so menacingly that Trickster drew back at once and fled from him. He ran with all his speed with the other behind him throwing objects at him which barely missed him. There seemed to be no escape. Only by making sudden and unexpected turns did Trickster escape being struck.

Thus did the man pursue Trickster. In desperation he thought of seeking refuge up in the sky or under the ground, yet he felt that there, too, he would be followed. 'Trickster, nowhere, no matter where you flee, will you be able to save your life,' shouted the man. 'No matter where you go, I will pursue and kill you. So you might as well give up now and be done with it. You are exhausted already as you see. You have nowhere to go. Indeed, you will not be able to find a refuge-place anywhere.' Thus spoke the man.

He pursued Trickster everywhere. It was only by adroit dodging that he escaped being hit by objects thrown at him. Then, suddenly, Trickster got frightened.[25] By this time he had run over the whole earth and he was now approaching the place where the sun rises, the end of the world.[26] Toward a pointed piece of land that projected, in the form of a steep wall of rock into the ocean, toward this he ran. It was the edge of the ocean.[27] He pressed up against it and finally jumped into the water. Right into the middle of the ocean he fell. 'Ah, Trickster, you have saved yourself! You were indeed destined to die!' Then the man gave up the pursuit. Trickster uttered an exclamation of heartfelt relief and said to himself, 'That such a thing should happen to Trickster, the warrior,[28] I never imagined! Why, I almost came to grief!'

9

There in the water he remained. As he did not however know where to find the shore, he swam along aimlessly. As he was thus moving about aimlessly, he suddenly saw a fish swimming. Him Trickster addressed, 'My younger brother, you have always had the reputation of being very clever, would you not tell me where the shore is?' 'I do not know, brother, for I have never seen the shore,' answered the fish. So Trickster went on again. Soon he came across a catfish and, addressing him, said, 'Brother, you have always had the reputation of being clever, do please tell me where the shore is.' 'I do not know,' answered the catfish, 'for I have never been anywhere near it, brother.' So again Trickster went on. Then he saw another fish, the *nasidjaga*,[29] and Trickster spoke to him, 'Brother, you have always been here in these waters, perhaps you could tell me where the shore is, for I cannot find it.' 'Alas, my brother, never, no, never, do I get anywhere near the shore,' the fish answered. And so the situation remained.

Trickster was forced to remain in the water swimming about aimlessly. As he was thus engaged, suddenly he came across a spoon-bill catfish and to him he spoke, 'Brother, O brother, you have always had the reputation of being clever, perhaps you can tell me where the shore is? I, myself, do not know.' 'Alas, brother, never indeed do I get anywhere near the shore,' answered the spoon-bill catfish. So again Trickster had to go on. Soon, unexpectedly, he came upon a yellow catfish. 'Brother, O brother, I have been told that you know everything, perhaps you know where the shore is? If you do, please tell me.' 'Alas, my brother, never indeed, have I been anywhere near the shore,' answered the yellow catfish. Again he had to go on. As he swam along, suddenly he came across another fish and said 'Brother, O brother, you have always had the reputation of being clever, perhaps you know where the shore is? I am lost, so please tell it to me.' 'Alas, brother, never, indeed, do I get anywhere near the shore,' answered the fish. And thus it continued as he encountered fish upon fish. Of all he made inquiries. There was the *witcugera*, the *hogagira*, the buffalo fish, the red-finned fish, the *hocdjagera*, the *howiregera*, the *homingera*, the *citcgagera*, the *hopagura*, the *wirara*, the *tcatutcgera*, the eel, the bullhead. Every fish imaginable he encountered.

Finally, quite unexpectedly, he came upon the white fish, a whole school of them, and them he addressed, 'My younger brothers, I know that nothing is unknown to you, perhaps you know where the shore is? If you do, do please tell me, for I, myself, do not know.' 'Why, older brother, the shore is right there, just exactly where you are,' answered the fish. And indeed he could see the shore from where he was swimming! It did not take him long to emerge from the water. 'Thank you, thank you, younger brothers!' Thus he spoke to the fish. He had actually been swimming along the edge of the ocean right along.

10

He was very hungry so when he got out of the water he hurriedly made a pail for himself, a clay pail. Then he went back to the edge of the ocean, for he coveted fish, the wonderful man that he was![30] He wanted to kill one very much. As soon as he saw one come running, he started after it. But it always got away from him. One ran very near him and he hurriedly started after it and dipped the pail in the water.[31] 'Ha, ha! From this one I will positively prepare soup for myself,' he said. So he built himself a fire, and boiled the water and drank it. 'My, my, what fine soup that was! The meat, I imagine, must be just delicious!'

Then he started off and all the way he managed to get fish[32] by dipping his pail into the water and preparing a soup from it. In this manner he filled himself to his utmost capacity. Indeed he made his stomach shine from being distended. Suddenly, he saw a red-finned fish drifting toward the bank. 'Well, well, my younger brother, your breathing must be entirely gone! Dead you probably are.'[33] Thus he spoke. 'Now I will put you aside and you will taste good to me after a while!' So he took it and went inland. There he dug a hole and buried it.

11

Again he wandered aimlessly about the world. On one occasion he came in sight of the shore of a lake. To his surprise, he noticed that, right near the edge of the lake, a person was standing. So he walked rapidly in that direction to see who it was. It was someone with a black shirt on. When Trickster came nearer to the lake, he saw that this individual was on the other side of the lake and that he was pointing at him. He called to him, 'Say, my younger brother, what are you pointing at?' But he received no answer. Then, for the second time, he called, 'Say, my younger brother, what is it you are pointing at?' Again he received no answer. Then, for the third time, he addressed him, again receiving no answer. There across the lake the man still stood, pointing. 'Well, if that's the way it's going to be, I, too, shall do that. I, too, can stand pointing just as long as he does. I, too, can put a black shirt on.' Thus Trickster spoke.

Then he put on his black shirt and stepped quickly in the direction of this individual and pointed his finger at him just as the other one was doing. A long time he stood there. After a while Trickster's arm got tired so he addressed the other person and said, 'My younger brother, let us stop this.' Still there was no answer. Then, for the second time, when he was hardly able to endure it any longer, he spoke, 'Younger brother, let us stop this. My arm is very tired.' Again he received no answer. Then, again he spoke, 'Younger brother, I am hungry! Let us eat now and then we can begin again afterward. I will kill a fine animal for you, the very kind you like best, that kind I will kill for you. So let us stop.' But still he received no answer. 'Well, why am I saying all this? That man has no heart at all. I am just doing what he is doing.' Then he walked away and when he looked around, to his astonishment, he saw a tree-stump from which a branch was protruding. This is what he had taken for a man pointing at him. 'Indeed, it is on this account that the people call me the Foolish One.[34] They are right.' Then he walked away.

12

As he was walking along suddenly he came to a lake, and there in the lake he saw numerous ducks. Immediately he ran back quietly before they could see him and sought out a spot where there was a swamp. From it he gathered a large quantity of reed-grass and made himself a big pack. This he put on his back and carried it to the lake. He walked along the shore of the lake carrying it ostentatiously. Soon the ducks saw him and said, 'Look, that is Trickster walking over there. I wonder what he is doing? Let us call and ask him.' So they called to him, 'Trickster, what are you carrying?' Thus they shouted at him, but he did not answer. Then, again they called to him. But it was only after the fourth call that he replied and said, 'Well, are you calling me?' 'What are you carrying on your back?' they asked. 'My younger brothers, surely you do not know what it is you are asking. What am I carrying? Why, I am carrying songs.[35] My stomach is full of bad songs. Some of these my stomach could not hold and that is why I am carrying them on my back. It is a long time since I sang any of them. Just now there are a large number in me. I have met no people on my journey who would dance for me and let me sing some for them. And I have, in consequence, not sung any for a long time.' Then the ducks spoke to each other and said, 'Come, what if we ask him to sing? Then we could dance, couldn't we?' So one of them called out, 'Well, let it be so. I enjoy dancing very much and it has been a very long time since I last danced.'

So they spoke to Trickster, 'Older brother, yes, if you will sing to us we will dance. We have been yearning to dance for some time but could not do so because we had no songs.' Thus spoke the ducks. 'My younger brothers,' replied Trickster, 'you have spoken well and you shall have your desire granted. First, however, I will erect a dancing-lodge.' In this they helped him and soon they had put up a dancing-lodge, a grass-lodge. Then they made a drum. When this was finished he invited them all to come in and they did so. When he was ready to sing he said, 'My younger brothers, this is the way in which you must act. When I sing, when I have people dance for me, the dancers must, from the very beginning, never open their eyes.' 'Good,' they answered. Then when he began to sing he said, 'Now remember, younger brothers, you are not to open your eyes. If you do they will become red.' So, as soon as he began to sing, the ducks closed their eyes and danced.

After a while one of the ducks was heard to flap his wings as he came back to the entrance of the lodge, and cry, 'Quack!' Again and again this happened. Sometimes it sounded as if the particular duck had somehow tightened its throat. Whenever any of the ducks cried out then Trickster would tell the other ducks to dance faster and faster. Finally a duck whose name was Little-Red-Eyed-Duck secretly opened its eyes, just the least little bit it opened them. To its surprise, Trickster was wringing the necks of his fellows ducks! He would also bite them as he twisted their necks. It was while he was doing this that the noise which sounded like the tightening of the throat was heard. In this fashion Trickster killed as many as he could reach.

Little-Red-Eyed-Duck shouted. 'Alas! He is killing us! Let those who can save themselves.' He himself flew out quickly through the opening above. All the others likewise crowded toward this opening. They struck Trickster with their wings and

15

scratched him with their feet. He went among them with his eyes closed and stuck out his hands to grab them. He grabbed one in each hand and choked them to death. His eyes were closed tightly. Then suddenly all of them escaped except the two he had in his grasp.

When he looked at these, to his annoyance, he was holding in each hand a scabby-mouthed duck. In no way perturbed, however, he shouted, 'Ha, ha, this is the way a man acts![36] Indeed these ducks will make fine soup to drink!' Then he made a fire and cut some sharp-pointed sticks with which to roast them. Some he roasted in this manner, while others he roasted by covering them with ashes.[37] 'I will wait for them to be cooked,' he said to himself. 'I had, however, better go to sleep now. By the time I awake they will unquestionably be thoroughly done. Now, you, my younger brother, must keep watch for me while I go to sleep. If you notice any people, drive them off.' He was talking to his anus.[38] Then, turning his anus toward the fire, he went to sleep.

13

When he was sleeping some small foxes approached and, as they ran along, they scented something that seemed like fire. 'Well, there must be something around here,' they said. So they turned their noses toward the wind and looked and, after a while, truly enough, they saw the smoke of a fire. So they peered around carefully and soon noticed many sharp-pointed sticks arranged around a fire with meat on them. Stealthily they approached nearer and nearer and, scrutinizing everything carefully, they noticed someone asleep there. 'It is Trickster and he is asleep! Let us eat this meat. But we must be very careful not to wake him up. Come, let us eat,' they said to one another. When they came close, much to their surprise, however, gas was expelled from somewhere. 'Pooh!' such was the sound made. 'Be careful! He must be awake,' So they ran back. After a while one of them said, 'Well, I guess he is asleep now. That was only a bluff. He is always up to some tricks.' So again they approached the fire. Again gas was expelled and again they ran back. Three times this happened. When they approached the fourth time gas was again expelled. However, they did not run away. So Trickster's anus, in rapid succession, began to expel more and more gas. Still they did not run away. Once, twice, three times, it expelled gas in rapid succession. 'Pooh! Pooh!' Such was the sound it made. Yet they did not run away. Then louder, still louder, was the sound of the gas expelled. 'Pooh! Pooh! Pooh!' Yet they did not run away. On the contrary, they now began to eat the roasted pieces of duck. As they were eating, the Trickster's anus continued its 'Pooh' incessantly. There the foxes stayed until they had eaten up all the pieces of duck roasted on sticks. Then they came to those pieces that were being roasted under ashes and, in spite of the fact that the anus was expelling gas, 'Pooh! Pooh! Pooh! Pooh!' continuously, they ate these all up too. Then they replaced the pieces with the meat eaten off, nicely under the ashes. Only after that did they go away.

14

After a while Trickster awoke, 'My, O my!' he exclaimed joyfully, 'the things I had put on to roast must be cooked crisp by now.' So he went over, felt around, and pulled out a leg. To his dismay it was but a bare bone, completely devoid of meat. 'How terrible! But this is the way they generally are when they are cooked too much!'[39] So he felt around again and pulled out another one. But this leg also had nothing on it. 'How terrible! These, likewise, must have been roasted too much! However, I told my younger brother, anus, to watch the meat roasting.[40] He is a good cook indeed!' He pulled out one piece after the other. They were all the same. Finally he sat up and looked around. To his astonishment, the pieces of meat on the roasting sticks were gone! 'Ah, ha, now I understand! It must have been those covetous friends of mine who have done me this injury!' he exclaimed. Then he poked around the fire again and again but found only bones. 'Alas! Alas! They have caused my appetite to be disappointed, those covetous fellows! And you, too, you despicable object, what about your behaviour? Did I not tell you to watch this fire? You shall remember this! As a punishment for your remissness, I will burn your mouth so that you will not be able to use it!'

Thereupon he took a burning piece of wood and burnt the

17

mouth of his anus. He was, of course, burning himself and, as he applied the fire, he exclaimed, 'Ouch! Ouch! This is too much! I have made my skin smart. Is it not for such things that they call me Trickster? They have indeed talked me into doing this just as if I had been doing something wrong!'[41]

Trickster had burnt his anus. He had applied a burning piece of wood to it. Then he went away.

As he walked along the road he felt certain that someone must have passed along it before for he was on what appeared to be a trail. Indeed, suddenly, he came upon a piece of fat that must have come from someone's body. 'Someone has been packing an animal he had killed,' he thought to himself. Then he picked up a piece of fat and ate it. It had a delicious taste. 'My, my, how delicious it is to eat this!' As he proceeded however, much to his surprise, he discovered that it was a part of himself, part of his own intestines, that he was eating. After burning his anus, his intestines had contracted and fallen off, piece by piece, and these pieces were the things he was picking up. 'My, my! Correctly, indeed, am I named Foolish One, Trickster! By their calling me thus, they have at last actually turned me into a Foolish One, a Trickster!' Then he tied his intestines together. A large part, however, had been lost. In tying it, he pulled it together so that wrinkles and ridges were formed. That is the reason why the anus of human beings has its present shape.[42]

15

On Trickster proceeded. As he walked along, he came to a lovely piece of land. There he sat down and soon fell asleep. After a while he woke up and found himself lying on his back without a blanket. He looked up above him and saw to his astonishment something floating there. 'Aha, aha! The chiefs have unfurled their banner! The people must be having a great feast for this is always the case when the chief's banner is unfurled.'[43] With this he sat up and then first realized that his blanket was gone. It was his blanket he saw floating above. His penis had become stiff and the blanket had been forced up. 'That's always happening to me,' he said. 'My younger brother, you will lose the blanket, so bring it back.' Thus he spoke to his penis. Then he took hold of it and, as he handled it, it got softer and the blanket finally fell down. Then he coiled up his penis and put it in a box. And only when he came to the end of his penis did he find his blanket. The box with the penis he carried on his back.

16

After that he walked down a slope and finally came to a lake. On the opposite side he saw a number of women swimming, the chief's daughter and her friends. 'Now,' exclaimed Trickster, 'is the opportune time: now I am going to have intercourse.' Thereupon he took his penis out of the box and addressed it, 'My younger brother, you are going after the chief's daughter. Pass her friends, but see that you lodge squarely in her, the chief's daughter.' Thus speaking he dispatched it. It went sliding on the surface of the water. 'Younger brother, come back, come back! You will scare them away if you approach in that manner!' So he pulled the penis back, tied a stone around its neck, and sent it out again. This time it dropped to the bottom of the lake. Again he pulled it back, took another stone, smaller in size, and attached it to its neck. Soon he sent it forth again. It slid along the water, creating waves as it passed along. 'Brother, come back, come back! You will drive the women away if you create waves like that!' So he tried a fourth time. This time he got a stone, just the right size and just the right weight, and attached it to its neck. When he dispatched it, this time it went directly towards the designated place. It passed and just barely touched the friends of the chief's daughter. They saw it and cried out, 'Come out of the water, quick!' The chief's daughter was the last one on the bank and could not get away, so the penis lodged squarely in her. Her friends came back and tried to pull it out, but all to no avail. They could do absolutely nothing. Then the men who had the reputation for being strong were called and tried it but they, too, could not move it. Finally they all gave up. Then one of them said, 'There is an old woman around here who knows many things. Let us go and get her.' So they went and got her and brought her to the place where this was happening. When she came there she recognized immediately what was taking place. 'Why, this is First-born, Trickster.[44] The chief's daughter is having intercourse and you are all just annoying her.' Thereupon she went out, got an awl and straddling the penis, worked the awl into it a number of times, singing as she did so:

'First-born, if it is you, pull it out! Pull it out!'

Thus she sang. Suddenly in the midst of her singing, the penis was jerked out and the old woman was thrown a great distance. As she stood there bewildered, Trickster, from across the lake, laughed loudly at her. 'That old naughty woman! Why is she doing this when I am trying to have intercourse? Now, she has spoiled all the pleasure.'

17

Again Trickster started out walking along aimlessly. After a while, as he went along, he heard something shrieking in the air. He listened and there to his great amazement was a very large bird flying above him. It was coming straight toward him. Then the thought suddenly struck him that it would be nice to be like this bird. So, when the bird, a turkey-buzzard, came close, Trickster spoke to it, 'My, my, my, younger brother! You certainly are a lucky one to have such a fine time! I wish I could be able to do what you are doing.' Thus he addressed it. Then, again, he spoke, 'Younger brother, you can carry me on your back if you want to, for I like your ways very much.' 'All right,' said the bird. So he got on the bird's back. The bird exerted himself to fly and, after a while, succeeded.[45] They were now high in the air and Trickster chattered contentedly, 'My younger brother, it is very pleasant. This is indeed a pleasant time we are having.' Then the turkey-buzzard began to fly sideways and Trickster, uneasy, appealed to him in a loud tone of voice, saying, 'Be very careful, younger brother, be very careful, for you might drop me.' So the bird continued to carry Trickster around properly, and the latter was enjoying himself hugely. The turkey-buzzard, however, was busily looking for a hollow tree. He wanted to play a trick on Trickster. After searching for a while he saw a hollow tree, one entirely without branches. He flew rather close to it and then dropped Trickster right down into it. That is exactly what happened. 'Alas! That horrible thing! He is indeed a very wicked being. He has turned the tables on me.'[46] Thus Trickster spoke.

18

After a while, he heard echoes sounding like the noise of trees being cut down. 'Oh! oh! I wonder whether these are people that I hear. But even if they are I don't suppose that they will come here,' he said to himself. Gradually the people came nearer and nearer and soon he could hear them talking. They were women conversing. Thereupon he sang:

'A bob-tailed racoon am I here!'[47]

One of the women heard it and said, 'Listen, there is someone here talking.' Then again he sang the same thing. Finally, when they came very close, the women said, 'Come let us cut it out.' So they began to cut him out of the tree. He held his racoon-skin blanket next to the hole and this it was the women saw. Finally the women said, 'Ah, it is going to be a fine, large racoon.' Hearing this, the so-called racoon spoke to them and said, 'As soon as my hiding-place has been plugged up by women's clothing, then leave me here and come back after me shortly. I assure you, I am very fat.' 'Yes, we'll do just that,' they answered. So they took off their clothing, plugged up the hole and went home.[48]

Then he came out and went on. When the women returned they found nothing.

19

As he continued his aimless wandering unexpectedly, much to his surprise, he met a little fox. 'Well, my younger brother, here you are! You are travelling, aren't you?' 'Yes, yes, here I am!' answered the little fox. 'The world is going to be a difficult place to live in and I am trying to find some clean place in which to dwell.[49] That is what I am looking for.' 'Oh, oh, my younger brother, what you have said is very true. I, too, was thinking of the very same thing. I have always wanted to have a companion, so let us live together.' Trickster consented, and so they went on to look for a place in which to dwell.

As they ran along they encountered a jay. 'Well, well, my younger brother, what are you doing?' asked Trickster. 'Older

21

brother, I am looking for a place to live in because the world is soon going to be a difficult place in which to dwell.'

'We are looking for the very same thing. When I heard my younger brother [50] speaking of this I envied him very much. So let us live together, for we also are hunting for such a place.' Thus spoke Trickster.

Then they went on together and soon they came across a *hetcgeniga* (nit).[51] 'Well, well, my younger brother, what are you doing?' they asked. 'Older brothers, I am looking for a pleasant place to live in,' the bird answered. 'Younger brother, we are travelling about looking for the same thing. When I heard these others saying that they wanted to live together as companions I liked it. Let us, therefore, live together,' said Trickster.

They were all agreed and soon they came to a place where the river forked and where there was a lovely piece of land with red oaks growing upon it.[52] It was indeed a beautiful place. This, they agreed, was a delightful place to live in, and so they stopped there and built themselves a lodge.

In the fall, when everything was ripe, they had, of course, all they wanted to eat. However, winter soon approached and not long after it began, a deep snow fell. The situation of the four now became indeed very difficult. They had nothing to eat and they were getting quite hungry. Then Trickster spoke, 'Younger brothers, it is going to be very difficult. However, if we do the thing I am about to suggest, it will be good. So, at least, I think.' 'All right, if it is indeed something good that our older brother means we certainly will do it, for otherwise some of us will starve to death. What is it that we should do that is good and by which we can get something to eat?' 'Listen. There is a village yonder, where they are enjoying great blessings. The chief has a son who is killing many animals. He is not married yet but is thinking of it. Let us go over there. I will disguise myself as a woman and marry him. Thus we can live in peace until spring comes.' 'Good!' they ejaculated. All were willing and delighted to participate.

20

Trickster now took an elk's liver and made a vulva from it. Then he took some elk's kidneys and made breasts from them.

22

Finally he put on a woman's dress. In this dress his friends enclosed him very firmly. The dresses he was using were those that the women who had taken him for a racoon had given him. He now stood there transformed into a very pretty woman indeed. Then he let the fox have intercourse with him and make him pregnant, then the jaybird and, finally, the nit. After that he proceeded toward the village.[53]

Now, at the end of the village, lived an old woman and she immediately addressed him, saying, 'My granddaughter, what is your purpose in travelling around like this? Certainly it is with some object in view that you are travelling!' Then the old woman went outside and shouted,[54] 'Ho! Ho! There is someone here who has come to court the chief's son.'[55] This, at least, is what the old woman seemed to be saying. Then the chief said to his daughters, 'Ho! This clearly is what this woman wants and is the reason for her coming; so, my daughters, go and bring your sister-in-law here.'[56] Then they went after her. She certainly was a very handsome woman. The chief's son liked her very much. Immediately they prepared dried corn for her and they boiled slit bear-ribs.[57] That was why Trickster was getting married, of course. When this food was ready they put it in a dish, cooled it, and placed it in front of Trickster. He devoured it at once.[58] There she (Trickster) remained.

Not long after Trickster became pregnant. The chief's son was very happy about the fact that he was to become a father. Not long after that Trickster gave birth to a boy. Then again he became pregnant and gave birth to another boy. Finally for the third time he became pregnant and gave birth to a third boy.

21

The last child cried as soon as it was born and nothing could stop it.[59] The crying became very serious and so it was decided to send for an old woman who had the reputation for being able to pacify children. She came, but she, likewise, could not pacify him. Finally the little child cried out and sang: -

'If I only could play with a little piece of white cloud!'

They went in search of a shaman, for it was the chief's son who was asking for this and, consequently, no matter what the cost, it had to be obtained.[60] He had asked for a piece of white cloud, and a piece of white cloud, accordingly, they tried to obtain. But how could they obtain a piece of white cloud? All tried very hard and, finally, they made it snow. Then, when the snow was quite deep, they gave him a piece of snow to play with and he stopped crying.

After a while he again cried out and sang:

'If I could only play with a piece of blue sky!'

Then they tried to obtain a piece of blue sky for him. Very hard they tried, but were not able to obtain any. In the spring of the year, however, they gave him a piece of blue grass and he stopped crying.

After a while he began to cry again. This time he asked for some blue (green) leaves. Then the fourth time he asked for some roasting ears. They gave him green leaves and roasting ears of corn and he stopped crying.

One day later, as they were steaming corn, the chief's wife teased[61] her sister-in-law. She chased her around the pit where they were steaming corn. Finally, the chief's son's wife (Trickster) jumped over the pit and she dropped something very rotten. The people shouted at her, 'It is Trickster!' The men were all ashamed, especially the chief's son. The animals who had been with Trickster, the fox, the jaybird and the nit, all of them now ran away.

22

Trickster also ran away. Suddenly he said to himself, 'Well, why am I doing all this? It is about time that I went back to the woman to whom I am really married. Kunu must be a pretty big boy by this time.' Thus spoke Trickster. Then he went across the lake to the woman to whom he was really married. When he got here he found, much to his surprise, that the boy that had been born to him was indeed quite grown up. The chief was very happy when Trickster came home. 'My son-in-law has come home,' he ejaculated. He was very happy indeed. Trickster hunted game for his child and killed very many animals. There he stayed a long time until his child had become a grown-up man. Then, when he saw that his child was able to take care of himself, he said, 'Well, it is about time for me to start travelling again for my boy is quite grown up now.[62] I will go around the earth and visit people for I am tired of staying here. I used to wander around the world in peace. Here I am just giving myself a lot of trouble.'[63]

23

As he went wandering around aimlessly he suddenly heard someone speaking. He listened very carefully and it seemed to say, 'He who chews me will defecate; he will defecate!' That was what it was saying. 'Well, why is this person talking in this manner?' said Trickster. So he walked in the direction from which he had heard the speaking and again he heard, quite near him, someone saying: 'He who chews me, he will defecate; he will defecate!' This is what was said. 'Well, why does this person talk in such fashion?' said Trickster. Then he walked to the other side. So he continued walking along. Then right at his very side, a voice seemed to say, 'He who chews me, he will defecate; he will defecate!' 'Well, I wonder who it is who is speaking. I know very well that if I chew it, I will not defecate.' But he kept looking around for the speaker and finally discovered, much to his astonishment, that it was a bulb on a bush. The bulb it was that was speaking. So he seized it, put it in his mouth, chewed it, and then swallowed it. He did just this and then went on.

'Well, where is the bulb gone that talked so much? Why, indeed, should I defecate? When I feel like defecating, then I shall defecate, no sooner. How could such an object make me defecate!' Thus spoke Trickster. Even as he spoke, however, he began to break wind. 'Well this, I suppose, is what it meant. Yet the bulb said I would defecate, and I am merely expelling gas. In any case I am a great man even if I do expel a little gas!'[64] Thus he spoke. As he was talking he again broke wind. This time it was really quite strong. 'Well, what a foolish one I am. This is why I am called Foolish One, Trickster.' Now he began to break wind again and again. 'So this is why the bulb spoke as it did, I suppose.' Once more he broke wind. This time it was very loud and his rectum began to smart. 'Well, it surely is a great thing!' Then he broke wind again, this time with so much force, that he was propelled forward. 'Well, well, it may even make me give another push, but it won't make me defecate,' so he exclaimed defiantly. The next time he broke wind, the hind part of his body was raised up by the force of the explosion and he landed on his knees and hands. 'Well, go ahead and do it again! Go ahead and do it again!' Then, again, he broke wind. This time the force of the expulsion sent him far up in the air and he landed on the ground, on his stomach. The next time he broke wind, he had to hang on to a log, so high was he thrown. However, he raised himself up and, after a while, landed on the ground, the log on top of him. He was almost killed by the fall. The next time he broke wind, he had to hold on to a tree that stood near by. It was a poplar and he held on with all his might yet, nevertheless, even then, his feet flopped up in the air. Again, and for the second time, he held on to it when he broke wind and yet he pulled the tree up by the roots. To protect himself, the next time, he went on until he came to a large tree, a large oak tree. Around this he put both his arms. Yet, when he broke wind, he was swung up and his toes struck against the tree. However, he held on.

After that he ran to a place where people were living. When he got there, he shouted, 'Say, hurry up and take your lodge down, for a big warparty is upon you and you will surely be killed![65] Come let us get away!' He scared them all so much that they quickly took down their lodge, piled it on Trickster, and then got on him themselves.[66] They likewise placed all the little dogs they had on top of Trickster. Just then he began to break wind again and the force of the expulsion scattered the things on top of him in all directions. They fell far apart from one another. Separated, the people were standing about and shouting to one another; and the dogs, scattered here and there, howled at one another. There stood Trickster laughing at them till he ached.

Now he proceeded onward. He seemed to have gotten over his troubles. 'Well, this bulb did a lot of talking,' he said to himself, 'yet it could not make me defecate.' But even as he spoke he began to have the desire to defecate, just a very little. 'Well, I suppose this is what it meant. It certainly bragged a good deal, however.' As he spoke he defecated again. 'Well, what a braggart it was! I suppose this is why it said this.' As he spoke these last words, he began to defecate a good deal. After a while, as he was

26

sitting down, his body would touch the excrement. Thereupon he got on top of a log and sat down there but, even then, he touched the excrement. Finally, he climbed up a log that was leaning against a tree. However, his body still touched the excrement, so he went up higher. Even then, however, he touched it so he climbed still higher up. Higher and higher he had to go. Nor was he able to stop defecating. Now he was on top of the tree. It was small and quite uncomfortable. Moreover, the excrement began to come up to him.

24

Even on the limb on which he was sitting he began to defecate. So he tried a different position. Since the limb, however, was very slippery he fell right down into the excrement. Down he fell, down into the dung. In fact he disappeared in it, and it was only with very great difficulty that he was able to get out of it. His racoon-skin blanket was covered with filth, and he came out dragging it after him. The pack he was carrying on his back was covered with dung, as was also the box containing his penis. The box he emptied and then placed it on his back again.

25

Then, still blinded by the filth, he started to run. He could not see anything. As he ran he knocked against a tree. The old man[67] cried out in pain. He reached out and felt the tree and sang:

'Tree, what kind of a tree are you? Tell me something about yourself!'

And the tree answered, 'What kind of a tree do you think I am? I am an oak tree. I am the forked oak tree that used to stand in the middle of the valley. I am that one,' it said. 'Oh, my, is it possible that there might be some water around here?' Trickster asked. The tree answered, 'Go straight on.' This is what it told him. As he went along he bumped up against another tree. He was knocked backwards by the collision. Again he sang:

'Tree, what kind of a tree are you? Tell me something about yourself!'

'What kind of a tree do you think I am? The red oak tree that used to stand at the edge of the valley, I am that one.' 'Oh, my, is it possible that there is water around here?' asked Trickster. Then

27

the tree answered and said, 'Keep straight on,' and so he went again. Soon he knocked against another tree. He spoke to the tree and sang:

'Tree, what kind of a tree are you? Tell me something about yourself!'

'What kind of a tree do you think I am? The slippery elm tree that used to stand in the midst of the others, I am that one.' Then Trickster asked, 'Oh, my, is it possible that there would be some water near here?' And the tree answered and said, 'Keep right on.' On he went and soon he bumped into another tree and he touched it and sang:

'Tree, what kind of a tree are you? Tell me something about yourself!'

'What kind of a tree do you think I am? I am the basswood tree that used to stand on the edge of the water. That is the one I am.' 'Oh, my, it is good,' said Trickster. So there in the water he jumped and lay. He washed himself thoroughly.

It is said that the old man almost died that time, for it was only with the greatest difficulty that he found the water. If the trees had not spoken to him he certainly would have died. Finally, after a long time and only after great exertions, did he clean himself, for the dung had been on him a long time and had dried. After he had cleansed himself he washed his racoon-skin blanket and his box.[68]

26

As he was engaged in this cleansing he happened to look in the water and much to his surprise he saw many plums there. He surveyed them very carefully and then he dived down into the water to get some. But only small stones did he bring back in his hands. Again he dived into the water. But this time he knocked himself unconscious against a rock at the bottom. After a while he floated up and gradually came to. He was lying on the water, flat on his back, when he came to and, as he opened his eyes, there on the top of the bank he saw many plums. What he had seen in the water was only the reflection.[69] Then he realized what he had done. 'Oh, my, what a stupid fellow I must be! I should have recognized this. Here I have caused myself a great deal of pain.'

27

Then he went on to the shore and ate as many plums as possible, and putting a belt around his racoon-skin blanket he filled it likewise with plums and proceeded downstream.

Much to his surprise as he travelled along he came upon an oval lodge. He peeped in and saw two women with many children. He took one of the plums and threw it through the top of the lodge. It made a great noise. The women grabbed it. This he repeated and soon one of the women came out and saw, unexpectedly, a man standing there. 'Aha, it is my older brother who is doing this.' She and her companion asked him to come in, and as he entered the lodge he gave a plum apiece to each of the women. Then they asked him, 'Where did you pick these, older brother?' 'There are many of these at a particular place, sisters, and if you wish to pick them I will tell you where to go.' 'We would like very much to have some, brother,' they said. 'However, we cannot leave our children alone for they are very disobedient.' 'Sisters, if you wish to go, I will take care of the children for you,' he said. 'You are very good, older brother,' they said. 'You cannot possibly miss the place,' he added, 'for there are so many plums there. You cannot really pick them all for they are too plentiful. If, toward evening, as the sun sets, you see the sky red, you will know that the plums are causing it.[70] Do not turn back for you will surely find it.'

They started out and as soon as they were out of sight, he killed the children, singed them, and then boiled them. They were racoons. 'Well, now, for once I am going to have a good meal,' he said. There he ate a good deal; he ate a good deal of singed racoon meat. When he was finished, he cut off the head of one of the children, put a stick through its neck and placed it at the door as though the child were peeping out and laughing.[71] After that he went to a hill that was not far off.

28

At this hill he encountered a female skunk and said to her, 'Grandmother, I wish to ask you to do some work for me right away.' 'What do you wish me to do?' said the female skunk. 'Grandmother, I want you to dig a hole through this hill and I

want you to dig it right away.' 'All right,' said the female skunk.
Immediately she began to dig. She was a very fast digger and dug
deeply. He sat down and watched her. As soon as she had dug
herself in fairly deeply, he followed her and then stopped and sat
down and watched her dig ahead. He told her to hurry. 'Hurry,
sister, hurry up, hurry up!' Thus he spoke. Then she dug deeper
and again he said, 'Hurry, sister, hurry up. The round vulva!'
Then the female skunk stopped and said, 'What did you say,
grandson? Did you say "round vulva"?' 'No, grandmother, I said
"Hurry up, hurry up! Tear up the earth, tear it up!" That is
what I said.' Then she started again and he again repeated what he
had said before. He sat there looking at her as he said it. She had
her anus turned toward him as she stooped to dig. He was watching her as he said it. Then again he spoke, 'Sister, hurry up, hurry
up! Vulva, round one!' 'Well, grandson, what did you say then?'
'Ah, grandmother, hurry up, hurry up and dig. I said I was getting warm.' Then she started again and again he said it and she
stopped and asked him what he had said. But again he said some-
this else. Four times he said this to her and by that time she had
burrowed through the hill. She did it very quickly, very quickly
indeed. Then he took some dry grass, brought it together and
placed it in each of the two holes that had been made in the hill.
Thereupon he went to the end of the hill nearest his road and
waited.

29

Soon the women came along. He saw them in the distance.
When they saw him he went inside of the hill. As they got
nearer home, they were getting quite angry for they had not been
able to find any plums. As they approached their lodge, much to
their annoyance, one of the children was peeping out of the door.
It was smiling at them. 'What kind of a joke is this? We were
not able to get any plums.' 'I am angry,' said one of the women.
So she slapped the child on the cheek and the head toppled over.[72]
There, much to her horror, she noticed that it was only the child's
head. Then both of the women cried out, 'Oh, my children! He
has killed them! It must have been Trickster! He must have been
the one who went into the hill!' They wept very much.
Soon Trickster came over to them again. He had changed him-

30

self into another person and his face was blackened.[73] When he got to them he said, 'Sisters, what are you crying about?' And they answered, 'Trickster has killed both of our children and has eaten them.' 'Oh, my, I wish I could get hold of him for you! When they tell me such things about him, I always long to get hold of him! In what direction did he go? Do you know?' They said, 'Some time ago a person went into the hill, that must have been he.' 'He is going to get it now! Which way do you mean? Come and show it to me.' So they went and there they saw a hole, a very large one, where the dirt had been freshly disturbed. 'Now he is going to get it! He is certainly the one that did it,' said the man. Then he went in the hole and after he was in a while he made quite a commotion as if he were striking something. Then they heard something like a groan inside the hill. Soon he came out all bloody. His nose was all covered with blood and bruised. He had, of course, bruised his own nose and then come out. 'My, what a large fellow he was! I suppose that is why they talk about him so much! He fought with great fierceness against me. But I killed him. I am sure you heard us inside. He is inside there. You ought to go and get him. He is dead so that you need not be in the least afraid of him.' Thus spoke Trickster to the women.

Then the women went in. After a few minutes, however, they turned back. 'He is inside, a little farther up. Don't be afraid of him.' So they went farther in and as soon as they were well in, he put some hay inside and set fire to it. Then he ran to the other side of the hill, put some hay in and set fire to it. When the hay was entirely burnt up he went inside and took the racoons out. They had been thoroughly singed. 'Now is the time that I will eat some fat,' he said.

30

But first he started for the water. When he had washed the racoons thoroughly he built a fire and boiled them. Then he took the one that was at the bottom and put it on top. After this he broke off some twigs and dished the food out. He was about to eat and put a piece in his mouth when he heard a squeaking noise above him. 'Well,' he said impatiently and did not eat the meat. Then, for the second time, he was about to put a piece of meat in his mouth and again he heard a squeaking noise. Again he did not put the food in his mouth. A third and fourth time this happened. Finally, he looked around and, much to his astonishment, saw a big tree whose branches were squeaking. So he climbed up the tree and said, 'Why, when I try to eat, do you tease me?' Thereupon he tried to split the fork of the tree but his arm got caught. It was held fast and do what he could he was not able to free himself.

31

Just then, unexpectedly, a pack of wolves passed by. He shouted to them, 'Say, go around a little farther back. I was just about to eat but I got my arm caught in the branches of this tree. This is why I am here now. Under the tree there is some meat which I had prepared for myself. Now don't you eat it.'[74] 'Well, there must be something of importance here,' the wolves said to one another. So they ran over there and when they got there they found food ready to be eaten. There was a good deal of food. 'Listen,' shouted Trickster from the tree, 'you can eat some of it, but you must leave me a little.' However, they paid no attention to him and ate everything there was. Then Trickster said, 'Now, don't drink the soup, for you have eaten the meat up entirely.' Then they took the soup and drank everything they found. When they were finished they ran away. 'My, how they have made me grieve, those covetous fellows! It is you who have caused me all this trouble,' he said turning toward the fork of the tree. He split it and it fell down.[75] Then he ran in the direction in which the wolves had gone.

32

As he was running along, he came to a valley. There he heard someone beating a drum, the drumming followed by many war whoops.[76] Somebody there was making a great noise. So loud was this noise that it seemed to reach the skies.[77] 'Well, I wonder what these people are up to? I guess I will go over and see for I have not had any fun for a long time. Whatever they are doing, I will join them. If they are going to dance, why I will dance too. I used to be a fine dancer.' Thus Trickster spoke. Then, as he walked across the valley, again and again he heard that noise.

Everyone was shouting with joy. It was wonderful! 'Ah! There must be many people over there,' he was thinking to himself. Again he heard them shout and, once again, when the drum was beaten, it seemed as if the heavens would burst asunder. Then again the people gave a tremendous shout. Now he became so anxious to join them that he began to run. The shouting was now quite close to him. Yet he could see no one anywhere. Again he heard the shouting. It was very loud. It sounded as if the sky would burst asunder.[78]

To him it seemed as if, even at that moment, he was walking in the midst of people shouting. Yet he did not see anything. Not far away, however, he saw, lying around, the bones of an animal and, farther still, he saw an object that turned out, on closer inspection, to be an elk's skull. It had many horns branching in every direction. He watched this head quite carefully and then he saw where the noise had come from and where the celebration was taking place. It was in the elk's skull. The head was filled with many flies.[79] They would go inside and then, when they rushed out, they made the noise that he had heard and which he had taken to be shouting. He looked at the flies and he saw that they were enjoying themselves greatly and he envied them.

'Well, I said that I would join in whatever they were doing and I am going to. I wonder what I would have to do in order to join them?' Thus pondered Trickster. Then he said, 'Younger brothers, you are certainly having a lot of fun. You surely are doing an important thing. I would very much like to be like one of you. How can I do it? Do show me how I can do it so that I, too, can join you.' Thus he spoke. Then they answered him, 'Well, there is no difficulty involved. We enter through the neck as you must have seen by this time.' Thus they spoke. Then Trickster tried to enter but failed. He wanted very much to enter but he was unable. 'How do you manage to get in, my younger brothers?' he asked. Great man that he was, he could not accomplish it, much as he wished to![80] Then they said to him, 'If you wish to come in just say, "Neck, become large!" and it will become large. In that way you can enter. That is the way we do it.' Thus they told him.

So he sat down and said, 'Neck, become large!' and the hole in the neck became large. Then he put his head in and entered. He put his head in up to his neck. All the flies ran away and the opening into which he had thrust his head became small again. Thus he was held fast. He tried to free himself exerting all his power but it was of no avail. He could do absolutely nothing. He was unable to free his head from the skull of the elk. When he realized that nothing could be done, he went down to the stream wearing the skull. He had long branching antlers, for he was wearing an elk's skull. When he came to the river he walked along the edge, and as he went along he came to a place inhabited by human beings. There he waited until night. The next morning he did the following. As soon as the people came to get water from the river, he stretched himself out and lay there with his racoon-skin blanket, quite a fear-inspiring object to look upon. His whole body was covered with the racoon-skin blanket and he had long branching horns on his head.

33

Early in the morning a woman came for water and saw him. She started to run back but he said to her, 'Turn back; I will bless you!'[81] So she turned back and when she got there, he said to her, 'Now, go home. Get an axe and bring it over here. Then use all the offerings that are customary, of which your relations will tell you. If you strike the top of my head with the axe, you will be able to use what you find therein as medicine and obtain anything that you wish. I am an elk-spirit. I am blessing this village.'[82] Thus he spoke to her. Then he continued, 'I am one of the great spirits living in these waters.'[83]

So the woman went home and when she got there she told all the people what had happened. 'There is a waterspirit at the place where we dip for water who blessed me. He told me that he had a "medicine-chest"[84] in the box that he carried and that if we brought an axe and suitable offerings, placed them there and then split his head open, what we found within his skull we could use for making various medicines.' Thus she spoke.

Thereupon the people went to the river with their various offerings and, sure enough, there they found him, quite fear-inspiring to look upon. The offerings—red feathers, white deer skin, and red-yarn belts[85]—they brought in great quantities.

34

After they had placed all these things before him, they selected a man who was to take the axe. He struck the skull and split it open and behold! there they found Trickster laughing at them. He arose and said, 'A nice head-dress I have been wearing but now you have spoiled it!' Then he laughed uproariously. When he got up the people said, 'It is Trickster!' However he spoke to them and said, 'Inasmuch as you have made these offerings to me they will not be lost.[86] For whatsoever be the purpose for which you use this head, that purpose will be accomplished.' So then they made themselves various medicinal instruments and afterwards found that they were efficacious. Then Trickster left and continued wandering.

34

One day he met a hawk flying about. He was looking for something dead or decaying. 'You ugly, good-for-nothing fellow, you once played a trick on me and I should like to return that compliment.' This is what was in Trickster's mind. So he lay down at the edge of the water where the waves come up and took on the form of a large dead buck-deer, one who had died but whose body had not yet decayed. The crows were already there longing for the carcass yet nowhere could they find a place at which to attack it for the hide was still tough owing to the fact that putrefaction had not yet set in. Then the hawk came and the crows shouted at him. They said to one another, 'He alone generally has a sharp knife.' They had to call for him repeatedly before he came. He was energetic and went all around the animal looking for a place at which to attack it. Finally he came to the hind part and began working his head into the rectum. He hurt Trickster so much in pecking at him that Trickster almost jumped up. Finally, however, he got his head into the rectum so that he could bite at some pieces inside. As soon as hawk's head was far in, Trickster closed his rectum tightly and arose. 'Aha, Mr. Hawk, you once hurt me a good deal and I thought to myself that some day I would get even with you.' Then he went on. The hawk tried to get free but all to no avail. He could not free himself. At first he kept his wings flapping all the time but, after a while, he only flapped them intermittently.

35

35

Then Trickster walked on. Soon he came upon a bear and the bear said to him, 'O, Kunu, how that tail becomes you!' Trickster made no answer but kept on. 'O, Kunu, how that tail becomes you! If only I were that way!' Then, after a while, the bear again spoke, 'O, Kunu, how that tail becomes you! I wish I could have one too!' Then Trickster answered and said, 'You are always talking in that way. What is the difficulty of obtaining one? Why don't you make one for yourself? When I saw one, a little time ago, I liked it and I had one made for me. Anyone who wishes to can get one.' 'All right, Kunu, since you think you can make me one, why I wish you would.' 'Good, that I will do for you. Now, look at the tail carefully and if anyone asks you to give him one like it, do the following.' Thereupon he addressed the hawk, 'Go, get out, for another tail is desired.' So he loosened his hold and there was an odour of foul air. The hawk got up and walked away. All his feathers were gone.

Trickster now turned to the bear, and said, 'Well, let me now first prepare you properly for the tail so that when the hawk comes back I can put him in your rectum.' Then he took a knife and cut out the bear's rectum and, pulling out his intestines, killed him. He built a fire and singed the hair off the bear. 'My, how long it has been since I have had the food that I like best! Now I surely will get my fill.' When he got through preparing the meat he put it on to boil.

36

Suddenly, however, he saw a mink at the edge of the water coming toward him. 'Ah, my little brother, I see you are walking about. Come over here, my younger brother, for I am about to eat. Let us eat together.' Thus he spoke. Then the mink came and he again spoke to him, 'My younger brother, a thought just occurred to me. Let us run a race and let the one who wins be the chief. The one who loses will then dish out the food.'[87] In imagination he was already thinking of how mink would dish out the food for him, for he felt positive he would unquestionably defeat him. He thought that if mink dished it out he would get his fill.

36

After a while he spoke to mink again, saying, 'Well, little brother, since the ground around here is not suitable for a race, let us run on the ice.' The river at that time was frozen. Both, accordingly, started off for a place in the river from which to start the race. The pot with the food in it was to be the goal and the one who would touch the food first was to be declared the winner.[88] Both agreed to all these things. Thereupon they started the race. Soon Trickster was left far behind. He, however, continued on until he came to a crack in the ice. There he stopped suddenly and spoke to the mink, 'My little brother, what is it you said when you came to the crack in the ice and walked on?' The mink replied, 'I said, "Crack in the ice, become large!" and then I jumped over it.' So Trickster said the same, 'Crack in the ice, become large!' Then he jumped over it. But the crack in the ice became quite large and he fell into the water. Immediately the edges of the crack joined again and Trickster was left under the ice. This is exactly what happened. With Trickster under the ice mink dished out the food for himself and ate it. He ate his fill of it.

Trickster, in the meantime, kept going under the ice until he got alongside of mink and said, 'My little brother, as you have eaten up the food alone, place a little piece in your mouth for me, a good piece.' He was speaking from under the crack in the ice. Then he put a piece in his mouth for Trickster. Then Trickster asked him to do it again and again he did it. The fourth time he asked him he put the last piece in his mouth. Then when the meat was entirely gone he drank up the soup and dropped a piece of bear's dung into Trickster's mouth.[89] 'My, what a bad fellow he is! He even abuses me! You will die for this!' Outraged, he broke through the ice, came out and chased the mink, but the latter finally got under the ice and escaped.

'It is a shame that he played such a trick on me, that despicable fellow! Some day I will get my revenge. He will have no place to which to escape.' Thus he spoke.

37

Soon he came to a human habitation and went to the village where he had previously married. He thought he would then be able to wreak his vengeance on the mink there. He borrowed a very good hunting dog and immediately started off in pursuit. But the mink would not come out from under the ice and there was thus no way in which he could get at him. Trickster did not care how he did it but he certainly wanted to revenge himself on the mink.

38

Then he continued his wandering. Suddenly he heard something singing:

'Trickster, what is it you are packing? Your penis it is you are packing!'

'My, what an awful thing he is saying, that contemptible person! He seems really to know what I am carrying.'[90] On he went. Shortly after this, and from a definite direction, he again heard singing. It was as if it was just at his side:

'Trickster, what is it you are carrying? Your testicles, these you are carrying.'

'My, who is this that is mentioning these things? He must indeed, have been watching me. Well, now I will carry these things correctly.'[91] Thereupon he emptied his box and threw everything out. Then he placed his testicles underneath next to his back. As he was doing this again, suddenly, he heard someone singing right at his side:

'Trickster, what is it you are packing? What is it you are packing? Your testicles underneath, your testicles underneath!'

'My, what a contemptible person it is who is thus teasing me! He must have been watching my pack.' So again he rearranged his pack. He now put the head of his penis on top. Then he went on but soon, unexpectedly, he heard the singing at his side again:

'Trickster, what is it you are packing? Your penis you are packing! The head of your penis you have placed on top, the head of your penis you have placed on top!'

'My, what an evil one it is who is saying this,' and he jumped towards him. But the one who had been singing ran away, exclaiming, 'Tigi! Tigi! Tigi!' It ran into a hollow tree. It was a chipmunk. 'I will kill you for this, you contemptible thing,' said Trickster. Thereupon he spoke to his penis, 'Now then, my

38

younger brother, you may go after him for he has been annoying you for a long time.'

So he took out his penis and probed the hollow tree with it. He could not, however, reach the end of the hole. So he took some more of his penis and probed again, but again he was unable to reach the end of the hole. So he unwound more and more of his penis and probed still deeper, yet all to no avail. Finally he took what still remained, emptying the entire box, and probed and probed but still he could not reach the end of the hole. At last he sat up on a log and probed as far as he could, but still he was unable to reach the end. 'Ho!' said he impatiently, and suddenly withdrew his penis. Much to his horror, only a small piece of it was left. 'My, what a great injury he has done to me! You contemptible thing I will repay you for this!'

39

Then he kicked the log to pieces. There he found the chipmunk and flattened him out, and there, too, to his horror he discovered his penis all gnawed up. 'Oh, my, of what a wonderful organ he has deprived me! But why do I speak thus? I will make objects out of the pieces for human beings to use.' Then he took the end of his penis, the part that has no foreskin, and declared, 'This is what human beings will call the lily-of-the-lake.' This he threw in a lake near by. Then he took the other pieces declaring in turn: 'This the people will call potatoes; this the people will call turnips; this the people will call artichokes; this the people will call ground-beans; this the people will call dog-teeth; this the people will call sharp-claws; this the people will call rice.' All these pieces he threw into the water. Finally he took the end of his penis and declared, 'This the people will call the pond-lily.' He was referring to the square part of the end of his penis.

What was left of his penis was not very long. When, at last, he started off again, he left behind him the box in which he had until then kept his penis coiled up.

And this is the reason our penis has its present shape. It is because of these happenings that the penis is short. Had the chipmunk not gnawed off Trickster's penis our penis would have the appearance that Trickster's had first had. It was so large that he had to carry it on his back. Now it would not have been good had our penis remained like that and the chipmunk was created for the precise purpose of performing this particular act.[92] Thus it is said.

40

Then Trickster started wandering around the world again. Soon he came across the coyote. 'It hardly seems possible for a person to go about but here is my little brother actually walking about.[93] Listen, little brother, I think there is something on the top of yonder hill. Let us go there,' said Trickster. So they both climbed to the top of the hill and when they got there they had a fine view of the surrounding country. 'Little brother, they say you have a keen scent. So at least you always gave yourself out to have. Let us play keen-scenter.[94] I, too am a keen-scenter. Let us try, therefore, to scent and see where the nearest people live.' Both, accordingly, held their noses up in the air and began to sniff. Indeed they were very diligent. Trickster, of course, was unable to scent anything. His plan was to behave as though he could and watch what coyote would do. He therefore went over to a certain place and then stopped for some time. The place he went to was in the direction of the timberland. 'He must be scenting something,' thought the coyote. Now Trickster spoke, 'My little brother, near the timber over there some people are living. You see, my little brother, you cannot scent as well as I can.' All this time, of course, he had not scented anything. He was simply imitating the actions of the coyote who seemed to scent something in that direction and indicated it by his actions. 'Why, my little brother, don't you scent anything?' continued Trickster. The coyote answered that he also believed there was something over there. Then Trickster said, 'Ah, my little brother, I see that you can scent a little too. Well, my little brother, let us go there.'

Then he went to the place he had meant. When he got there, truly enough there was a human village. In this village he remained and there after a while he got married. After some time had passed a child was born to him. As this was the time for the tribe to go on their fall move, he left for another place where he lived alone. There he remained and there he made his permanent home. He never went back to the village where he had first married. One day he spoke to the coyote and said, 'My little brother, it is about time for me to go and pay a few visits.'[95]

41

He first went to the village of muskrat. All its inhabitants were very happy at his arrival. The children exclaimed, 'Our uncle has come!' This they repeated again and again. Then the old muskrat spoke to him, 'Ah, my older brother has come! It is good.' Turning to his wife he said, 'Old woman, prepare some food for my older brother right away. Boil him some roots, some roots of the lily-of-the-lake.' Thereupon she handed him a pail which he took and went out and brought back some ice. Then taking a sharp instrument, an awl, he whacked away at the ice. After a while the pail was full of ice. This chipped ice he brought to his wife. She took it and put it over the fire, hanging it on a hook. After a while, amazingly enough, she dished out some lily-of-the-lake roots. The kettle was now filled with these although ice had been put in it originally. Trickster was delighted and ate a great quantity of them. When he was finished he left, but purposely forgot one of his mittens under the mat so that he would have an excuse for calling back to the muskrats that he had forgotten something. When he had gone but a short distance he shouted back, 'Say, younger brother, I left one of my mittens at your house. Let one of the children bring it over to me.' When the old muskrat heard this he said to one of his children, 'Say, take this mitten over to your uncle. Remember he always talks a good deal. Go only part of the way and throw it at him.' So the young muskrat went only a part way and was about to throw the mitten over to Trickster, when the latter said, 'Bring it over to me. I dread going back. That is why I am asking you to bring it over.' Then he took the mitten over to Trickster and the latter said, 'Tell your father that in the morning he is to come over to see me.' When the little muskrat got back he told his father, 'Father, you are to go over to visit my uncle tomorrow morning.' 'I knew he would say something like that and that is why I asked you to throw it at him.' 'Well, I did go part of the way and wanted to throw it at him but he told me not to, that he dreaded to go back. For that reason, he asked me to bring it to him. I, therefore, took it over to him.'

Now when Trickster had left he had been asked to take some lily-of-the-lake roots with him for his wife but he refused and said, 'Never mind, my younger brother, remember we have something to eat at our house too.'[96] He was lying, however, for they were entirely out of food just then and it was, of course, for this reason he had gone out to visit muskrat.

The next morning the muskrat went over to Trickster's. 'Well, younger brother, it seemed impossible for anyone to travel on such a day but you have come! Well, younger brother, what do you want to eat? Old woman give me my bag and my sharp instrument.' The old woman was embarrassed at the request but, at last, gave him the things he had asked for. Thereupon he went to the ice and whacked away at it for quite a while. He filled his bag with ice and brought it back. Then he put a kettle on the fire and poured the ice into it. All this time his wife felt very much ashamed at his actions. 'Brother-in-law, he must have seen you do something and that is why he is acting in this manner,' she said. After a while the water got warm and the ice began to melt and the water began to run out of the kettle. There was so much water that it put out the fire. In fact they had to empty the contents of the kettle outside.

Trickster stood there unabashed and said, 'I wonder why it acted in this strange way? I have always been able to do it before.' Muskrat now took the bag, went outside, and brought it back full of ice and poured the contents out on the side of the lodge. The ice turned into lily-of-the-lake roots. Then he went out again and came back with a bag full of ice. This, likewise, he poured out and it turned into lily-of-the-lake roots. Four times he did this. Trickster's wife thanked him very much. 'You wicked old woman, what are you saying? How often have I done this for you, yet you never thanked me for it! Yet you thank this man!' Then muskrat went home. Trickster said to his wife, 'Well, this is the way you are supposed to act in order to have plenty of lily-of-the-lake roots, so muskrat told me. At any rate, old woman, this ought to suffice us and the children for some time. They will indeed have food for many days to come now.'

42

After some time had elapsed and they had eaten up all the food, Trickster said, 'Well, old woman, I am going to visit one of my younger brothers.' 'All right, go ahead,' said his wife. So he went to the place where snipe lived. When he got there, snipe said, 'Aha, my older brother, I thought it was quite impossible to walk about but you seem to have done it.' Snipe and his children were happy at seeing Trickster. Then snipe said to his wife, 'Say, old woman, what is my brother-in-law going to eat?' 'Well, why don't you try to get some fish for him?' said the old woman. 'Well, hand over the fibre-twine to me,' said the old man. Then he took it and went outside with it. He went to a place where a tree was leaning over the edge of the water. To that he walked and, standing there, he cried, 'Riririgi,' and soon many fish came along. From among these he selected the largest one. Waiting for it to open one of the gills, he entered it, coming out at the other gill. Thus he strung it and brought it back with him. Trickster was delighted. They boiled it immediately and soon Trickster was able to eat as much as he wished. When he finished eating he thanked them and said, 'Ah, my younger brother, it is good that you have all the fish you want.' 'Older brother, take some fish along for the children. I can go out and get some for you.' 'Younger brother, we have some fish to eat at home,' answered Trickster with pretended dignity. As a matter of fact, of course, they were keenly in want of food. He said this simply to make an effect.

Then he purposely forgot one of his mittens under the mat and went away. After he had gone a short distance he shouted back, 'Younger brother, let one of the children bring me the mitten that I have forgotten at your house. It is under the mat.' Then old snipe said to one of his children, 'Take this mitten but stop at some distance from him for he is a great talker.' Then the little snipe brought the mitten to him and was about to throw it when Trickster said, 'Here, here, my child, I dread to turn back and that is why I want you to bring it over here.' Then the little snipe took it over to him and Trickster said, 'Tell your father that tomorrow morning he is to come over to visit me.'

When the little snipe got home he said, 'Father, you are to go over to our uncle's house tomorrow morning.' 'Now, that is exactly the reason why I told you not to go over to him.' 'Well, I stopped some distance from him and wanted to throw it at him but he told me that he dreaded to turn back and that was why he asked me to bring it clear over to him. So I did.'

43

In the morning snipe went over to Trickster's house and Trickster said, 'Is it possible! I hardly expected anyone to travel at such a time and yet you have come over the road!' The children were also delighted. 'Our uncle has come,' they said. 'Well, old woman, hand me the fibre-twine so that your brother-in-law can have something to eat.' She did not know why he wanted it but, finally, she gave it to him anyhow. He took it and went out. He went and stood at the edge of the river and said, 'Tcigirixidjeje.' 'Well, he is making some strange sounds,' thought the old woman. The fish came in great numbers. He selected the biggest and, when this fish opened its gills, he intended to enter one of them. But, by mistake, he entered its throat. And thus Trickster was swallowed by a fish. The children all began to cry and the woman said to snipe, 'Brother-in-law, he must have seen you do something and that is why he is acting in this strange way. Never before have I seen him do this.' Then the latter said, 'Sister-in-law, have you any fibre-twine left?' She gave him a piece immediately and he went to a place where a tree was leaning over the edge of the water and began to shout. Many fish came to him but not for some time did the big fish that had swallowed Trickster come. Finally he came, the *cawawankce*. Snipe watched him carefully and, finally, a small opening became visible where the gills were. This place he immediately entered and soon brought out Trickster. Trickster laughed, 'Younger brother, never before did this happen to me. This is the first time. I thought that you were probably very hungry after your journey so I hurried and that is how this accident occurred.' Then snipe caught many fish and they had plenty of food for a long time. After snipe had gone home, Trickster said, 'Well, old woman, am I not a good provider? We will have fish now for a long time.' Then they barbecued the fish on a frame. And thus they ate barbecued fish for a long time, for a very long time indeed.

43

After some time the fish were all gone and Trickster said, 'Well, old woman, I must visit one of my younger brothers again for it is only then that I will be able to get some food. I am going to visit my younger brother woodpecker.' 'You may go,' said the old woman. So he went to visit his younger brother. After a while he got there and woodpecker said, 'Well, well, my older brother! I thought it was quite impossible to travel on the roads but yet you have made the journey.' 'Well, younger brother, I have been about a good deal.' Then woodpecker's wife said, 'Well, old man, what is our brother-in-law going to eat? The fresh meat is all gone.' 'Well, old woman, give me my awl.' Then she gave him his awl and he fastened it on his bill. Thereupon he went to the middle of the lodge where the centrepole stood and, hopping on it, exclaimed, 'Kowank, kowank, kowank!' and looked all around the pole. Then he pecked the pole with his bill exclaiming, 'Koko!' Immediately a bear fell down. They put it in the fire and singed the hair from its body. Then they cut the body up and put it in a kettle. It was not long before it was cooked. Immediately they dished it out. Trickster ate very much for he was really quite famished. When he had finished woodpecker said, 'My older brother, you may take some home with you for your children.' But he said, 'My younger brother, I know you mean well but never mind. I also use my awl at times.'

Then he purposely secreted one of his mittens under the mat and went out. He had not gone very far before he shouted back, 'Younger brother, I put one of my mittens under the mat and forgot it. Let one of your children bring it over to me.' Thereupon the woodpecker said to one of his children, 'Take this mitten over to your uncle but stop some distance away and throw it at him. He talks a good deal.' Then the child went over there and stopped and wanted to throw it over but Trickster said, 'Here, here! Bring it over, my child, for I dread to turn back and that is why I asked you to bring it over to me.' So he took it over to him and Trickster said, 'Tell your father to come over to my place tomorrow morning.' When the child came back, he said, 'Father, you are to go over to uncle's place tomorrow morning.' 'Now, that is exactly why I wanted you not to go too near him and throw the mitten at him,' replied the father. 'I wanted to throw it over to him when I was quite some distance away but he forbade me and said that he dreaded to turn back and wanted me to bring it to him in person. Then I took it over to him.'

The next morning, early, he went over to Trickster's. The latter

45

was anxiously waiting for him but he spoke as though he were surprised. 'My, my! Is it possible that my younger brother has come, with the roads in so impossible a condition!' Then the old woman said, 'Well, brother-in-law, what will you eat?' Then Trickster interrupted and said, 'I think the old woman is out of fresh meat. Give me my awl,' he said to her. As, by this time, she knew why he spoke thus she gave it to him. He stuck it into his nose and climbed to the top of the lodge centrepole and said, 'Kowank, kowank, kowank!' Then he pecked at the upper part of the pole and made a loud sound. He knocked the awl into his nose and made himself unconscious. He was thrown down from the pole and fell to the ground unconscious, his nose bleeding profusely. The children all began to cry. When the old man finally came to, the old woman said, 'O, my, my brother-in-law, he must have seen you do something and that is why he is acting in this strange way. He never did this before.' 'Younger brother,' exclaimed Trickster, 'never before did this happen to me. This is the first time. It is too bad that it just occurred when you were here.'

Then woodpecker asked for the awl and they gave it to him. He took it, hopped to the top of the centrepole, looked around and said, 'Kowank, kowank, kowank!' Making a loud sound at the top of the pole, he knocked down a racoon. It fell to the ground with a thump. Then he did it a third time and another fell down. Then he did it a fourth time and knocked down four bears. After he had done all this he came down and went home.

Then Trickster said, 'Well, old woman, this is what real men do when they want to eat fat.[97] We will now have plenty of white lard.'

Now they skinned the animals and made robes from the skins. Some of the skins they singed. They also prepared the entrails so they could put them to some use and they carefully washed the intestines. They even cleansed the rectum. There was plenty of lard. Even the bones were used for making soup. In short, they threw nothing away except the dung.[98] Thus they had plenty of bear meat. They ate and feasted continually and their life was pleasant and enjoyable.

44

After a time they had eaten up everything. It must have been a long time for bears are large animals. Then Trickster said, 'Well, old woman, we have lived a long time on these animals. I think it is about time for me to visit one of my younger brothers again. I am now going to visit my younger brother polecat.' 'Go ahead and do so, if you wish to obtain something for the children to eat for they have finished all the fat. Otherwise they will have nothing.'

So Trickster went to visit his younger brother polecat. When he got there polecat said, 'My, my! My older brother has come! It seems hardly possible that anyone could travel around now and yet our older brother has done it! That is true, my older brother.' The children were also glad. Polecat's family was a very good-natured one. They could hardly do enough for Trickster. Then the old woman said, 'What will our brother-in-law eat? The fresh meat is all gone. Why don't you do something,' she said to her husband. 'Well, old woman, are there any acorns left?' 'Yes, there are some left,' she said, and handed them to him. Then he took the acorn bag and opened the door and said, 'Come here, deer, and eat!' Soon many deer came from all the different directions and he scattered the acorns in the yard. He did it himself as he spoke. As soon as there were many deer in the yard he pointed his anus toward them and broke wind in their direction. In this way he killed many. Then both the polecats prepared the deer that had been killed. Some of the meat they put in a pot for boiling. Soon it was cooked and served to Trickster. Thus Trickster ate very much deer meat. When he was finished they said, 'Older brother, take with you as much as you can carry. Take it along for the children.' However Trickster answered, 'We still have enough as I did what you have done before I left the house. As a matter of fact I shot off all of my ammunition before I came here. That is why I came and I want you to give me four rounds.'[99] 'All right,' said the polecat and did something to the Trickster's rectum. Then Trickster went home.

After he had gone a short distance he said to himself, 'Polecat used to be unreliable. Perhaps he has fooled me and I have not discovered it yet.' It so happened that right near him was a knoll and so he thought it would be a good thing to shoot at it. Thereupon he turned his anus in that direction and broke wind and the knoll disappeared. 'Well, that unreliable fellow told the truth after all!' After a little while he again became suspicious of polecat's gift, thinking that perhaps it was only the first round that worked. So he thought that he would test it again. There was a big tree near the place he had come to so he decided to shoot at it. He turned his anus toward it and broke wind in that direction and the tree was knocked over and destroyed, roots and all. 'Well, the little fellow, he told the truth after all!' exclaimed Trickster. Then he went on and again got nervous thinking that perhaps only the first two loads were good. 'Well, what am I worrying about? I can try it.' Near him was a big rock and at that he decided to shoot. So he turned his anus toward the rock and broke wind and the rock was blown to pieces. 'Well, the little wayward fellow did tell the truth after all!' Then he went on again and soon he was quite near his lodge. 'I am sure that he did not give me the full amount,' Trickster again said to himself, 'for he is a very peculiar fellow. He did more than I expected in giving me three rounds of ammunition. However, there is no need of my talking about it, for I can soon find out.' Right near him was a pointed hill and a very rocky one. At this he would shoot, he thought. Then he turned his anus toward the hill and broke wind and the hill disappeared. 'Well, well, my little brother did tell the truth and I was wrong in doubting him.'[100] Then he went home.

Early the next morning polecat came to Trickster's house. 'My, my! I thought it was impossible for anyone to go about and yet here is my little brother!' Everyone was delighted. 'It is our uncle,' they told each other. They had found out that when they were told that an uncle had arrived, that this meant food for them and for that reason they had learned to like anyone who was called uncle.[101] Then the old woman said, 'Well, brother-in-law, what do you want to eat?' Then Trickster said, 'Are there any acorns left?' Sure enough some of the acorns that they were accustomed to boil were left. 'There are some of them here,' said the old woman, 'but perhaps he does not eat such things,' she added. 'Give them to me and I will try to do something with them. That is why I asked for them.' She gave them to him and he opened the door and scattered the acorns in the yard. Then he hid himself and pointed his anus outside and said, 'Deer, come here and eat.' 'Why, Trickster is acting as though he really had something to say!' exclaimed the old women. Then many deer came running and even entered the lodge for food. They could not, however, see anything. All of a sudden they saw him standing near the door, with his anus turned toward them, trying to expel gas. He strained himself very much but with each straining simply soiled himself all the more. Indeed how could he help it? Then all the deer left. They even stepped on him and bruised him. There he was all covered with blood and filth.

Then polecat said, 'Sister-in-law, have you any acorns left?' 'I have a few,' she answered. 'Well, give them to me,' said polecat. Then she handed him the acorns and he opened the door the least little bit and scattered them in the yard saying, 'Deer, come here and eat.' Then many deer came and he expelled some gas from his anus into their midst and killed many of them. Only a few escaped. Thus he did and went home. [102]

'Well, old woman, so must one act in order to obtain many deer.' Then they began to skin, to barbecue, to broil and to boil them. They surely had many deer. Then they rendered some deer-fat and froze it in holes in the ground. Out of the bones they made soup. The deerskins they tanned and the deer-hoofs they singed. Then they packed the meat and placed it here and there. They also obtained plenty of fresh lard. Of the fat around the intestines they made deer-sausage. [103]

45

One day Trickster said, 'Well, I think it is about time that we went back to the village. Perhaps they are lonesome for us, especially for the children.' [104] 'Well, let us do that. I was thinking of it myself,' said his wife. When they were ready to go back, they packed their possessions and began to carry them away. It required many trips. Trickster would go for a short distance. The children helped but there were so many packs that they did not get very far in a day. After a while they got near their home and all the people in the village came out to greet and help him with the packs. The people of the village were delighted. 'Kunu is back,' they shouted. The chief lived in the middle of the village and alongside of him they built a long lodge for Trickster. The young men would gather there at night and he would entertain them, for he was a very good-natured fellow. [105] The

49

young men always liked to gather around him and, when they were out courting women, he would go along just for the fun of it.

One day a traveller came to the village. The Trickster knew who he was.[106] The other young men tried to get the stranger to go out courting the girls but he would not do it. However, Trickster said to him, 'Say, the chief's daughter is in love with you. That is what the old woman told me she had told her.' 'Well,' said the stranger, 'it is on account of the other young men that I don't go out courting although I am perfectly willing to do so. However, don't say anything about it. I will try it tonight.' Then Trickster took some fish-oil and some artichoke roots, pounded them together and gave them to the young man to eat. He did this purposely in order to play a trick on him. That night he went courting with the stranger and, when they got to the place where the chief's daughter was accustomed to sleep, he showed the place to him. Then the young man went inside and stayed there all night. Trickster watched him all that time. About daybreak something terrible happened! The young man was just about to go away when the oil that he had eaten caused him to have a passage. He did not know, however, that it was Trickster's doing. He soiled the chief's daughter. Then Trickster shouted, 'The traveller has soiled the chief's daughter!' He went through the entire village announcing it. The traveller was very much ashamed for he was no other than the mink and that is why Trickster played this trick on him. He was just going to marry the chief's daughter when this happened to him. Mink then went into the brush and did not return. Trickster laughed heartily at him. 'What a funny fellow! When you escaped from me I just ached to get hold of you and now you have come right here!' Thus he spoke.

46

In the village in which they were staying the people owned two horses. The coyote had married into the village. Trickster was very desirous of revenging himself on him and coyote, on his side, had the desire of playing a trick on Trickster. However, Trickster discovered what coyote intended to do and did not like it. 'Many times he has done me wrong and I let it pass, but this time I am not going to overlook it. This time I intend to play a trick on him,' said Trickster.

Then he went into the wilderness,[107] to the place where the horses belonging to the village generally stayed. He found one of them and put it to sleep. When he was quite certain that the horse was asleep he went after mouse and said, 'Say, there is an animal dead here. Go to coyote and tell him, "My grandson, there is an animal dead over there and I was unable to move him. It is over there near the village. Pull it to one side and then we will be able to have it to ourselves."' Mouse was quite willing and ran over to coyote and said, 'Grandson, I know you are very strong and therefore I wish to tell you that there is an animal over there near the village, lying dead. If you will push it aside, it will be good. I wanted to do it myself but I was unable to pull it and that is why I have come over here to tell you, for I have compassion upon you.'[108] Coyote was very much delighted and went to the place. Trickster, at the same moment ran back to the village and waited for them. The mouse and the coyote soon arrived and the mouse tied the horse's tail to the coyote. Tightly she tied the two together. Then the coyote said, 'I am very strong and I know that I can pull this animal. The animal that I am about to pull is called an elk or a deer.' 'Well, everything is ready, you may pull it now,' said the mouse. 'All right,' said the coyote and tried to pull it. He woke the horse up and it got scared. Up it jumped and finding an animal tied to its tail it got even more frightened and began racing at full speed. Coyote was pulled along looking as though he were a branch being dragged. The horse ran to the village and Trickster shouted at the top of his voice, 'Just look at him, our son-in-law, coyote! He is doing something very disgraceful. Look at him!' Then all the people ran out and there, unexpectedly, they saw coyote tied to the horse's tail bouncing up and down. The horse finally went to its master and there it was caught. They untied the coyote and his mouth just twitched as he sat up. He was very much ashamed. He did not even go back to his lodge. He left the village and was not more seen. He had a wife and many children but those too he left. From that time on he has not lived among people.[109] If a person sees him anywhere he is ashamed of himself and when one gets very close to him his mouth twitches. He is still ashamed of what happened to him long ago.

47

Trickster stayed at that village for a long time and raised many children. One day he said, 'Well, this is about as long as I will stay here. I have been here a long time. Now I am going to go around the earth again and visit different people for my children are all grown up. I was not created for what I am doing here.'[110]

Then he went around the earth. He started at the end of the Mississippi river and went down to the stream. The Mississippi is a spirit-village and the river is its main road. He knew that the river was going to be inhabited by Indians and that is why he travelled down it. Whatever he thought might be a hindrance to the Indians he changed. He suddenly recollected the purpose for which he had been sent to the earth by Earthmaker. That is why he removed all these obstacles along the river.[111]

As he went along he killed and ate all those beings that were molesting the people. The waterspirits had their roads only at a short distance below the surface of the earth so he pushed these farther in. These waterspirit-roads are holes in the rivers. Many rivers have eddies which it would be impossible for a boat to pass through and these he pushed farther down into the ground.

48

He went all over the earth, and one day he came to a place where he found a large waterfall. It was very high. Then he said to the waterfall, 'Remove yourself to some other location for the people are going to inhabit this place and you will annoy them.' Then the waterfall said, 'I will not go away. I chose this place and I am going to stay here.' 'I tell you, you are going to some other place,' said Trickster. The waterfall, however, refused to do it. 'I am telling you that the earth was made for man to live on and you will annoy him if you stay here. I came to this earth to rearrange it. If you don't do what I tell you, I will not use you very gently.' Then the waterfall said, 'I told you when I first spoke to you that I would not move and I am not going to.' Then Trickster cut a stick for himself and shot it into the falls and pushed the falls on to the land.[112]

49

Finally he made a stone kettle and said, 'Now for the last time I will eat a meal on earth.[113] There he boiled his food and when it was cooked he put it in a big dish. He had made a stone dish for himself. There he sat and ate. He sat on top of a rock and his seat is visible to the present day. There, too, can be seen the kettle and the dish and even the imprint of his buttocks. Even the imprint of his testicles can be seen there. This meal he ate at a short distance from the place where the Missouri enters the Mississippi. Then he left and went first into the ocean and then up to the heavens.

Under the world where Earthmaker lives, there is another world just like it and of this world, he, Trickster, is in charge. Turtle is in charge of the third world and Hare is in charge of the world in which we live.[114]

II

NOTES TO PAGES 3-53

1. The Winnebago tribal chief cannot under any circumstances go on the warpath.
2. A man's sisters' sons are always asked to bring the food for a feast.
3. It is strictly forbidden for men starting on a warpath to have sexual intercourse.
4. The giver of a feast must always be the last one to leave.
5. This is, of course, correct. The point, however, is that the guests had not finished their meal.
6. At the ceremony given before starting on the warpath, i.e. the warbundle rite, the choicest part of the animal, the head, is given to distinguished warriors.
7. This is to be contrasted with the four male bears served at the third feast.
8. As custom demanded. The listeners now know that the warriors are ready to start out.
9. Really a quiver.
10. This exclamation is to prepare one for the destruction of the arrowbundle.
11. A typical ritualistic understatement. This refers to the well-proved warriors who had taken part in the warbundle rite.
12. Meant ironically, of course, for the chief never goes on the warpath.
13. This ridiculous action is part of his method for discouraging anyone to accompany him.
14. An inconceivably sacrilegious action designed to discourage those who are still accompanying him.
15. He has deprived himself now successively of the means of transportation, of the guarantee of success and of the weapons for defence and offence.
16. This is really in the nature of a narrator's comment. They are, of course, not his younger but his older brothers. However, since he

54

is called Kunu, older brother, that is, strictly speaking, his name. As such he is frequently addressed by animals.

17. This was the approved Winnebago method of capturing buffaloes.
18. Of course he understands very well what they are saying.
19. It is very bad form to attempt to speak to a person when he is busy.
20. It is Trickster, of course, who is hungry.
21. In sarcastic imitation of the solicitude which the father of the children had exhibited.
22. He wished to get rid of his companions so that no one could watch him and identify him. Yet the world of his self-styled younger brothers sees him and mocks him.
23. Enormous because, after all, it is meant for him.
24. It is difficult to determine here whether this is meant to be sarcastic or as an indication of Trickster's complete insensitiveness.
25. 'To get frightened,' implies the beginning of awareness of wrong, a vague conscience.
26. That is, the east. The Winnebago conceive our world to be an oval-shaped island. The east is called the end of the world because Trickster has now been chased completely around it.
27. According to Winnebago cosmological notions our world and all the other three worlds are islands.
28. There is a double sarcasm here. First of all Trickster is always thought of as the antithesis of a warrior; secondly, warriors pursue an enemy. They are not themselves pursued.
29. I do not know the English equivalent of the fish. The same holds for those given in Winnebago further on.
30. Comment of the narrator.
31. A method used only for catching small fish in shallow water.
32. That is, he was not getting any fish at all but simply boiling the water through which the fish had been swimming.
33. When he finally succeeds in catching a fish, it is a dead one. Even this, however, he cannot enjoy for he is now filled to his utmost capacity with water. Since it is not customary to eat fish that have already died in the water, the idea of burying a dead fish to save it for a future meal is doubly absurd.
34. This indicates the beginning of his awareness of the nature of what he is doing. On pp. 8 and 10 the animals call him Trickster. Now he himself applies it to his actions.

35. The ridiculous answer Trickster gives is possibly meant either as a take-off on the prevailing Winnebago theory that songs appear to one in dreams or that people own them and can disgorge them. The whole episode is clearly a travesty on festal dancing and singing.

36. Sarcastic reference to a warrior's shout at the moment of victory.

37. The two approved methods for roasting and boiling animals.

38. Throughout he endows the various parts of his body, but more particularly his anus and his penis, with independent existence.

39. He, of course, knows very well what has happened.

40. He is now publicly admitting that he knows what has happened and is preparing the listeners for the punishment he is going to mete out to his anus.

41. Cf. in connection with this remark, the interesting justification of Trickster by a Winnebago, p. 147.

42. This is one of the few explanatory motifs in the Trickster cycle. Cf., however, episodes 34 and 46.

43. At the feasts given by the two chiefs of the tribe, the chief of the Thunderbird clan—he is likewise the tribal chief—and the chief of the Bear clan, carry their tokens of office, two long crook-shaped staffs, two apiece, with feathers attached to them. In spite of the fact that chiefs are mentioned he is clearly referring to the great peace feast given by the tribal chief—and this makes this whole incident doubly scurrilous and blasphemous.

44. Trickster is frequently called First-born with no other designation.

45. He had difficulty in rising from the ground on account of his enormous size and weight.

46. There is no intimation that Trickster intended to play a trick on the turkey-buzzard, but tricks are always to be expected of him.

47. This is a take-off on a racoon hunt with the racoon telling the hunters where he is.

48. It is considered a most shameless thing for women to undress in public.

49. That is, a sacred place where one can feel secure.

50. That is, fox.

51. English equivalent not clear, possibly a nit.

52. This is the stereotyped description of a beautiful place.

53. Women never went visiting alone. This and the whole of the next paragraph is a parody on the conventional type of folktale which always has an old woman living at the end of the village.

54. She takes upon herself the function of the public crier, a person, always of considerable social standing and one which she, of course, does not possess.

55. The opposite, of course, of what is the proper course.

56. Nothing could possibly be so ridiculous as these words of the chief. The children of a chief held a very high social position and were not married to strangers.

57. The proper food for a 'bridal' meal.

58. It is completely against Winnebago etiquette to eat in this fashion. This is only permitted in the so-called 'fast-eating' contest at the warbundle ceremonies.

59. It is not usual for Winnebago children to cry. Continuous crying implied something serious and had to be interpreted.

60. Definitely meant to be ironical.

61. Teasing and the playing of practical jokes on one another is quite common between sisters-in-law.

62. Quite the reverse, of course, of the proper behaviour. It is the boy who should start travelling.

63. I.e. taking on responsibility.

64. A parody on the habit of warriors to publicly announce every exploit they perform.

65. An absolutely ridiculous request. First of all, the lodge serves as protection in case of sudden attack and, secondly, it would take some time to pull down a lodge.

66. People are not supposed to run away from their village when it is attacked and certainly not in mere anticipation of an attack.

67. The term 'old man', instead of First-born, is occasionally applied to Trickster.

68. In which he carried his penis.

69. This episode is possibly of European origin.

70. In a number of Winnebago folktales, a red sky is the stereotype symbol for death. This is what it should have meant to the foolish women for their children are about to be killed.

71. This is a Winnebago war-custom which, however, they ascribe to their enemies.

72. Children are never slapped among the Winnebago.

73. In mock sign of mourning. The women, of course, should have blackened their faces.

74. The humour here, from the Winnebago viewpoint, is that he gives the wolves all this precise information as though they could not find it out for themselves.

75. The point is that he should have become angry and split it before, since, as we have seen, even so slight an annoyance as the squeaking of the branches interfered with his eating.

76. I.e. some social dance was taking place. War-whoops are not given at such a dance, but people make as much noise as they do when they give war-whoops.

77. This is a stereotyped phrase for describing the pleasure experienced from hearing dance songs. The narrator, Blowsnake, uses it often.

78. Another stereotyped phrase. Blowsnake was a well-known dancer and singer and always loves to describe in detail the pleasure experienced on such occasions.

79. The point is that dancers at a social ceremony are like flies in the skull of a dead animal.

80. This is the narrator's sarcastic comment to indicate first, that although Trickster thought he could do everything, he could not do so slight a thing as enter the orifice of an elk's skull and, secondly, to point a moral: Large people should not try to get into small holes.

81. He is impersonating an elk spirit. This is indicated by the phrase 'fear-inspiring object'.

82. So spirits frequently speak when they are bestowing their powers upon human beings.

83. He is impersonating a waterspirit. However, elk are supposed to come from the waters according to Winnebago mythology.

84. This is the technical term for the receptacle in which magical powers, particularly those obtained from waterspirits, are kept.

85. The approved offerings for elk-spirits.

86. According to the theory of the ordinary man, after offerings have once been made, the blessings follow automatically. This is not the priest's theory.

87. This is a parody on the myth explaining how the Thunderbird clan obtained the chieftainship of the tribe. In that myth a member of the Thunderbird clan, representing the upper phratry, races with a member of the Bear clan, representing the lower phratry,

for the chieftainship. To dish out the food implies that you are the host and etiquette demands that the host at a feast eats last.

88. A pot of food is substituted for the regular goal-post.

89. In short, a man whose mind is always centred on food is likely to get just this, a piece of dung.

90. This pretended ignorance on the part of Trickster of something known and visible to all is a humorous motif occurring throughout this cycle.

91. We have here the first intimation that the penis and scrotum are now to be given their normal position and the penis to receive its normal size.

92. The special creation of an animal to perform a particular act is not an old Winnebago concept.

93. A stereotyped compliment implying that the one addressed can overcome all obstacles.

94. There is, of course, no such game.

95. The narrator's device for introducing the next episode, that of the bungling host, which really belongs almost anywhere in the cycle.

96. It is proper etiquette to say this just as it would be inconceivably bad manners for a guest to offer to bring food to the place where he is invited. The humour of the situation here is, of course, that both persons know all the circumstances and motives involved.

97. Bears are always associated with fat.

98. Dung, of course, had very unpleasant associations for Trickster.

99. This is, of course, something that he cannot imitate without help.

100. A rocky hill is the stereotyped description for a sacred hill.

101. The phrase 'our uncle has arrived', taken from this episode, was used by the Winnebago with the meaning, 'we're going to have good food today'.

102. In every one of the four incidents the guests leave before the food is cooked. This is very bad manners and is obviously meant to indicate how much they despise Trickster and his subterfuges.

103. I have no other reference to the Winnebago ever having had such a thing as deer-sausage.

104. Of course his desire is to return home in order to show all the food he has obtained.

105. Trickster is never pictured as malicious but always as good-natured and entertaining.

106. He recognizes him as mink and thoughts of revenge immediately rise up in his mind.
107. Wilderness here simply means the area outside of the village proper. This whole episode is of European origin.
108. This is a phrase used only in connection with the granting of benefits (blessings) to fasters by the spirits.
109. Another of the very few explanatory motifs to be found in this cycle.
110. The reference is, of course, to the fact that, according to the Origin Myth of the Medicine Rite, Trickster was created to destroy the evil spirits who were molesting man.
111. In his capacity as a culture-hero. There is no other reference in any other myth to his performing such actions.
112. This is, of course, meant half humorously.
113. I suspect that this last scene really represents an element borrowed from the *Twin Cycle*.
114. The narrator has left out the name of the spirit in charge of the second world. He is Bladder.

Part Two

———

SUPPLEMENTARY
TRICKSTER MYTHS

I

THE WINNEBAGO HARE CYCLE

1

ONCE an old woman lived together with her young daughter. The latter was a virgin and she tended the fires for her mother. One day the young girl became pregnant although she was not married and although she had not had sexual intercourse with anyone. She finally gave birth to a child, a boy, after only seven month's pregnancy. Soon after that she died,[1] leaving the child to be taken care of by his grandmother. So the grandmother raised him. When he became big enough he played outside the lodge and was always intractable and mischievous. Finally he began playing at some distance from the lodge. Day after day he did this, going farther and farther away from his home every time.

2

One day, the child, Hare, went farther than usual and suddenly came upon a being walking on two legs. It seemed so weak that he expected it to fall over at any moment.[2] Hare ran ahead of it and waited. When it came near he blew at it, thinking he could thus blow it over but he did not succeed. Again and again he blew at it, in each case without avail. The fourth time he did it, the being walking on two legs became aware of something white (namely the hare) and shot at it with an arrow. Hare cried out in pain as he was hit and ran home to his grandmother. She pulled the arrow out of him and said, 'It must have been one of your uncles[3] and you must have been annoying him for otherwise he would not have shot at you.' 'What great people my uncles must be,' said Hare, 'for he shot me when I was quite some distance away from him.' 'Grandson, that is the weapon these people use for killing game,' she said. Hare then seized the arrow and took great care of it.

63

3

The next morning he took the arrow and went out to the woods. There he came upon an elk. He put the arrow in the fork of a tree in line with the elk and said, 'Arrow, go!' Then he pushed it but it would not go. He flattered it and tried again to direct it but it would not go. So he went home and spoke thus to his grandmother: 'Grandmother, the arrow would not obey me and so I could not kill an elk. I pleaded with it repeatedly but still it would not go.' Then his grandmother said, 'My grandson, that is not the way hunters act. They send the arrow off by means of an object they call a bow.' 'Make me one, grandmother,' said Hare. Thereupon the old woman answered, 'Grandson, the human beings make bows out of a substance called the hickory tree. The hickory tree is a tree with smooth bark. If you will go and get some of it for me I will make a bow for you.' 'There are many such trees right around here, grandmother,' said Hare, and ran out to fetch some. He came back soon with some poplar twigs. 'This is not the right kind, this is what we call poplar,' said the old woman. Then he went out again and brought some hickory twigs[4] and with these she made a bow. Then she told him the kind of wood to use for arrows. In order to get these he had to go out four times before he brought the right ones.

After she had made some arrows for him she sent him out to get some turkey-feathers, telling him what they were like. He went out and caught a turkey alive and when he brought it home he asked her what he was to use with which to kill it. She answered, 'a frog-tree'. Then he went in search of a frog-tree. But he only succeeded in obtaining one after four attempts. The old woman then told him that she would have to have some glue and that he could get some from the vertebrae of a long fish, the sturgeon. After four attempts he got some. Then the old woman completed making the arrows for him. He immediately took them and began shooting holes into the lodge.[5]

4

One day he went out to get some feathers, on the way he had to climb a high hill. When he reached the top he shouted. 'What a nice toy bird!' But then, after a while, from above there came a roaring sound and suddenly a bird swooped down upon him and carried him away, upwards. Be it remembered that he was in the form of a white hare.[6] The bird carried him away upwards to a place where two eagles had their nests. In this nest were four little eagles who looked very pretty. Whenever the young eagles spread out their tail-feathers he noticed they were very white.

Then he said to them, 'When do your parents come home?' 'Not until night,' they answered. Thereupon he killed them, took their feathers and skinned one of them. Then he put the skin of the one he had killed over himself and started to fly down toward the earth. 'What a fine sensation,' he said to himself as he came flying down in a circle just as the eagles do. Finally he reached the earth.

When he got near his lodge he put his feathers in the hollow of a tree and went home. 'Grandmother,' he said, 'I have obtained some fine feathers but I left them in the hollow of a tree outside. I wish you would go and get them for me.' So she went out in search of them. But when she got there and peeped in, a streak of lightning shot forth from the feathers and she ran back and said, 'Grandson, I could not get them for you. I was afraid of them.' He told her to go again but, again, she came back without them and it was only after the fourth attempt that, with eyes closed, she seized them and brought them back to him. They were very beautiful and she asked for one but he refused.[7] After that he made his own arrows.

5

One day Hare said, 'Grandmother, where will I be able to get arrow-points?' 'Grandson,' she answered, 'from your grandfather. He does not live far from here. Go first and ask him for some tobacco. Take this tobacco to your other grandfather who does not live far from him and then ask him for some arrow-points. He will unquestionably give you a few.' So he went over to his first grandfather, singing the following song as he approached him:

'Grandmother sent me for some tobacco; that is why I have come!'

Thus he sang, coming nearer and nearer to his grandfather each time. He had made himself very tall when he started. Then, suddenly, he heard a mighty noise and he saw an old man appear, very much frightened. 'What is this? As long as I have lived here I have never seen so mighty a spirit as you. Whatever spirit you are, I give you a pipeful of tobacco.'

But Hare did not accept it and sang again:

'Grandmother sent me for some tobacco, that is why I have come!'

'Hiyi!' Hare shouted and jumped up in the air and landed a little closer to the old man. The latter now offered him two pipefuls of tobacco but Hare refused these likewise and came still closer. Then he offered him three pipefuls of tobacco but again he refused them and came closer and closer. Then, as Hare approached him the fourth time, he offered him four pipefuls of tobacco. Then Hare cried, 'Hiyi! Hiyi' and chased the old man all over the earth. As he ran, he scattered his tobacco all over the ground. Finally Hare caught up with him and killed him. He turned out to be a huge grasshopper.

Then Hare took some tobacco and went home with it. 'Grandmother,' he said, 'my grandfather would not, at first, give me any tobacco.' 'That is just like him! He is a bad-natured fellow,' the old woman replied. 'Don't worry about that, grandmother, because I made myself very large before I left and when I got to him I took my club and scattered that old man all over the earth.' 'Oh, you ugly big-eyed creature,[8] you must have killed my brother,' she shouted. 'Well, you evil old woman, I will get my club and scatter your over the earth too.' 'Oh, grandson, I meant that only as a joke. I am really very glad you killed him because he was witholding from your uncles the tobacco belonging to them and you were right in killing him.'

6

Shortly after this Hare went to Flint and approached him in the same way as he had approached the first old man. He transformed himself into a tall being and sang as he came near the lodge of Flint. At the end of his song he would always exclaim, 'Hiyi! Hiyi!'

When he finished the song for the first time, Flint said: 'Whatever spirit you are, I give you an arrow-point from my wrist, one that I value very much.' The second time Flint said, 'Whatever spirit you are, I give you a flint from my ankle, one that I value very much.' The flints from his wrist and ankles were actually his poor ones.

Finally after Hare had sung for the fourth time, he jumped toward him and chased him all over the earth, clubbing him and forcing him to scatter his flint arrow-points all over the earth.[9] Then he killed him. Thereupon he picked up some of the flint arrow-points that he found. The best ones were blue.[10] Those that came from his stomach were white, while still others were red and black.

With these he returned to his grandmother and said, 'Grandmother, for a long time my grandfather refused to give me any arrow-points.' 'Yes, grandson, that is his nature; he is a cross man.' 'Don't worry about that grandmother; don't mind his crossness for I made myself large and, using my club, I scattered his body all over the earth.' 'Oh, you ugly, big-eyed, big-eared creature, I hope you did not kill my brother,' said the old woman. 'You evil old woman,' said he, 'I'll go after my club and scatter you all over the earth too.' 'Grandson, I only said that in fun. Actually I am glad. You have really helped your uncles, for my brother had been keeping these flint arrow-points from them.' Then Hare made some arrows for himself. They looked most fear-inspiring. Whenever he pressed one very tightly the lodge would be filled with lightning.

7

The next morning he went out hunting again and, on the way, came across an animal, a straight-horned elk. He shot it and told it to fall down dead on the outskirts of Sharp-elbow's[11] village. Then Hare came home. When he got home he told his grandmother than he had shot an elk in the belly and that he would go and trail it in the morning.

The next morning he took up the trail and finally came to the place where he had ordered it to fall dead. To his surprise it had been dressed and nothing remained of it except the entrails. So he continued on to the village. There, on the outskirts, lived an old woman.[12] Her lodge he entered. 'Grandmother,' he said, 'yesterday I wounded an elk and my coming here is for the purpose of finding it.' 'Grandson, this is what happened. A great number of warriors were gathered here. In fact they have just left. When they were here a wounded elk with an arrow in it came by and fell dead just outside the lodge. All of them tried to pull it out. I, too, went over but you might know that a person like myself would hardly get permission from those people to try to pull it out. So all I could obtain was a little blood. From that blood I am now making some soup.' Thus she spoke.

'Grandmother, who pulled out my arrow?' inquired Hare. 'Grandson, the chief, Sharp-elbow, pulled it out.' 'That arrow is mine. It is a fear-inspiring thing. I don't suppose you have any such arrows around here?' 'Indeed it was fearful. However, let me see one of your arrows,' said the old woman. So he took one out. As he did so the entire lodge became filled with lightning.[13] 'Oh, grandson, put your arrow back in its quiver,' she said. 'Now I know,' she added, 'that the arrow which was pulled out was yours.' 'Grandson,' so she continued, 'I have made some broth from the blood of the elk and here is a little for you.' After she had handed him a bowl of soup, she said, 'You can warm your arrow-quiver with it.' 'Very well,' said Hare, and was about to pour it into his arrow-quiver[14] when the old woman stopped him and said, 'Grandson, I did not mean that. I meant that you can warm up your ribs with it.' So he took it up again and was about to draw up his clothes and pour it upon his ribs. But, again she stopped him, and it was only at the fourth time that he finally did what she meant and drank it.

'Now, grandmother, let my friend go after my arrow.' 'Oh, grandson, he will be killed,' she answered. 'I thought you said he was a chief? How, therefore, can he fight and be killed?'[15] Then turning to the young man in question he said, 'Young man, go after my arrow.' Now the young man was a grandson of the old woman and yet here he was calling him friend![16]

The friend started out and when he came to the village of Sharp-elbow, he said, 'My friend wants his arrow.' But the chief did not so much as answer him and so he went back without it. 'Go again,' said Hare. Three times he went back. At the fourth time Sharp-elbow said, 'There it is, take it!' The friend went forward and tried to reach it but the chief, Sharp-elbow, using his elbows, thereupon tore him open and said to his attendants, 'Hang him up to dry. I will soon make a nice meal of him.'

Someone ran over to the old woman and told her that her son had been killed by Sharp-elbow. Then Hare, who was present, turned to the old woman and said, 'I thought you told me your grandson was a chief and yet this man says he has been killed. However, I will now go over and see this chief Sharp-elbow myself. Have you a whetstone, grandmother?' 'Here is one,' she said. Taking it, he went over to Sharp-elbow's village and when he got there he found the chief in a long lodge full of the best-looking women, all of them his wives.[17] 'Say,' said Hare, 'I understand my arrow is here. I sent for it before but I hear that you are killing people on account of it, killing them because they ask for it. So, therefore, I thought I would come for it myself.'

The arrow was stuck between the lodge wall and the poles, just above where Sharp-elbow was lying. 'There it is,' said the latter. 'You can get it.' Then Hare put the whetstone between himself and the chief and bent forward to reach it. As he did so Sharp-elbow jabbed him with his elbow but he struck the whetstone and broke his elbow. 'Well,' said Hare, 'if you have any more jabs just come on with them.' 'All right,' said Sharp-elbow and jabbed him with his other elbow. But he broke that too so then he used his knees and broke those. 'Well!' said Hare, 'now I will show you how to kill people.' So he shot him, the arrow going clear through him. Then Hare took his friend down from where he had been hung and throwing the body aside said, 'What makes you go to sleep here? I sent you for my arrow, not for you to go to sleep.'[18] Immediately his friend came to life again and went home. Hare then took his arrow down and told the people to burn up all of Sharp-elbow's children and all of his wives who were pregnant.[19] This they did. Then the people said to Hare, 'We would like to go over to the place where you live and take care of the village for you.'[20] But Hare answered, 'No. You can have your old chief back again and live as you used to for I have killed the one who was abusing you.' So the people thanked him and Hare returned home.

When he got home he said to his grandmother, 'Listen, grandmother, I went to trail my elk, but Sharp-elbow's people had already taken it when I reached his lodge. What a great man Sharp-elbow is!' 'Yes,' said his grandmother, 'Sharp-elbow is one of the great spirits.'[21] 'Oh,' said Hare, 'I think you make too much of him, for I took grandmother's whetstone and let him break his elbows on it and then I killed him and had him burnt up.' 'Oh, you big-eyed, big-eared, big-footed creature, you have killed my brother,' she exclaimed. 'Oh, you evil old woman, I will shoot you and burn you up also,' he answered. 'Ah, grandson, I only said that in fun. I am really glad, for my brother had been abusing your uncles and aunts and you did a good thing in killing him.'

8

One day, shortly after this, Hare said, 'Grandmother I am going over to my grandfather, the bear, to pay him a visit.' 'It is good, my dear grandson,' said the old woman, 'you may go and he will be glad to see you.' 'Grandmother, I will take a sack of acorns for him.' 'All right, you may do so.' So Hare went off. When he got there he placed the sack of acorns outside of the lodge and went in. 'Oh, my dear grandson,' exclaimed the bear, 'so you have come at last!' 'Yes, I have come,' said Hare, 'and I have brought you a sack of acorns which I have left outside.' After a while, Bear walked out and came back and asked, 'Grandson, where is the sack?' 'Why, I left it right outside,' said Hare. After the bear had come back for the fourth time Hare went out to show him but it was nowhere to be found. So he said, 'Grandfather, you have eaten it up already.' 'Grandson, I found a half of an acorn out here and I took it up with my left hand and ate it. Is that what you meant? You said that you had brought a sack full of acorns and it is for that I have been looking,' said the bear. 'Yes, that is what I meant,' said Hare, 'and it was a sack full.'

The Bear spoke to Hare saying, 'Grandson, I don't suppose you have had your meal yet.' So he put a kettle full of fat to boil and soon Hare had a big meal.

After the meal Hare suddenly said, 'Grandfather, you have been living here a long time, have you not?' 'Yes, grandson, I have been living here for a long time.' 'Don't you ever get frightened?' 'No, grandson, I am not afraid of anything.'[22] Then, after a pause, Hare said again, 'Grandfather, do you know that the country is full of wars?' 'Yes, indeed, grandson, but I am not afraid of it.' 'Well, grandfather,' said Hare, 'I feel rather uneasy about it and that is why I am talking in this way.' Then Hare went out and scattered dung all around the lodge, stuck feathers in the dung and told the piles of dung to give the war-whoop early in the morning. Thereupon he went back and said, 'Grand-father, aren't you really afraid of this?' and he took out one of his arrows and showed it to him. 'No,' said he. Then he took out another, but it was only when he took out the fourth one that the old man said, 'Grandson, put that away quickly for of that one I am afraid.'

As soon as night came they went to bed. During the night the old man had a nightmare and yelled in his sleep, so Hare called to him, 'Grandfather, wake up, you are having a nightmare!' The old man woke up immediately and said, 'Grandson, I had a night-mare. I dreamt that I was shot under the arm with an arrow like the one that you showed me.' 'Now, there you are, grandfather. I told you that I have been feeling uneasy ever since I came here this evening.'

Early in the morning the war-whoop was given outside. It was so loud that it seemed as if the enemy were right upon them. 'Oh!' said Hare and rushed outside and waited at the door for the old man to come out. When finally he did come Hare took aim and shot him under the arm, the arrow going clear through him.

Then Hare went home and said, 'Grandmother, what a great man my grandfather is!' 'Yes,' said she, 'he is one of the great spirits.' 'Oh, I wouldn't praise him too much. This is what I did to him.' And he went through the motions of shooting. 'Oh, you big-eyed, big-eared, big-footed creature, you must have killed my brother,' she exclaimed. 'Well, you evil old woman, I will wait for you outside and shoot you under the arm just as I did him,' said Hare. 'Oh, I only said that in fun. Actually I am glad, for now we shall have plenty of fat to eat,' she said.[23]

9

They went over to pack the bear home. They skinned him and cut him into pieces. After this was done Hare said, 'Grand-mother, will you carry the head?' 'No,' said the old woman, 'I am not a man that I should be carrying heads.[24] He who does the killing is the one to carry the head.' 'Well, grandmother, will you carry the hind-end then?' 'How could I carry a bear's hind-end with such a back as I have?'[25] 'Well, grandmother, will you carry the ribs then?' 'If I were to do that I am sure my ribs would grow long.'[26] Thereupon she began to sing:

> 'Grandson, that I will pack;
> Grandson, that I will pack.'

Then she began to dance. However, he let her pack the hind-end[27] and she started off right away. He followed her but after a short time she turned off the road. Then he began to think and wonder what grandmother was up to by turning off the road.

Now the old woman had a deer-skin with her which she took up to the top of a hill and upon which she slid down, pack and all. When at last she got home she told her grandson that she had lost her way and had finally turned up in a village where they had used her pack for a ball. That is why it was dirty she explained. Continuing, she said that one of Hare's friends, who happened to be there, finally got the pack back for her, whereupon she came home. Then Hare asked, 'Grandmother, was it my friend *Gicoknuxgiga*?' 'Yes, yes, grandson, he is the one I mean.' Now there really was no such person. Hare had merely invented the name to see what she would say and to find out what she had been doing all the time. Suddenly Hare said, 'Grandmother, you must cook for yourself and I will do the same.'[28] So they each cooked for themselves and each had plenty of fat to eat.

10

'Grandmother,' said Hare one day, 'I am going over to visit my uncles.' 'You may go,' said she. So he left. On the way he came to a large river and he shouted, 'Crabs, come here!' Immediately a large number of crabs came over to him. He caught a large one and said, 'Lend me your boat!' Then he skinned the crab and, turning up its tail for a sail, exclaimed, 'Blow me across!' Then the wind changed and blew him across the river. So he sailed across in the shell of a crab, singing as he proceeded.

Finally he got to the other side and, pulling his boat to one side, went on. Soon he came to a lodge and this he entered. Those within said, 'Haho! our grandson has come.' Those within were people without bodies; they consisted only of heads. All in turn stopped to greet him and said, 'Our grandson must indeed be

72

hungry.' So they boiled something for him to eat. They boiled
bear ribs with corn. This he ate and he thought it delicious, and
he ate a great deal of it. In eating he used a knife that they
handed him. He would first bite a piece of meat and then cut it
off. Suddenly, accidently, he cut a slit in his nose. Blowing his
nose, he yelled with pain.[29] 'Our grandson has cut himself. Give
him another knife.' He was very much pleased with the new
knife they gave him and did not seem to mind the fact that he had
cut himself.

Soon Hare went home. When he got home his grandmother
said, 'Oh, my grandson has disfigured himself while visiting.'
Ever since that time, even to the present day, whenever anyone
goes visiting his uncles, they say he is going somewhere to slit his
nose.

II

One day Hare went to visit his uncles or, as they say, to slit his
nose. He came to another long lodge full of the same kind of
people as before, that is, people without bodies. He went in and
again they said, 'Oh, our grandson must be hungry. Let us boil
something for him.' This they did and he ate large quantities of
food again.

When he was finished, the heads said, 'Let us eat our grandson.
He looks so good to eat.'[30] So they closed the doors and blocked
all other possible places of exit. However, he spied a little opening somewhere and ran out there. One of the heads said, 'He has
gone. Run after him!' So they all pursued him. One in particular
followed behind the rest, shouting, 'Catch him! Catch him!'
Finally Hare got tired so he ran up a tree. But the head behind
came up and said, 'Gnaw the tree down!' So all encircled the tree
and began to gnaw it down. But Hare got away again. 'Oh, he has
got away again!' So they spurred one another on again and
shouted, 'Chase him!' They chased him and he ran up a tree
again. Again they gnawed it down and again he ran away. Now,
for the fourth time, he went up a tree and again they began to
gnaw at it. Suddenly one of them said, 'Ah, it is bitter! It is
bitter!' and began to spit. But another one spurring the others on
to continue, said, 'Wait till he comes down.' So they stopped and
waited till he would have to come down. Finally Hare got tired

of staying there and pondered to himself, 'What shall I do now?'
Then he began to sing:

> 'Bodiless heads, I want to go by,
> Go to sleep! Go to sleep!'

And so they said to one another, 'Our grandson says sleep, so let
us sleep.' Thus they spoke but they only feigned sleep. Finally,
however, after he had sung the song four times, they actually
went to sleep. Then he came down very quietly. However, when
he reached the ground he made a noise. Immediately he rushed
away. The heads woke up and shouted, 'Our grandson has gone!'
and gave pursuit. Hare kept running until he came to a creek over
which he jumped. Then the pursuers yelled, 'He has jumped
across!' and the last one exclaimed, 'Jump across too!' So all
tried. But they failed and fell into the creek and were drowned.
Hare thereupon chased the dead heads down the stream, built a
fire and threw them in. Then he took some stones, ground their
remains very finely and threw them back into the creek saying,
'You tried to abuse people. From now on the people will call you
fast-fish and when they step into the water you will nibble at
their ankles.'[31]

Then he went home to his grandmother. She scolded him again,
as on former occasions and said that the heads were her brothers.
But he told her that he would make fast-fish of her and, thereupon, as always, she said that she was really glad that he killed
them because they were abusing his uncles and aunts and that he
had done a good thing.[32]

12

One day as Hare was wandering about in his usual fashion he
heard something moving, so he went to see what it was. It turned
out to be a tall man with a big cane and very small about the
waist.[33] Hare thought to himself, 'How is it he does not break
in two?' So he blew upon him and tried to break him in two.
After each attempt—he tried three times and failed—he would
run ahead and wait for him and blow upon him again. The fourth
time the tall being noticed a small white object sitting on the
ground, so he placed his cane upon it and smashed it flat.

As Hare did not come home for some time, his grandmother

began to worry and went to look for him, saying to herself, 'That grandson of mine must be up to one of his foolish tricks again.' Finally she came to where the tall being was living and said, 'Brother, my little grandson is missing and I am looking for him. He is full of mischief so I thought you might, without intending it, have harmed him in some way. That is why I have come to see you.' Then she went over to the place where he had placed his cane and she found him. 'Oh, you big-eyed, big-eared, big-footed, slit-nosed, evil creature, get up and come away from here,' and she took him by the arm and lifted him up.[34] 'Grandmother,' replied Hare, 'I was sitting far away from this being yet he could do this to me. What a great man grandfather must be!'

The next morning Hare started for the home of his grandfather but this time he made himself very tall, even taller than the tall being itself. He also took a cane with him. Then he went looking around for him. The cane that he took along was a big cedar tree which he had pulled up by the roots. Finally, as he came near the tall being, that one was singing:

'Who is the equal of me? Who is the equal of me?'

Then Hare likewise began to sing the same song. The big being saw him and exclaimed, 'Well, well! In all my life I have never met anyone equal to me.[35] Where did you come from?' he asked. Then Hare asked the same question. 'Well,' said the other, 'come we will walk together.' So they walked on together and as they were going, Hare placed his cane on the tall being and smashed him to pieces. And the tall being turned out to be a large ant. Then Hare spoke, 'You were trying to abuse human beings and, for that reason, you will henceforth remain down there close to the earth and the people will tramp upon you.'

13

Then Hare proceeded on until he came to a nice road. 'Now, what kind of a being constructed this road?' he mused. 'Whoever it was I am going to catch him,' he thought to himself. So he took some nettle-weeds and made a trap. The next morning he went to inspect it but whoever it was who was walking along this road had broken the trap. So he made another trap, this time of sinew strings and, in the morning, he went over to inspect it but again the trap was broken. So, again, he made some rope, this time out of basswood bark and set up another trap. But that which he was trying to trap broke away again. Finally, he went to his grandmother and said, 'Grandmother, will you make me a very strong rope?' She agreed and took some of her hair and braided it. With this he made another trap. The next morning he heard someone singing:

'Hare, come and untie me; Hare come untie me!
Hare, what will the people do?
Hare, come and untie me! Hare, come and untie me!'

'So you are up to your tricks again, you big-eyed, big-eared, big-footed, slit-nosed, evil object,' exclaimed his grandmother and taking a wooden poker she hit him with it.[36] Hare cried out in pain, 'Ouch! Ouch!' and ran away in the direction of the singing. When he got near he saw something shining. He tried in vain to untie it so he went home, borrowed a knife from his grandmother, and ran over to the object he had captured. When he got there he closed his eyes and, running up as far as he could, cut it loose. However, his buttocks got thoroughly scorched and sore for what he had trapped was the sun. And thus he was scorched by the sun.[37]

14

One day as he was walking along in his accustomed way, he saw an object on which there appeared many people. They were riding on top of it and crying as they rode along. 'I wonder what they are doing?' he mused. So he got on and rode with them but they said to him, 'You had better get off for we are not having any fun here.' 'Why,' answered Hare, 'it is fun to sit still and yet be moving.' Just then he was engulfed by something and found himself in an enclosure from which he could not get out. The old woman, thinking something was wrong, went over to the being on which they had been riding and asked, 'Brother, my little grandson is lost, so I came over here to look for him.' So he vomited Hare up for her and she brought him home. 'Grandmother,' Hare was saying as he went home with her, 'I was far away when this being engulfed me.'

The next morning Hare went out and, gathering some flint

arrow-points, covered himself with them. Then he went on top of a hill and sang:

'You who can lap them in;
You of whom it is said, you lap them in;
Lap me in! Lap me in!'

Thus he sang. Then this being came at him as fast as a flame shoots upward.[38] But Hare jumped aside as he attempted to lap him in and he missed him. Then when this being came back again, Hare sang the same song again. This being was loaded with people. As he was sitting there and singing, the being spoke, 'I thought I lapped you in once.' He tried again to lap him in but always missed him. Three times he missed him. The fourth time, however, Hare allowed himself to be lapped in voluntarily.

Inside he found many people who were crying. 'What are you crying about? Is it not fun to ride in a carrier like this?' 'Hare,' they answered, 'we are all going to die, that is why we are crying.' Then Hare said, 'Don't cry. We are not going to die and, besides, it is such fun to ride in a carrier like this. So why are you crying?' Then they were swallowed again.[39] Inside there were many people, some dead and some dying; some were still strong and some were very weak. Then Hare began to play inside this being and it said, 'I don't feel quite well. I guess I must have swallowed something evil that I ought to vomit up again.' So he vomited and Hare was thrown up but he was immediately washed back and swallowed again. Four times he was vomited up. Only after he had been washed back and swallowed for the fourth time did Hare speak to the people. Then he said, 'If any of you can find something in my head you will live.' So they looked all over his head. Finally one of them said, 'We have found this,' and handed him pieces of flint. 'Good, you will live,' said Hare. Then he made a large arrow-point and said, 'There is plenty of fat in here,' and began cutting out fat from the insides of the object and eating it. The object began to groan and Hare kept right on until he got to the place where its heart was throbbing. This he cut to pieces and then cut a hole through the side of the being and led the people out. There they found a long lodge full of women that the being had forcibly taken from the people and married.[40] They killed all the children and all the women that were pregnant and burnt them up.

Thereupon Hare went home and told his grandmother about it. The old woman scolded him and he threatened her but, at the end, as usual, she thanked him, saying that she had only been joking and that Hare had really saved the lives of his uncles and his aunts.

15

One day Hare said, 'Grandmother, I am going to the place where one can get rope-grass.' The old woman said, 'All right, grandson, you may go.' So he started out. Soon he came to a big ravine along which he walked for some distance. He knew that someone was there in front of him so he sang as he walked along:

'If one of my uncles is at the rope-grass place,
I will fight with him.'[41]

The one that was there heard and inquired, 'Hare, what did you say?' So the Hare repeated, 'I said that if there is anyone at the place where rope-grass is collected, I will play with him.' 'No, Hare, that is not what you said,' that being answered. 'You said you would fight with him. 'No,' said the other, 'you said "I will fight with him," you big-eyed, big-eared, big-footed creature!' 'No,' continued Hare, 'I did not say that. I said I would play with you, you homely bob-tailed, ring-eyed object,' replied Hare and started to run. 'Oh, Hare, you will die for this!' exclaimed the other and ran in pursuit of him. Whenever he was about to overtake him, Hare would jump aside and thus escape. Finally when Hare was tired out he came to a hole in the ground and into this he escaped. 'Hare you have saved yourself,' the being told him. Shortly after, however, the being said to Hare, 'Hare, how do objects get out when, like you, they crawl into a hole?'[42] 'Well,' answered Hare, 'they get some of grandmother's reed-matting and smoke me out with it. Then I always come out.' 'Good,' said the other, 'you stay right here and don't go out for I wish to go and get some of this matting.' 'Certainly,' said Hare, 'where could I go to? I will remain here.' So the other one went away and as soon as he went away Hare also left. Then he got four acorns from an oak tree and put them in the hole. To one of them he said, 'If this being talks to you, you must answer.' Then he taught it what to say and, taking a forked stick, hid himself near by.

Finally the being came back and asked, 'Hare, are you still in there?' 'Yes,' came the answer. 'Where else could I go? I am still here for you told me to remain here.' One of the acorns was speaking. Then the being stuffed the hole with the matting, lit it and stood there waiting for Hare to come out. It began to burn inside and soon one of the acorns burst, making a loud report. 'There,' said the being, waiting, 'one of Hare's eyes has burst.' After a while there was another report and he said, 'There goes the other eye.' Then there was another report from within and he said, 'Aha, there goes one of Hare's testicles.' When he heard a fourth report he said, 'There goes the other testicle.' Now Hare, taking his forked stick and sneaking up behind him, placed the fork over his neck, pushed this being into the fire and burnt it to death. Hare, taking some basswood bark, then tied its remains to the stick and took them home.

16

When he got home he said, 'Grandmother, we are going to have some soup for I have brought a wildcat with me that I killed. 'Ah, grandson, I am glad of it.' So they both dressed it and singed it nicely. Suddenly Hare took some blood and threw it at his grandmother's legs, saying to her at the same time, 'Grandmother, you are having your menses! You are going to kill my war-weapons!'[43] Thus he shouted. So she looked down and the blood was flowing down her legs. 'Oh, dear! I must have killed my grandson's war-weapons,' she said, and she went out immediately. After she had gone some distance away she shouted, 'Grandson, where shall I make my lodge?' and he shouted back, 'A little farther back still. There you may make your lodge.' Instead of going farther away, however, she really came nearer to the lodge and said in a low voice, 'Where?' and he shouted back, 'A little farther still.' The fourth time she came right up to the lodge and said almost in a whisper, 'Where?' 'Just where you are,' he said. So there she made her lodge. Then Hare said, 'Grandmother, we were just about to have some meat but as it is impossible for you in your present condition to eat any I will not eat any of it either and instead give a feast with it.'[44]

Then he went outside and shouted, 'Come, you are all invited to a feast!' After a while he pretended that someone had come and began talking but, of course, he was only feigning. Actually he changed his voice so that he could fool his grandmother and thus be able to eat the food alone. When the meat was cooked he made a long festal speech and ate up everything alone. 'Grandmother,' he said afterwards, 'a large number of people came to the feast and among them was an old man who said that he was coming over to court you. I told him he might do it. Now I hope you will let him for we are all alone and it does not look nice. Indeed, people might talk about us if we continue living here all alone for the rest of our lives.' 'All right, grandson, if that is your desire, it shall be as you wish.' The Hare said again, 'Grandmother, you will easily be able to recognize the old man when he comes, because he has only one eye.'

When night came Hare took out one of his eyes and leaving it outside entered the lodge and stayed with his grandmother all night.[45] Early in the morning he left and went back to his own lodge. But when he got to the place where he had left his eye he had great trouble in finding it and when he found it he saw that mice had gnawed at it. The next morning he told his grandmother that she might come in. He had, of course, eaten all the meat. That was the only reason that he had wanted her to go away.[45]

17

One night something came outside of Hare's lodge and sang:

'You who live with your grandmother, wherever you go I will trail you with dogs and crush you in my mouth.'

'Oh, grandmother, we are in a bad fix! Now we shall surely die,' said Hare. 'Only if we hide between the reed mattings will we be able to save ourselves.'[46]

'You who live with your grandmother, if you hide between the reed matting I shall find your scent with dogs,' it sang.

'Oh, grandmother, we are in bad straits! The only place we can hide is under the floor mattings.'

But the being sang:

'You who live with your grandmother, if you hide under the floor mattings, I will find your scent with dogs.'

'Grandmother, we are in bad straits! Let us change ourselves into charcoal and sit under the embers,' said Hare.

'If you change yourselves into charcoal and sit under the embers, I will find your scent with dogs.'

'Oh, grandmother, the only thing we can do now is to go up to the sky.'

But the being said:

'If you go up to the sky, I will find your scent with dogs.'

Then Hare got angry and went outside and looked around the lodge but could see nothing. So finally he asked his grandmother whether she knew where the being was who was speaking and she answered, 'Over in that direction.' He looked in the direction she mentioned and there he saw a little frog. 'So it is you? How come you to speak in such a fashion?' he said and smashed it with his club. Yet he wondered how it had been possible for such an object to speak in this way so he opened its mouth and he saw that it had long teeth. Then he knocked out the frog's teeth, burned the frog up and exclaimed, 'You talk too much and you scare people. Henceforth you will never be able to harm anyone.'

18

One day as Hare was ambling along again he heard some people shout at him, 'Look, there is a little Hare!' So Hare ran away to seek shelter in a thicket. But again they said, 'Little Hare has run into a thicket.' So Hare ran away again and hid under a log. But again they said, 'The little Hare is hiding under a log.' Hare, then, ran away again and went into a hole in the ground. But they again called out, 'The little Hare ran into a hole in the ground so give chase to him.' Hare then ran up a hollow tree but they said again, 'The Hare has gone up a hollow tree.' Finally Hare ran away until he came to a lodge where someone from within spoke to him, 'Grandson, come in!' So he went in and there he found an old man with his head bandaged up. 'It was I who caused you to come here for I want you to do something for me. This, grandson, is what brought you here,' and he took a woodtick from Hare's ears. 'This is the one that was always telling me where you were going whenever you tried to hide, so how could you ever have succeeded?' Then the old man continued, 'Grandson, you must be hungry.' 'Kettle, get some water in yourself and hang yourself over the fire!'[47] Immediately the kettle began to move about and do as it was told. It went after some water and then hung itself on the kettlehook all by itself. 'Now, plate, put some dried sweet corn in the kettle,' and, immediately, the plate began to move and put some corn in the kettle. 'Now put some bear-ribs in the kettle,' and it did so. The old man seemed to be working his mouth only and whatever he said took place. 'Now, plate, put some of the food on yourself and come before Hare,' and it did as it was told. Hare was very much surprised at the way orders were being given and obeyed. When he was through eating, the plate went on, got a watermelon and set it before Hare.

Finally the old man said to Hare, 'Grandson, I want you to do something for me. You see me now with my head bandaged up. That is because my scalp has been taken away. Those who have taken it, carried it across the ocean and are keeping it there. A great many people have tried to get it and failed. Now, I would like to have you try to get it and that is why I asked you to come here. I believe you could get it for you are a smart and clever fellow. If you get it for me I will give you the power to order things about as I do and you will then be able to pass on that power to your uncles and aunts.'[48] Then Hare said, 'Grandfather, I will try it.' 'Ah!' said the old man, 'grandson, it is good. You can start in the morning. Now, when you get to the edge of the lake you will find the home of your grandfather, beaver, and you must ask him to take you across.'

19

In the morning Hare departed taking with him a hoe and an axe. He came to the place where beaver lived with his wife and his children. 'Oh, my grandson has come!' said beaver. 'Well, I am sure you did not come without some reason. You certainly must have something on your mind.'[49] 'Yes, grandfather, I have. I wish to stay here overnight with you and I want you to take me across the lake in the morning. That is why I have come. For your troubles let me present you with a hoe.' 'Oh, grandson, this is good. I have been carrying people across for nothing and was glad to do it. This is indeed great. In the morning I will take you across.' Then said the female beaver to her husband, 'Old man, I think I had better take our grandson across. He has treated us well and you are so slow that I think it would suit him better if I carried him.' 'All right,' said the male beaver.

Then the old couple said to their children, 'Which one of you shall our grandson eat?'[50] 'Me,' they all shouted in chorus. Thus the young beavers shouted. There were some very large ones and some very small ones so they selected one of medium size and boiled it for Hare. When it was cooked they put it on a plate and gave it to him. Then the old man said, 'Grandson, do not separate the bones but pick the meat off very carefully and leave all the sinews attached.' Hare, however, was very hungry and was therefore not very careful and broke some of the sinews of the forepaw. When he had finished, the bones were taken and put into the water. Soon after, a beaver came in crying, and when his parents looked him over they noticed that the sinews in his forepaw were broken and that he was crying for that reason. And this is why beavers' paws to this day are drawn together. 'I am very sorry,' said Hare, 'I really tried to be careful.'

20

In the morning when he was ready to leave, the female beaver took him and carried him across the ocean on her back. Then she said, 'Grandson, you have a hard task but I will concentrate my mind on the matter in order to help you.[51] Over there where you are going, you will find a village near the ocean. The son of the chief of that village wears on his head the scalp you are after. If anything happens to you[52] or if you succeed in seizing the scalp, you must run to the ocean and jump far out in it. I will be there waiting for you. In the meantime I will gnaw holes in all of the boats.'[53]

Then he went ashore and walked toward the village to look around. After a while, he saw on the outskirts of the village, a place where they kill birds and he walked over and scared away some birds congregated there. Unexpectedly someone peeped out of a hiding place and said, 'Young man, come in! You have scared the birds away for me.' Then the birds came back again and this man shot them with arrows.

In the meantime Hare was asking all sorts of questions, such as 'Who is the chief of the village?' and 'What do you usually do?' The man answered, 'I am the chief of the village and I usually get four braces of birds and then go home. I go to a place where some women are watching a field and I give each of them one pair.

They always ask me to stop but I always refuse and go right on to the outskirts of the village where an old woman lives. There I leave another brace and go to a large lodge in the centre of the village. When I get home, I throw my arrows to the rear of the lodge. They always fall even. My mother always notices this. Then I take off my moccasins and throw them up on the lodge-poles and they always fall even. My mother always notices this, too. Then she gives me something to eat. I eat just a little and stop. Sometimes I say to my father that my head aches and that I would like to put on my head-dress provided the people dance. Thereupon the cooks and attendants get ready and the crier announces throughout the village that a dance is to be given. Then I put on my head-dress and dance.'[54] Thus Hare asked him all about himself. Suddenly, when he had turned around for a minute, Hare struck him dead. He skinned him and put the skin over himself and thus he was exactly like the young chief in appearance.

Soon he shot four braces of birds and took the route indicated by the chief he had killed. After a while he reached the place where the women were watching the field and gave them two braces of birds apiece. 'We have boiled some food and it is ready now, so you had better eat before you go,' they told him, but he refused and said he had to proceed home directly for he he was expected there for the meal. Then he went to the old woman's lodge, gave her a brace of birds and started for the lodge in the centre of the village.

As soon as he entered the lodge he threw his arrows in the back of the lodge and they all fell even. However, the mother said, 'Oh, I wonder if this really is my son, for I believe one of the arrows sticks out just a little more than the other.' But the old chief said, 'What do you mean by making our boy nervous, you evil old woman,' and addressing himself to Hare he said, 'Don't mind her but throw your arrows any way you please.' Then Hare took his moccasins and threw them over the lodge-poles and they caught and hung there. The mother gave him food and he ate a great deal as he was hungry. 'Well,' said the mother, 'this cannot be my son for he never eats so much food.' 'What is the matter with that evil old woman?' said the old chief. 'Why don't you let our child eat in peace? You will make him nervous with your

84

talk. Besides, he has not had any food all these days and he has a right to be hungry.' After a while, Hare said to the old man, 'Father, my head aches and I would like to wear my head-dress. If you will tell the attendants to get everything ready I will put it on.' So the attendants were told and they prepared everything and made the announcement in the village. When the crowd had gathered he took the head-dress, which consisted of a human scalp the hair of which was red, put it on, and danced with the crowd. Finally, he danced toward the door and, when he got near it, he ran out. 'The chief's head-dress is being taken away!' everyone shouted and gave chase. On he ran until he came to the ocean. He jumped far out in it and landed on the shoulders of his grand-mother, the beaver. Immediately, she started off. The pursuers got into boats to follow them but the boats soon began to fill up with water. Then the pursuers thought of two boats that were inland and went for them and again they started after Hare. They finally caught up with him and drew their boats up on each side but the beaver said, 'Grandson, hold tight on to me,' swung her tail up in the air and then brought it down on the water. The waves rolled up very high and overturned the boats of the pursuers. 'Now, grandson,' she said, 'we are rid of them. We need fear nothing else.' Thus they finally got back to their own shore.

The old male beaver was very glad that they had returned. Hare then went to the lodge of the old woman and when he was quite near he shouted, 'Grandfather, I am coming, so be ready!' The old man took off the wrappings around his head and sat in the door of the lodge, waiting. When Hare got near he took hold of the scalp by the hair and threw it at the old man's head. Im-mediately it united with the head. There he sat, a handsome man with his scalp intact again. The old man thanked Hare very much and said, 'It was for this reason that I sent for you. I knew you were very bright and I thought you would therefore be the only one who would be able to get the scalp for me. Now, grandson, just as I promised, you shall have all those things over which I have power and that you saw me use the other day. Whatever you wish for will be yours. But about one thing I would like to warn you. Never ask for the same thing four times in succession. Above all, never harm the woman who lives in the partition of this lodge in any way for she is in charge of all these things. If you care to sleep with a woman you may do so and this woman, by her power, will help you to get any woman you want. Now then, grandson, since I am likely to be in the way here on earth, I will go home.' Saying this he went upwards towards the sky, making a noise as of thunder as he disappeared.[55] Soon he passed out of sight.

21

In the night Hare tried his power on the things that the old man said would be his and everything that he had told him proved correct. When he was ready to go to sleep he said, 'Now I would like to have a nice-looking woman to lie with.' Immediately one came. She was very beautiful but Hare spoke again and said, 'I meant a beautiful woman.' Then the one that had come left and another came in still more beautiful than the former. But Hare said again that he had called for a beautiful woman so she, too, left and another came in still more beautiful. Again he called for a beautiful woman and, again, she left. Finally one came who was superlatively beautiful. With her he had sexual intercourse. Now he had been told not to call for anything four times in succession and yet he had done it. He had been told not to harm the woman in the partition, and yet he was even now having sexual intercourse with her!

It appears that he should have taken any kind of a woman for he had even lain with his grandmother.[56] In spite of it all he lay with the one woman that had been forbidden to him. It is because of his disobedience that we have to work at the present time for everything we want. If Hare had done as he had been told we would have the powers that he had been given up to the present day. He obtained a good thing for us and he lost it. That is why we cannot order things about today as the old man did.

The next morning when Hare got up the woman got up also and went into the partition. Hare went to the partition and peeped in to see her. She was lying in the midst of white feathers and the only thing dark were her eyes.[57] After a while the lodge began to roar and the noise became louder and louder. Hare began to get frightened and ran out of the lodge. After a while the roaring stopped and when he came back the lodge was nowhere to be seen. Then Hare began to repent of what he had done, saying, 'Oh, dear, when will I be of any use in this world?[58] I had obtained a good thing for my uncles and my aunts but I lost it again for them.' Saying this he started for his home.

When he got home he said to his grandmother, 'I have done an awful thing, grandmother. I went to grandfather's place and I found him without a scalp. It had been taken away from him and carried across the water. He sent many people for it but no one was able to bring it back to him, so he sent for me. In his lodge he commanded all the things to do whatever he wished and they always obeyed. These powers he gave to me and he told me not to ask for anything four times in succession. But I did by mistake. I asked to lie with a woman and I asked for a beautiful one but none of the kind that I am accustomed to lie with came, so I asked four times and thus I lost all that had been given to me, the lodge with it.' 'Oh, you big-eyed, big-eared, burnt buttocks, evil creature, you! A good thing you had obtained for your uncles and aunts which they would have had for all times and now you have lost it for them. They will always be sorry for this, you evil creature, you!' Then, taking a wooden poker she whipped him. 'Ouch! Ouch!' said Hare. 'I said I lay with a woman and you are jealous because of that.'

22

Then Hare began to think of the work he had been appointed to do and he said to himself, 'By this time I must have trampled upon all the evil beings that were abusing my uncles and aunts. That is what Earthmaker sent me here for.' Thus he mused. 'My uncles and my aunts will now live on earth as peacefully as myself since the evil beings that had been abusing them are now all dead.' Then all the birds that had been abusing the human beings he pushed higher up into the sky and he trampled upon and pushed under the earth the evil spirits who had inhabited the the earth so that the people might live in peace here.

Then he thought to himself, 'Those that I have destroyed were all bad animals. Now I must prepare some for the human beings to eat.'[59] So he decided to ask the animals themselves. All the animals gathered together not only the large but also the small ones such as the racoon, the skunk, the muskrat, etc. Then Hare got some oil ready. With this he intended to fatten those animals that were going to be used as food by human beings.

He asked the elk first, 'How do you wish to live?' and the elk answered, 'I wish to live by eating human beings.' So Hare asked him to show his teeth. The elk's teeth were long and fearful to look at. 'Well,' said Hare, 'if that is your wish, take this and eat it. It is blood from the human beings.' He then gave him some kind of fruit which was so sour that it knocked the elk's teeth out so that only a few of his front teeth remained. The elk wept and said, 'Hare, I take back what I said for I was wrong. Your uncles may kill me and eat me at all times.' Then Hare thanked him and said, 'It is good.'

Then the bear was asked. He said that the people could eat him, but that they would have to fast before they could find him[60] and that if anyone tried to find him without having fasted, he would not be successful for he would hold his paw in front of the opening of his cave. 'Bear, you ought not to have said that,' said Hare, 'because my uncles have medicine that is hard to overcome and they have dogs that can find anything.'

Then the horse[61] was asked, and he answered, 'Hare, with your uncles and aunts will I ever live and I will work for them. Whenever they have anything heavy I will carry it for them.' Hare thanked him, saying, 'It is good. You have proved yourself a chief and you will be a great help to the people throughout their life. I knew that you would do something good because you are good natured. For that reason I dreaded to ask you for fear you would say that you wanted to eat human beings. It is good.'

Then Hare said to the other animals, 'All of you who said you were willing to be eaten by the people may take a bath in this oil. You will be fattened thereby.' So the bear went in first and rolled himself in the oil, and that is why he is so fat. Then the mink jumped in. But they said he was not fit to be eaten so they fished him out and wrung him dry and that is why he is so thin and lean. Then the skunk jumped in without being asked and they said that he was not fit to be eaten because he smelled so badly. But the skunk said that if anyone ate him when he was ill he would drive away his illness. So Hare told the people to let him alone if he kept his promise to prolong their life. They all agreed to let him go. Then all the rest who were to be eaten took their baths of fat and went to their homes.

After they were gone Hare took two dogs and prepared some medicine for he was going to show how bears were to be hunted. Then he heated some stones and prepared a vapour-bath lodge. When it was ready he entered it and 'concentrated his mind.'[62] He had also boiled a kettle of dried corn. In the vapour-bath he communed with all the trees and with all the grasses and weeds, with all the stones and even with the earth.[63] Then he poured tobacco as an offering and began the ceremony. He started to sing and asked his grandmother to sing along with him to which she consented. He began with blackroot songs.[64] As he proceeded the bear was seized with a great desire to look towards him. Finally the bear did look in his direction. Then Hare cried out, 'Grandmother, someone's mind came to me just then!' But she only said, 'Try harder!' The bear in his cave could hear all that was said and regretted what he had said on the previous day.

Then Hare started to sing again. This time he sang his dancing-songs. Again the bear was seized with a strong desire to dance. Finally he was seized with the desire to come over to where Hare was singing for the savour of the food was so enticing that he wished to have some of it.[65] Thus he could not keep his mind off Hare and the things Hare was doing.

Now Hare knew when the bear's mind[66] had come to him. At that very point he stopped and retired. The next morning he took his dogs and started for the bear. 'In this direction there came a mind to me last night,' he said to his dogs, urging them on. Finally one of the dogs started toward the bear's cave. The bear put his paw in front of the opening in order to close it but the dog found it anyhow. Finally the bear said to the dog, 'Don't tell on me and I will give you a piece of fat.' But the dog began to bark at him and the other dog came up. They both tried to pull him out of the cave. Just then Hare came up. 'Oh, it is good,' he said. 'Now come out of this cave' and poked the bear until he came out. Thereupon Hare pointed an arrow toward his side. The bear looked askance expecting to be shot at any minute. But Hare instead ran around ahead of him and waited for him while the dogs chased him. Indeed Hare stood there and waited. Finally the bear came right up to where Hare was standing.

Again Hare pointed his arrow at him, right at his heart. The bear now stopped running and simply walked. But Hare did not shoot him. The fourth time Hare pointed the arrow at the bear he began to cry.[67] Then Hare began to make fun of him saying, 'So you are not as strong-minded as you thought? Why do you cry? This is what human beings could do to you even if you did put your paw in front of the opening of your cave. If I had been one of your uncles you would have been killed by this time.' 'Hare,' said the bear, 'you were right. From now on the people will be able to find me whenever they hunt for me.' Then the bear gave himself up, and the people to this day do as Hare did when they want to hunt bears.

23

Then Hare thought to himself, 'Now the people will live peacefully and forever.' But the old woman, his grandmother, said, 'Grandson, your talk makes me sad.[68] How can your uncles and aunts live as you do? Earthmaker did not make them thus. All things have to have an end. You yourself in your travels around the country must have seen trees fallen to the ground. That is their end; that is their death. And when you see grass lying flat on the ground, it is dead. Everything will have an end. I also will have an end as I am created that way.' Then Hare looked in her direction and some of her back caved in just as the earth does sometimes. That was what he saw. And he saw people cave in with the earth. 'Grandson, thus it is,' said the old woman, 'I have been created small and if all the people live for ever they would soon fill up the earth. There would then be more suffering than there is now, for some people would always be in want of food if they multiplied greatly. That is why everything has an end.' Then Hare thought for a long time. 'A good thing I had obtained for my uncles and my aunts but my grandmother has spoiled it.' So he felt sad, took his blanket, covered himself with it, lay down in the corner and wept.

24

He wept for the people. It was at that time that he thought of creating the Medicine Rite.[69]

Now this is the story of the origin of the Medicine Rite. All the birds of the air that were evil or abusive of man Hare killed. That is why it is said that he pushed them farther up into the air. All the evil spirits that lived on this earth he also killed so that they could not roam over it any longer. This is what is meant when they say that he tramped down deeper those whose backs protruded through the earth.

Hare was sent by Earthmaker to teach the people on earth a better life. That is why he roamed over its whole extent. As soon as he grew up he did away with all the things that were hindrances to the people.[70]

The reason why he called the people his uncles and aunts is because his mother was a human being. He was born of an earthly and human mother and that is why he called the men uncles. As his mother was a virgin he could have no other relatives except these uncles and aunts. All the hares are sons of all the women and the nephews of the men.

II

NOTES TO PAGES 63–91

1. In many versions of this very widespread episode she is torn to pieces in giving birth to the child.
2. The human beings whose ritualistic name is 'two-legged walkers'.
3. 'Uncles and aunts' means human beings.
4. The narrator has omitted the second and third attempt.
5. This is what children do when they are first given a small bow and arrow.
6. Throughout the myth the two forms of Hare, one, his true form, the other, his more general theriomorphic form, interchange.
7. Women are not supposed to handle arrows, especially sacred ones.
8. With every new adventure an additional adjective is used by Earth in scolding Hare until all his physical traits have been included.
9. The Winnebago claim that they never made flint arrow-points like their neighbours but that they found them in the ground.
10. That is, holy and powerful.
11. Sharp-elbow is a figure occurring in the oldest stratum of Winnebago mythology and always associated with evil.
12. Cf. note 53 of the Trickster Cycle.
13. Cf. end of episode.
14. Arrow-quiver with the symbolic meaning of ribs is quite unusual.
15. As already pointed out, the chief of the tribe is forbidden to go on the warpath or kill anyone.
16. This is, of course, a comment of the narrator. The establishment of the bond of friendship between a chief's son and an orphan is a very common motif.
17. All evil spirits in Winnebago mythology have polygamy as one of their outstanding characteristics. It may be associated with an older Winnebago cultural trait which has been lost.
18. This motif is used extensively in the Twin Cycle.
19. It was a Winnebago custom to kill all captured enemy male children

and pregnant women. Female children and other women were generally spared.

20. I.e. have him as chief.

21. He is possibly identical with Bladder, supposed to be the third of the heroes created by Earthmaker but who has, in some myths, been merged with one of the evil spirits.

22. Bear is supposed to be fearless and, as we shall see later on, originally unwilling to permit himself to be used by man for food.

23. For the association of bear with fat cf. Trickster Cycle, note 97.

24. That is, she is not a warrior returning with a scalp.

25. Here for the first time Earth is referring to herself as the earth proper and not as an anthropomorphic being.

26. The meaning of this statement is not clear to me.

27. This incident has been greatly foreshortened in this version. To understand it, it should be remembered that Bear is really Earth's husband. Hare gives her the hind end, which she really wishes but which she is afraid to ask for because it contains Bear's penis.

28. The reason for this is not clear. Winnebago women and men always eat together. It is best to take Hare's statement as a stylistic device for indicating that he is beginning to realize that she is a woman who has not yet reached her climacteric (cf. episodes 9 and 16) and that he, now grown up, should not be living with her any more. In fact there is still a saying, among Winnebago—'Stay with your grandmother!'—which implies that a man is still not grown up.

29. This, of course, gives Hare another of his physical traits.

30. This splitting of the bodiless heads episode is quite unusual. The slit-nose motif, incidentally, does not belong here. In practically all other versions the bodiless heads are always evil beings.

31. An example of the explanatory motif with which this cycle, in contrast to that of Trickster, abounds. The reduction of the destructive traits of animals or evil beings, from killing to harmless biting, is also quite characteristic of this cycle.

32. Apparently the narrator got tired of repeating the proper details. This would never have happened had he been telling the story to an audience.

33. This is the characteristic description of human beings from the animals' viewpoint. Here it is applied to an ant.

34. Shaking a dead person in order to restore him to life again is an exceedingly common motif.

35. Boasting is always used as a literary device to imply weakness. Every Winnebago would know immediately that the tall being is going to be killed because he has boasted of his powers.

36. Only twice, in the whole cycle, does Earth strike Hare, here where he has interfered with the proper functioning of natural phenomena, and in episode 21 where he has, by his action, deprived mankind of gratifying all its desires without any effort on its part.

37. This gives Hare his final physical trait, his 'burnt' buttocks.

38. A stock metaphor for tremendous speed.

39. The water monster has a number of stomachs.

40. Cf. note 19.

41. This expression, which is a form of boasting, immediately brings dire consequences upon Hare. In his case, however, these consequences cannot be the same as with other beings. It is quite significant to notice that Hare himself is aware of the danger to which he has exposed himself by his boasting and immediately corrects 'fight' to 'play'.

42. This type of question and answer is a favourite literary device for plot elaboration among the Winnebago.

43. Cf. note 28. The first thing Hare thinks of is not that Earth should immediately retire to a menstrual lodge but the danger to the efficacy of his war-weapons through their being in contact with a menstruating woman. As a rule the Winnebago think mainly of the danger to the warbundles under these circumstances. Since, however, Hare has no warbundle he substitutes war-weapons, i.e. his bow and arrows. According to Winnebago conceptions contact with a warbundle would kill everyone except a menstruating woman. In her case it is just the reverse.

　　The lodge to which Earth refers in the next few sentences is the menstrual lodge.

44. Menstruating women must observe a number of food taboos. The prohibition of eating meat is among them.

45. The incident described in the last three paragraphs constitutes the official origin myth of the menstrual period and the customs connected with it. As stated before (cf. note 28), Hare's staying with his grandmother so long has led to a well-known taunt, commonly used, that implies not merely impropriety but the suspicion of incest.

46. The particular motifs that follow are quite stereotyped and are

94

used whenever a person wishes to hide from an evil being. The fact that threats, definitely in the nature of boasts, are made indicates, of course, that the person uttering them is to be killed. We must not be surprised, then, at Hare's anger and sudden action.

47. This motif and the one that follows seem definitely to be of non-Indian origin.

48. That is, human beings.

49. This frequent greeting to people paying visits sounds worse than it is. First of all, it is quite stereotyped and, secondly, it never means that you have an ulterior motive in coming but, on the contrary, that you are bringing news, etc., to the person you are visiting. Here, of course, the plot elaboration demands that Hare have a motive. Presents, naturally, are always exchanged. The statement of beaver, a few sentences later, that he is always glad to take people across even without a present, is simply a polite phrase.

50. The beaver was one of the animals who had, according to Winnebago mythology, immediately consented to serve as man's food. Here this belief is combined with the origin of the shape of their paws.

51. This concentration of mind was regarded as essential for the success of any rite or undertaking.

52. That is, if you are detected and are unsuccessful.

53. This is a well-known motif connected specifically with beaver's activities.

54. With the exception of the headache this whole incident appears in a number of totally unrelated myths.

55. This is the stereotyped ending for folktales dealing with deities who have become incarnated in order to help human beings.

56. This is, of course, a comment of the narrator.

57. This description might fit either a night-spirit-woman or a water-spirit-woman. It is, however, clearly a waterspirit-woman here for only they are supposed to be superlatively beautiful.

58. This remark is to prepare us for the complete change in Hare's character in the next episode.

59. What follows is an excellent illustration of what was unquestionably the prevalent theory, among the people at large, of the origin of the present physical traits of animals. It was definitely not the priest's or thinker's theory.

60. Bears cannot be hunted unless an elaborate rite is performed first. It is described on pp. 87ff.

61. The horse, of course, is not a native animal.
62. This was necessary for all ceremonies but vital in this particular one. In the preparations for the bear-hunt it was customary for the prospective hunter to gaze steadily at the burning fire-logs until he thought an ember had flow toward him. This ember flying toward him was interpreted as the bear's mind turning in his direction. Cf. the end of this paragraph.
63. He means the objects on the earth.
64. These songs were generally connected with the curing of disease. Some, however, had magical efficacy.
65. One of the theories of why animals are killed is because they, more particularly, their spirit-prototypes, cannot resist the odour of the food sacrificed to them. The same theory holds for the granting of power from the spirits. Only there it is the tobacco whose fumes the spirits cannot resist.
66. Cf. note 62.
67. This is regarded as a sign of weakness and complete powerlessness.
68. Cf., in this connection, The Origin Myth of the Medicine Rite in my *Road of Life and Death*, New York, 1945, pp. 22 ff.
69. Cf. the Origin Myth mentioned in note 68.
70. This and what follows is a comment of the narrator.

III

SUMMARY OF THE ASSINIBOINE TRICKSTER MYTH[1]

1. The earth is flooded. Sitconski[2] makes the muskrat dive for mud, and fashions the earth out of it. He makes the muskrat and beaver change tails.

2. The muskrat brings up mud, from which Inktonmi shapes the earth. Inktonmi debates with Frog on the length of the winter season, and finally agrees to have seven winter months. He creates men and horses.

3. The earth is covered with snow, for the summer is kept in a bag tied to a medicine-man's lodge-pole. Inktonmi is hired by supernatural beings to secure the summer for the people. He stations animal helpers one behind another. The fox steals the summer and passes it on to his associates, who escape while Inktonmi engages the owner in conversation. Inktonmi joins his comrades, and makes summer by opening the bag. A council is called to decide the length of the winter. Frog proposes six months, and is knocked down by Inktonmi, but then Inktonmi pities him and fixes the period at six months. There is a debate whether men are to return to life after death. Inktonmi decides that they are to die forever. Inktonmi makes all animals plunge into a hole with fat.

4. Inktumni plays with rocks and leaves the impress of his body on them.

5. Sitconski discovers women who have never seen men. He informs his fellow-men, who follow him to the women's camp. The women choose husbands. The chieftainess chooses Sitconski,

---

1 Cf. R. H. Lowie, *The Assiniboine, Anthrop. Pap. Amer. Mus. Nat. History*, Vol. IV, New York, 1909, pp. 239–244.

2 *Sitconski* and *Inktonmi, Inktumni, Inktomi* are the same personages.

who refuses to marry her. She forbids her subjects to marry him, and he remains single.

6. Inktonmi goes paddling with a young man, lands, and discovers women's camp. He explains sexual matters to the two chieftainesses and other women. When he has gratified his desires, he wishes to retire, but the women as yet uninitiated hold him back. At last he makes his escape.

7. Inktumni wishes to fly with the geese. The birds take him up, but drop him in a mud-hole, where he is left sticking for several days.

8. Sitconski wishes to travel with the eagle. Eagle abandons him on a mountain top. Sitconski tumbles down head foremost, and sticks in a swamp. When he frees himself, he turns into a moose to entice the eagle down. When the eagle eats of the meat, Sitconski kills him.

9. Sitconski wishes to travel with the geese, is warned of dangers, but insists on joining them. The Indians shoot at the geese, who drop Sitconski into a mud-hole.

10. Inktumni refuses to present a rock with a gift, and is captured by it. He calls on birds to help him, promising them his daughter. The birds cause a wind that shatters the rock. Inktumni announces that he has no daughter.

11. Inktonmi suffocates a bear in a sweat-lodge. He wishes to distribute the meat among the animals, but is suddenly seized by a rock and held fast. Frog informs other animals. They devour all the meat. Finally Inktonmi is released by birds who break up the rock.

12. Fisher has escaped with some of Sitconski's meat. Sitconski sees Fisher in the water, dives after him, but misses him. He discovers that it is only Fisher's reflection, and finds Fisher on a tree. Fisher offers to give him some meat if he shuts his eyes and opens his mouth, then drops a knife and kills him.

13. Inktumni plunges into the water to get berries, but the real berries are above him and he has been deceived by their reflection.

14. Sitconski meets a chicken and abuses it. The chicken flaps its wings, frightening him so that he falls into the water. He gets out and by a ruse gets two fish to fight and kill each other. Mink steals the meat. Sitconski angrily calls on Thunder, who causes a flood. All unwinged animals perish. Thunder stops the rain, and Sitconski revives the animals.

15. Sitconski arouses geese's curiosity by packing two sacks. He invites them to dance with closed eyes, and wrings their necks. He cooks the dead geese. Fox approaches, pretending to limp. Sitconski proposes a race for the food. Fox wins, and eats up all the food.

16. Inktonmi pretends to mourn his brother's death and induces the ducks to accompany him on a warparty. First he bids them dance around Turtle with closed eyes. While they are dancing, he kills most of them. The rest escape. Turtle tries to flee, but is slain, after warning Inktonmi not to drink water for four days. Coyote approaches, pretending to limp. Inktonmi offers to give him food, provided he gets a bucket for him. Coyote gets several buckets, but Intonmi is not satisfied with them and sends him off again. Finally, he obtains the desired vessel, and Inktonmi sits down on a rock, which holds him fast. Coyote notifies other animals, and they eat up all the food. Inktonmi begs birds to free him, promising to paint their wings. They shatter the rock, and he fulfils his promise. Inktonmi recollects Turtle's warning, and is afraid to drink. When he stoops down at last, a large turtle seizes his lip and hangs on, until Inktonmi burns it with his pipe. Inktonmi lays it on its back and makes it promise never to bite people.

17. Fox pretends to be lame. Inktumni challenges him to a race, offering to tie a stone to his foot. Fox outruns him, and devours all his food. Inktumni vainly tries to kill him.

99

18. Inktumni asks his rump to guard his eggs and wake him if anyone should approach. The rump fails to do so, and the eggs are eaten up by a stranger. Inktumni angrily burns his rump and walks off. He returns to the same place, mistakes his flesh for meat, and eats it.

19. Sitconski passes a sleeping marten and lynx. .

20. Sitconski hears people dancing, and finds mice dancing in a buffalo skull. He puts his head in and cannot get it out for some time.

21. Sitconski puts his head into dancing mice's buffalo skull. He falls asleep. The mice chew up his hair, and when he wakes up he cannot pull his head out. Finally he breaks the skull against rocks.

22. Sitconski learns an eye-juggling trick of some birds. When he throws both his eyes on a tree, however, they remain there, and he is obliged to make new eyes of pitch.

23. Inktonmi learns the eye-juggling trick of four boys, who warn him not to practise it too frequently. They also show him the trick of whittling off his feet and catching game, but warn him not to perform it when alone. He tries the eye-juggling trick once too often, and loses his eyes; the boys restore them to him, but take away his power. He also disobeys the second warning, and gets stuck in a tree. The boys rescue him, but take away his remaining powers.

24. Sitconski bids a bird transport his mentula to a sleeping beaver on the opposite side of a creek. The bird puts it in the wrong place. Then the beaver wakes up and dives into the water.

25. A mink has intercourse with a beaver. Sitconski sees them and requests the mink to act as his go-between (like the bird in 24).

26. Sitconski abducts young beavers. Fear of the old beaver deters him from drinking, and he perishes of thirst. Magpie restores him to life.

27. Sitconski stays with Beaver for a time. He abducts and eats the young beaver. Beaver bites him when he tries to drink. He howls with pain.

28. Sitconski abuses a rock and is pursued by it. It catches him and rolls over him. He begs Thunder for aid, and the rock is burst asunder.

29. Sitconski marries a girl, but infringes nuptial taboo and his wife disappears. He meets and follows a buffalo cow to her camp, and is caught in a pen with the buffalo.

30. Sitconski suspects wolverenes of wishing to steal his coat. They actually take it. He gives chase, but fails to overtake them. In the spring he tracks them to their camp, and holds one of the thieves over the fire, burning his hair.

31. Sitconski is pursued by a bear, kicks up a buffalo skull, puts on the horns, and then pursues the frightened bear.

32. Sitconski is plagued by mosquitoes.

33. Sitconski repeatedly kicks and pulverizes a buffalo skull in his path, but it invariably resumes its former shape. Finally it turns into a buffalo that pursues him. Sitconski conciliates it with tobacco.

34. Inktumni proposes to Rabbit that whichever of them falls asleep first may abuse the other. Inktumni falls asleep first, and is abused. When easing himself, he drops little rabbits, but when he tries to catch a rabbit he soils his blanket.

35. Four Cree set out to visit Sitconski. They hear his drum near by, but fail to reach him for several days. When they arrive at their destination, one of them asks for eternal life, another for Sitconski's daughter, the remaining two for medicines. The first man is transformed into stone. The second Cree weds the girl, but breaks nuptial taboo, and his wife disappears. The. other visitors receive medicines. They believe they have stayed only four days, but in reality they have been away for as many years.

36. (Begins like 35.) Sitconski kills his sisters' children. The women pursue him. He builds a tunnel and suffocates them in it.

37. Sitconski feigns death, after giving his wife instructions. He is buried, but returns to marry his daughters. He is detected and obliged to flee.

38. Sitconski travels in female garments, and is married by a young man. He pretends to give birth to a child, but actually packs a fox. When his trickery is exposed, he flees.

39. Sitconski leaves his old wife to go travelling. He puts on women's clothes and marries a young man. (The story continues as in 38.) He ultimately returns home, and lies to his wife about his long absence.

40. Sitconski finds berries and asks them for their second name. They are called Scratch-Rump. He eats of the berries, and is obliged to scratch himself until the blood begins to flow. He angrily builds a fire, burns his buttocks, and walks away. Returning to the same spot, he puts his burnt flesh on the trees, forming gum.

41. Sitconski finds roots, named Wind. After eating them, he breaks wind and is carried up into the air. He is carried higher and higher. Trees which he tries to cling to are carried up with him. He finally falls into a mud-hole. When he gets out, he finds many snakes. He uses them as whips, killing one after another.

42. (Similar to 41.) Sitconski packs an old woman to stop her ascending, but both rise into the air. The woman is killed in falling down; Sitconski sticks in the ground.

43. Sitconski borrows some of Skunk's power, but wastes it, splitting a tree stump. He is killed trying to steal Skunk's wife, but revives. A passer-by captures him and makes him pile up firewood. Sitconski begs Weasel to crawl into his captor's body and eat his heart. Weasel obeys, killing Sitconski's enemy. By way of compensation, Sitconski washes him in snow to make him white.

44. Inktonmi teaches the Indians to hunt buffalo, to eat the various parts of the animal, and to make knives.

45. Inktonmi warns ten women of the approach of Disease, and instructs them how to be saved. He profits by their obedience, playing the part of Disease.

46. Inktonmi distributes ceremonials to various animals, bidding them appear to the Indians in their dreams and to pass on the ceremonials to them.

47. Inktonmi helps a calf out of the mire. They travel together. The calf rolls over several times on the way and becomes a very large bull. Inktonmi is also transformed into a well-sized buffalo. They steal two women from the buffalo camp, and have to fight two of the bulls. They defeat their enemies. The calf and Inktonmi separate, the calf promising plenty of buffalo for the Indians.

48. Inktonmi pretends to guard a man's rattle, while the owner is sleeping, but tries to steal it. He is overtaken, and pleads as an excuse that he was only trying to preserve the rattle from winged thieves.

49. Sitconski roasts and eats one of his boys. His second son escapes.

50. Sitconski has been refused by a chief's daughter. By magic, he transforms rags into fine clothes, and in this guise lures her from home. On the way he disappears, leaving his clothes, which turn into excrements.

51. Inktumni tries to visit another man's wife, but gets stuck in the ground as he crawls toward her lodge.

52. Sitconski fails to cross a swamp, until he begs a stick to act as a bridge. He is doctored by a bear. In return, the bear asks him to fill several pails with berries for him. Sitconski gets tired and fills them partly with moss. Travelling on, he meets beavers pretending to be dead. He packs one, and cuts sticks to roast it on. In the meantime, the beaver swims out on the lake with Sitconski's pouch, but returns it when Sitconski begins to cry.

IV

SUMMARY OF THE TLINGIT TRICKSTER MYTH [1]

Raven was the son of a man named Kit-kaositiyi-qa, who gave him strength to make the world. After he had made it he obtained the stars, moon and daylight from their keeper at the head of Nass by letting himself be swallowed by the keeper's daughter and be born of her. He obtained fresh water by tricking its owner, Petrel. As he was flying out through the smoke hole, however, Petrel made his smoke-hole spirits catch him and lighted a fire under him, turning him from white to black. Raven scattered the fresh water out of his mouth to make rivers and streams. Because some people who were fishing for eulachon would not take him across a river, he let the sun forth, and they fled into the woods or ocean, becoming such animals as the skins they wore had belonged to. Next Raven stole fat from some boys who were throwing it back and forth. He found a piece of jade bearing some design, stuck it into the ground, and pretended to a spring salmon that the object was calling it names. The salmon came ashore, and Raven killed it. Then he got the birds to procure him skunk cabbage so that they might eat the fish, but instead of feeding them, he sent them away a second time and ate it himself, burying the bones in the ashes. After that the birds dressed and painted themselves up.

Raven came to the bear, and the latter fed him on some of his own flesh, a proceeding which Raven tried to imitate in vain a little later. Then Raven went out fishing with Bear and Cormorant, killed the former by cutting off a piece of flesh, and pulled out Cormorant's tongue so that he could not tell anybody. Afterward he killed Bear's wife by inducing her to eat halibut

[1] Cf. J. R. Swanton, *Tlingit Myths and Texts*, Bur. Amer. Ethn. Bulletin 39, Washington, D.C., 1909, pp. 416-419.

bladders which he had filled with hot stones. He came to some fishermen and stole the bait from their hooks, but was finally hooked in the nose and had to recover his nose disguised as another person. Now he came to some deer with fat hanging out of their nostrils, pretended that it was mucus, and obtained it. He started along by canoe, and all of the animals wanted to accompany him, but he accepted only Deer. Coming to a deep valley, he laid some dried celery stalks across, covered them with moss, and induced Deer to try to walk across. Deer did so and was precipitated to the bottom, where he was devoured by Raven. Afterward Raven began mourning for him.

Now he met the old woman who controls the tide, and forced her to let the tide fall and rise as it does today. At the same time he told Mink to live on sea-urchins. Then he went on crying, 'My wife, my wife,' and, when he saw some gum on a tree, thought that the tree also was mourning. Coming to Petrel again, he contended with him as to which was the older, but finally Petrel put on his fog-hat so that Raven was unable to find his way out and had to admit Petrel was older than he. He induced Petrel to let his hat 'go into the world', so that when people see fog coming out of an opening in the woods and going right back, they know it will be good weather. He obtained fire with the help of a chicken-hawk whose bill was burned off in getting it, and he put the fire into red cedar and some white stones.

Coming to the great house containing all fish, he brought it ashore by means of a cane carved to resemble the tentacle of a devil-fish, and gave a feast for his dead mother out of part of its contents. The other fish spread throughout the world. He invited the killer whales, pretended that he was going to show them how to stick canes into their necks, and stuck sharp-pointed sticks in instead, thus killing all but one. When Raven and another person were boiling down the grease from these killer whales, he stole all from the other man. Then this man shut him up in a grease-box and kicked it off a high cliff, but Raven had induced him to fasten it with a piece of straw instead of rope, and immediately flew out. He flew inside a whale, and lived on what it swallowed and its insides. At last he cut out its heart and killed it. After he had floated ashore the people cut a hole through and he flew away. Returning to the same place, he persuaded them that this was a bad portent, so they left the town, and Raven consumed what they had abandoned.

Once Raven went to a calm place just outside Sitka and made many waves by rocking his canoe, since which time it has always been very rough there. Next he set the heron and seagull to quarrelling in order to obtain a herring which the former had swallowed. Having stolen a salmon from some people when they were asleep, they in turn discovered him asleep and wrenched off his gizzard. He went after it, found them using it as a polo ball, and recovered it, but ever since the Raven's gizzard has been big and dirty. Next he married the daughter of Fog-on-the-salmon, and they put up many salmon eggs and dried salmon. When it became stormy the salmon eggs helped him paddle. Afterward he carried up the dried salmon and dumped the salmon eggs overboard, so that people do not care much for salmon eggs nowadays. He met a man whose club would go out to sea and kill seal of itself, stole this club, and tried to make it do the same thing for him, but it would not, and he broke it in pieces on the rocks. He tried to make a certain place like Nass, but the clams shooting upward drowned his voice and he was unsuccessful. He turned to stone two brothers who had started to cross the Stikine. Coming to the ground-hog people, he tried to make them believe that the spring snowslides had begun so that they would throw their surplus food out of doors, but in vain. He had to wait until spring, when they threw it all out, and he gave a feast for his mother with it. Before this took place, however, he obtained the female genital organs from a certain island and put them in their places. Then he invited everybody in the world to his feast because he wanted to see a dance hat and Chilkat blanket which were owned by the Gonaqadet. Since then people have liked to attend feasts.

Raven put a woman under the world to attend to the rising and falling of the tides. Once he wanted to go under the ocean, so he had this woman raise the waters, and they went up to the tops of the mountains. They went up slowly, however, so that people had time to load their canoes. The bears which were walking around on the tops of the mountains tried to swim out to them, and those who had dogs were then well protected. Some people walled about the mountain tops and kept their canoes inside. All who survived were without firewood, however, and died of cold, except some who were turned to stone by Raven along with many animals and fishes. Then the sea went down so far that it was dry everywhere. Raven and another bird-man went about picking up fishes to boil the grease out of them, but Raven took only small fishes like sculpins while the other took whales, etc. Raven scared his companion away and began drinking his grease, but he came back, put Raven into a grease-box, and kicked him off from a high cliff as had happened before. Raven also escaped in the same manner.

One time Raven invited the bears to a feast, and induced the wren to pull out the entrails of one of them through his anus and thus kill him. Raven had become so great an eater from having eaten the black spots off his toes. After everybody had been destroyed at the time of the flood, Raven made a new generation out of leaves, and so it happens that at the time when leaves fall there are many deaths. He made a devil-fish digging stick and went around to all things on the beaches, asking them if they were going to hurt human beings. If they said 'No,' he left them; if 'Yes,' he rooted them up. In his time fern roots were already cooked, but he made them green; while devil-fish, which were fat, he made hard.

On one occasion he invited all the tribes of little people, and, when they were seated upon mats, he shook them, and the little people flew into people's eyes, becoming their pupils. He tried to capture a sculpin in order to eat it, but it slipped between his fingers, and its tail became slender as it is today. He threw his blanket upon the sea, let it float ashore, and threw it upon a bush where it became *Rebis bracteosum* (cax). Drinking water he called *catk*. He placed a woman at the head of a creek and said that the salmon should go up to see her. He made the quills of the porcupine out of yellow cedar bark. He made the west wind, which he placed in a house on top of a mountain, and decreed that it should hurt nobody. He also told a person how to obtain strength enough to paddle home by taking up a piece of red salmon and blowing behind him. Raven made also the south wind and the north wind. He made all the other native races of people. The dog was at first a human being, but Raven altered him because he was too quick. One time Raven came to a thing called fat-on-the-sea. He made it go underwater and come up again, and every time it came up he cut some of it off with his paddle. The eighth time it went under for good. At one place a person came out and spoke angrily to Raven, whereupon he turned him into a wild celery plant. He tied something around the head of a clam and gave it the same name as a man's privates.

After having tried every sort of contrivance for supporting the earth, Raven drained a sea-water pond when the tide was out, killed a beaver living at the bottom of it, and used its foreleg. Old-woman-under-the-earth has charge of it. Afterward Raven killed a big whale and tried to have it towed into the pond where the beaver had been. Finally he got tired out and turned it into stone along with the four canoes that were towing it. He gave names to several other places in this neighbourhood.

Part Three

THE NATURE
AND THE MEANING
OF THE MYTH

By Paul Radin

1

THE TEXT

THE Winnebago Trickster myth which follows was obtained by one of my principal informants, Sam Blowsnake, in 1912, from an old Winnebago Indian living near the village of Winnebago, Nebraska. It was written down in the Winnebago syllabary, a script that had been introduced about a generation before that time and which, up to the time of my coming to the Winnebago, had been used exclusively for the writing of letters. It was known only to a relatively small number of people.

Since it is quite essential to be certain of the authenticity of the document I am presenting here, a few words about Blowsnake seem in place. Sam Blowsnake was a full-blood Winnebago belonging to the Thunderbird clan. His father was a prominent individual who, until his conversion to the Peyote religion around 1909–1910, had steadfastly adhered to every aspect of the old Winnebago culture. All his children were carefully taught this old way of life. They fasted at the proper time, were initiated into the ancient rites and were told the traditional myths, sacred and profane. The elder Blowsnake was a well-known raconteur, so his son, Sam, had ample opportunity for becoming acquainted with most of the important myths of the tribe in an authentic form.

That the elder Blowsnake knew the Trickster myth is unquestioned. This does not mean, however, that he would narrate it, even to his children, unless, traditionally, he had the right to do so. He did not have this right apparently. Sam Blowsnake accordingly, at my suggestion, approached an older individual who did know it. Who this individual was I do not know. There were a number of reasons, into which I cannot enter here, why it was inadvisable for me to ask, the most important being that the myth was a sacred one and that I was a stranger and a white man. It clearly must have been told by someone who accepted it as true. The narrator certainly could not have been an individual who had joined the new semi-Christian Peyote cult that was sweeping through the Winnebago tribe when I was there.

The identity of the narrator is, however, not really of great importance. What is important is whether it was obtained under the proper conditions and whether Sam Blowsnake wrote it down as it was told to him. By proper conditions I mean that adequate offerings of tobacco were presented to the narrator and gifts commensurate with the traditionally accepted value of the myth given to him. This I know was done. That Sam Blowsnake recorded it as he heard it, I am certain for a number of reasons. It would never occur to a Winnebago to alter, in any appreciable manner, a narrative told to him by one who had the traditional right to tell it and for which he was paying. Quite apart from that fact, Sam Blowsnake was a highly conscientious person whom I had tested repeatedly for his accuracy. But the best proof that he had injected nothing new into the text and made no changes is the manner in which the myth was told and the vocabulary used. I knew Blowsnake's style very well, for he had dictated to me and written down for me innumerable texts.

The initial translation was made by two younger Indians, John Baptiste and Oliver Lamere, both of whom knew English very well, particularly the former. It was then revised by myself. I could read the syllabary with some ease and knew Winnebago well.

We can thus begin our analysis with the certainty that the text is authentic, obtained in an authentic manner, is adequately translated and that it represents an accepted version of the Trickster myth as it was to be found among the Winnebago in 1912. We can safely assume, moreover, that it had the same form one hundred years or so ago as it had then. But before we attempt this analysis a few words about the Winnebago and their culture are necessary.

II

WINNEBAGO HISTORY AND CULTURE

THE Winnebago belong to the far-flung Siouan-speaking peoples whose members at one time inhabited an area which extended from South Carolina and the lower Mississippi River northward and westward to the states of Wisconsin, North and South Dakota and Montana, and the provinces of Saskatchewan and Alberta in western Canada. Apart from certain secondary changes the culture of these tribes was basically alike. The centre of this Siouan civilization at one time lay, presumably, somewhere along the Mississippi River, extending from St. Louis southwards and eastwards.

The Winnebago themselves are most closely related, linguistically and culturally, to those Siouan tribes who lived in the state of Iowa and in south-eastern Nebraska and the region immediately to the south, that is, the Oto, Iowa, Omaha and Osage, to name the most important ones. No later than A.D. 1000, so the archaeological evidence seems to indicate, these tribes were living close to the centre of that area where the oldest complex American Indian cultures first took on their mature forms and became differentiated. That all of these cultures owed many of their basic characteristics to the influence of the great civilizations of Mexico there can no longer be any question.

The Winnebago were first discovered by the French in 1634, at the western end of Green Bay, Wisconsin, completely encircled by simpler non-Siouan speaking tribes. How long they had been living in this region we do not know, but it could not have been very long for, on the basis of the archaeological evidence, they did not reach Wisconsin much before A.D. 1400. This same archaeological evidence indicates that they must have pushed their way northward, at first together with their close kin, the Iowa and Oto, and entered Wisconsin at the south-west end of that state and the north-western edge of Illinois. It was during the early part of this northward thrust that the Iowa and Oto split off from them. The northward progress of the Winnebago, it would seem, was bitterly contested by the Central Algonquian tribes living in this area. After entering Wisconsin the Winnebago were completely surrounded by Central Algonquian tribes, with whom they waged ceaseless warfare and by whom they were finally forced into the general area of south-eastern Green Bay.

Thus, for three hundred years before the French found them they were in contact with cultures much simpler than their own. In some ways this was fortunate, for it was this fact which enabled them to keep their older culture fairly intact. Yet this did not prevent influences from these simpler peoples manifesting themselves, despite wars and antagonisms. These influences were strengthened after the establishment of the French missions in this general area in the middle of the seventeenth century. The coming of the French had, however, one beneficial effect upon the Winnebago; it permitted them to break out of the very circumscribed area in which they had been confined by their enemies, so that they could spread over the whole of southern Wisconsin and establish autonomous villages where much of the old distinctive Winnebago culture could flourish and reassert itself. That it brought about entirely new conditions and led to innumerable crises is, of course, another matter.

For the purpose we have in mind, the elucidation of *The Trickster Myth*, the reader must then always remember that the Winnebago culture, as studied in the early twentieth century, is a compound of three distinct elements: an old basic culture, going back to at least A.D. 1000 and possibly much earlier, which has been repeatedly reorganized to meet new situations and new challenges; a considerable number of borrowings from Central Algonquian tribes after A.D. 1400; and a few borrowings from the Whites and from Christianity beginning with the middle of the seventeenth century but not becoming of any real importance until a century later.

There is no need here for giving more than the briefest account of Winnebago culture,[1] and I shall confine my remarks almost entirely to those features of their culture which find reflections in the Trickster myth. The social organization contained two structural patterns characteristic of many North American Indian tribes: first, the division of the tribe into two phratries, among the Winnebago called Upper and Lower, and second, the clan, with descent in the male line. The chief was selected from the Upper phratry, from the clan generally regarded as the most important, the Thunderbird. He, in contradistinction to all other Winnebago, could not go on the warpath. One of his most im-

[1] Those who are interested in studying it are referred to the author's monograph on the Winnebago in the 37th *Annual Report of the Bureau of American Ethnology*, Washington, 1923, and to the summary to be found in *The Road of Life and Death*, New York, 1945, pp. 49–77.

portant functions was to succour the needy and plead for clemency in all cases of infractions of tribal law and custom, even in case of murder. His lodge was a sacred asylum and absolutely inviolable. If a murder had been committed he not only interceded for the life of the murderer but actually, if need be, offered to take the place of the malefactor.

In contrast to the role and functions of the chief of the Upper phratry were those of the chief of the Lower, who belonged to the Bear clan. In him were centred pre-eminently the police, the disciplinary and the war powers. He and his associates policed and guarded the village, inflicted punishment for transgressions of law and custom, took charge of the whole tribe when it was on a warpath or when engaged in hunting or other communal activities. It was in the official lodge of the chief of the Lower phratry that prisoners were confined before being killed, and it was in his lodge where the sacred warbundles of the tribe were stored and guarded against contamination.

The Winnebago believed in a large number of spirits, some defined vaguely, others sharply. The vast majority were depicted as animals or animal-like beings. The main trait of these spirits was their ability to take on any form they wished, animal or human, animate or inanimate. To these supernatural beings man made offerings of various kinds which were always accompanied by tobacco. In a class by himself was the supreme deity, Earthmaker. While the conception of earthmaker had probably been influenced by the Christian concept of God, there is little question but that it antedated the coming of the Europeans and belongs to the oldest stratum of Winnebago beliefs.

The relationship between the spirits and deities and man was a very personal one. Every child, male and female, fasted between the ages of nine and eleven, and tried to acquire what was to all intents and purposes a guardian spirit upon whom he could call in any critical situation throughout life. This acquisition of a guardian and protective spirit at puberty was one of the fundamental traits of Winnebago culture as it was that of numerous other American Indian tribes. According to Winnebago ideas, without it a man was completely unanchored and at the mercy of events, natural and societal, in their crudest and most cruel forms. When they lost their belief in the efficacy of fasting and the spirits no longer vouchsafed them visions, Winnebago culture rapidly disintegrated.

In addition to this guardian spirit every individual attempted, by the proper offerings and propitiations, to obtain protection and specific powers from a large variety of spirits and deities. A man could not, for example, go on the warpath unless he had prayed to one of the deities controlling success in war, and had bestowed upon him by such a spirit certain gifts and had been promised success. These gifts were symbolized by material objects, paint, feathers, flutes, bones and so forth.

There were three fundamental types of ritual: those in which only members of the same clan participated; those performed by individuals all of whom had obtained visions from the same spirit; and the Medicine Rite, where membership was based upon personal conduct and achievement other than war. Only the warbundle rituals require a few words here.

Each Warbundle Rite or Feast, as it was technically called, was divided into two parts, the first presided over by the Thunderbird spirits and the second by the Night-spirits. However, all the great spirits of the Winnebago pantheon had their place in it, and, to all, offerings were made. Although in the eyes of the Winnebago the warbundle ritual was devoted entirely to the glorification of war, it is interesting and significant to see that, besides the great patrons of war, the Thunderbird spirits, Night-spirits, Sun, Morning Star, Evening Star, Disease-giver, Eagle and Black Hawk, specific peace deities like Earthmaker, Earth, Moon and Water were also included, and, at times, even hero-deities like Turtle and Hare, and even Trickster himself. From this we can infer that even in a ceremony devoted pre-eminently to the enhancement of the importance of the warrior and of warfare, deities symbolizing peace and the antithesis of violence and force could not be entirely left out.

Admittedly their inclusion had little effect upon the one and insistent prayer of the participants, war. Indeed, even Earthmaker was represented as bestowing success on the warpath, a function unquestionably completely new to him. Yet the mere fact that Earthmaker was included did act as a reminder that the pursuit of war was not regarded as the exclusive purpose of man.

The warbundle rituals represent the classic and most complete expression of the war spirit, the glorification of the viewpoint of the chief of the Lower phratry of the tribe, namely, that one goes out to combat evil, militantly and with violence. Even orgies, where all self-control was abandoned, were permitted to a limited degree, something that was always abhorrent to the normal Winnebago and greatly dreaded.

Only such individuals as possessed warbundles—there was theoretically only one in each of the twelve clans—could participate actively in the warbundle rites.

The warbundle itself consisted of a deerskin wrapping enclosing a strange assortment of objects. One of those used by the Thunderbird clan, for instance, contained the following: the desiccated bodies of a black hawk, of an eagle and of a snake, a weasel skin, a number of eagle feathers, a deer-tail head-dress, two wolf tails, a buffalo tail, a war-club, three flutes and various kinds of 'paint-medicine'. The black hawk body was to enable its possessor to fly when leading a war party; the wolf tails would give him the power of running; the buffalo tail, fleetness; the snake and weasel skins, the gift of dodging and wiggling; the paint, when smeared over the body, would make him invisible and prevent fatigue; and the flutes, when blown during a fight, would paralyse the running powers of the enemy and make them easy victims.

The warbundle was the most prized of all Winnebago possessions. It was carefully concealed and guarded not only because of its sacredness but because of the dangerous emanations which flowed from it, and which could destroy those who approached it. Only one thing could destroy its power, contact with menstrual blood.

To be a successful warrior was the highest ideal of a Winnebago, and it was in the warbundle rites that this ideal received its greatest glorification. It has, therefore, a very deep significance, psychologically and culturally, that the Winnebago Trickster myth should begin with what is essentially a satire on the warbundle ritual. The same significance attaches to the fact that of all Winnebago religious beliefs and practices the only one mentioned in the Trickster myth, and satirized, is the acquisition of a guardian spirit.

III

WINNEBAGO MYTHOLOGY AND LITERARY TRADITION

LIKE most American Indian tribes, the Winnebago divided their prose narratives into two types: those that dealt with a past that was irretrievably gone and which belonged to the realm of things no longer possible or attainable by man or spirits; and those which dealt with the present workaday world. The first is called *waikan*, what-is-sacred, and the second *worak*, what-is-recounted. No *waikan* could be told in the summertime or, at least, when the snakes were above ground. *Waikan* could not end tragically, that is, the hero could not be represented as dying or being killed except temporarily. Such an ending was, of course, conditioned by the fact that the heroes of a *waikan* were always divine beings, and divine beings among the Winnebago were regarded as immortal unless they belonged to the category of evil beings. The *worak*, in contrast, could be told at any time and had to end tragically. No *worak* could ever become a *waikan*, but a *waika* could, under certain circumstances, be placed in the category of a *worak*. The heroes of the *worak* were always either human beings or, very rarely, divine beings who had thrown in their lot with man.

The heroes of the *waikan* were either spirits and deities like Thunderbird, Waterspirit, Sun, Morning Star, or vague semi-deities like Trickster, He-who-wears-human-heads-as-ear-pendants (also called Red Horn) and Bladder, or animals like Hare, Turtle, Bear, Wolf. These animals were, however, really regarded as spirits. The Winnebago made a clear distinction, at least the Winnebago 'theologians' did, between the animal-deity who presided over all the animals of a given species and the concrete animals themselves. It is those presiding animal-deities who appear in the *waikan*. Certain of the animals belong to a special category, for instance, Hare, Turtle and possibly Bear, for there is some reason for believing that the first two at least were once deities who have secondarily lost their primary divine traits.

Like their close kinsmen, the Iowa, and their more distant relatives, the Ponca, as well as their non-Siouan speaking neighbours, the Ojibwa and Menominee, the Winnebago had a marked tendency to group the adventures of their heroes into large units, into cycles. The most important of these myth-cycles were those connected with Trickster, Hare, Red Horn, the Twins and the Two Boys.[1] Perhaps it is best to give a summary of the contents of the Red Horn and Twin cycles in order to contrast the episodes found therein with those of Hare and Trickster. For the Hare cycle, see pages 63–91.

The Red Horn Cycle

First Episode

1. All but the youngest of ten brothers are invited to participate in a race, the chief's daughter being the prize. The youngest, however, joins them and discloses himself as Red Horn. Red Horn wins the race.

Second Episode

2. All the brothers are invited to go on a warpath. Red Horn obtains the first war honour.

Third Episode

3. Orphan girl is told by her grandmother to court Red Horn.

Fourth Episode

4. Red Horn pulls out an arrow from a wounded man.

Fifth Episode

5. Red Horn and his companions go to the aid of human suppliants to defend them against giants. They defeat the giants in a ball game.

6. They defeat the giants in a game called *Who can shoot farthest*.

7. They defeat the giants in a dice game.

8. They defeat the giants in a game called *Who can stay under water longest*.

9. They are defeated and killed by the giants in a wrestling game.

[1] Cf. P. Radin, *Winnebago Hero Cycles*, Indian University Publications in Anthropology and Linguistics, Memoir I, Baltimore, 1945, and *The Evolution of an American Indian Prose Epic*, in Special Publications of the Bollingen Foundation, No. 3, Basle, 1954.

Sixth Episode
10. Red Horn's two wives give birth to two boys.
11. Red Horn's children restore their father and all the other inhabitants of the village to life, after killing all the giants.

Seventh Episode
12. Red Horn's children obtain a warbundle from Storms-as-he-walks, and attack two spirits whose bodies are made of iron (copper).

Eighth Episode
13. The younger of Red Horn's sons is enticed by a woman who pursues him and is demeaned.

Ninth Episode
14. The companions of Red Horn return to their homes.

The Twin Cycle

First Episode
Father-in-law ogre kills his daughter-in-law. Removes from her body two children. He throws one into the corner of the lodge, the other into the hollow of a tree stump. Father returns and finds the first child, Flesh, and rears him.

Second Episode
The second child (Stump) appears and plays with his brother. Father finally captures him.

Third Episode
Father warns his sons not to go to certain places.

Fourth Episode
The Twins kill the snakes.

Fifth Episode
The Twins kill the leeches.

Sixth Episode
The Twins kill the thunderbirds.

Seventh Episode
The father flees from the Twins.

Eighth Episode
The Twins direct their father to a village.

Ninth Episode
Twins visit and kill the ogre who killed their mother.

Tenth Episode
Twins visit the evil spirit, Herecgunina.

Eleventh Episode
Twins visit Earthmaker.

Twelfth Episode
Twins visit Herecgunina again.

Thirteenth Episode
Twins visit their father and mother.

Fourteenth Episode
Twins go on warpath with Red Horn.

Fifteenth Episode
Twins destroy a beaver, one of the foundation-posts of the earth.

Sixteenth Episode
Earthmaker sends his messenger to frighten the Twins and stop their wandering.

We are probably dealing in these cycles with an old Siouan literary form for, to a certain extent, we find it among some of the western Siouan tribes, such as the Hidatsa and the Crow. It is quite clear that, originally, many of the incidents and adventures recounted in these cycles, particularly in that of Hare, were independent myth-incidents. As such they are found throughout aboriginal North America. Nor have they always been combined in the same manner, even where cultural similarities were as close as among the Iowa and the Omaha. In fact, even among the Winnebago themselves, different raconteurs, while in agreement about what incidents and exploits were basic and had to be included in a given epic as well as about the sequence in which these had to follow one another, frequently added certain incidents and omitted others. This variability, large and small, must not be dismissed as accidental or as due necessarily to a faulty recounting of the myth or myth-cycle. It generally had some real significance. What we always have to determine then is, first, what incidents and exploits, in a given tribe, were regarded as fundamental and could not be omitted and what were regarded as secondary and could be. These same considerations hold for the various themes, for the way in which the actors of the plot are characterized, and for the identity of the actors. And this brings us to one of our fundamental questions: what role are we to assign the narrator in accentuating changes and even, at times, in bringing about new styles and suggesting new interpretations? This question must be answered if we wish to understand the nature and significance of the Trickster myth-cycle.

It can be safely asserted that there exists no aboriginal tribe in the world where the narrating of myths is not confined to a small number of specifically gifted individuals. These individuals are always highly respected by the community, and they are permitted to take liberties with a given text denied to people at large. In fact they are sometimes admired for so doing. While unquestionably the accepted theory everywhere is that a myth must always be told in the same way, all that is really meant by theory here is what I have stated before, namely, that the fundamental plot, themes and *dramatis personae* are retained. In short, no marked departure from a traditional plot or from the specific literary tradition is countenanced. The liberties that a gifted raconteur is permitted to take with his text vary from myth to myth and from tribe to tribe and, within the tribe itself, from period to period.

Among the Winnebago the right to narrate a given myth, that is, a *waikan*, belongs, as I have already indicated, either to a particular family or to a particular individual. In a certain sense it is his 'property', and as such often possesses a high pecuniary value. Where the myth was very sacred or very long, it had to be purchased in instalments. The number of individuals, however, to whom it would be sold was strictly limited, because no one would care to acquire the right to tell a myth out of idle curiosity nor would it be told by its owner to such a one. What actually occurred was that a *waikan* passed, through purchase, from one gifted raconteur to another. This meant that its content and style, while they may have been fixed basically and primarily by tradition, were fixed secondarily by individuals of specific literary ability who gave such a *waikan* the impress of their particular temperaments and genius. That they would attempt to narrate it as excellently and authentically as their most gifted predecessors had done stands to reason. The strict conformists and 'classicists' among the raconteurs would manifestly try to preserve the exact language of a predecessor. However, fidelity was not demanded of him. In fact, an audience generally preferred and valued a raconteur in terms of his own style and phrasing, that is, in terms of his own personality. We must never forget that we are not dealing here with narratives that were written down. Every narrative was, strictly speaking, a drama where as much depended upon the acting of the raconteur as upon his actual narration. This may seem an unnecessarily elementary point for me to stress, but it is frequently forgotten.

Only an example, however, will make clear the nature of the variations a raconteur can introduce without it being felt that he had departed from the traditional manner of telling a given myth. Two Winnebago, Sam Blowsnake and his older brother, Jasper, gave me versions of *The Twin Myth* which they had obtained from their father, a well-known raconteur who owned the right to narrate it.[1] Of the seventeen episodes included in the myth by Sam Blowsnake, Jasper Blowsnake had fifteen. The latter, on the other hand, had two not mentioned by his brother. Both of those added by Sam Blowsnake clearly do not belong to the traditionally accepted plot, yet they clearly were not added without a specific reason. The first was introduced to add a humorous note to a humourless plot, the second, to bring the heroes of the myth into relationship with certain hero-deities in order to increase the prestige of the former, who were not deities. Of the two Jasper Blowsnake included which are not found in his younger brother's version, one definitely belongs to the *Twin Cycle* and was accidently omitted by Sam, the other was quite unimportant and belongs to an entirely different myth-cycle.

The differences between the two versions are thus quite minor as far as the exploits of the Twins and their sequence are concerned. Apparently little deviation was countenanced in this respect. When, however, we compare the two versions from the point of view of narrative style or with regard to the motifs employed, the subthemes and the precise characterizations of the *dramatis personae*, then numerous differences, some of considerable

[1] Cf. *Winnebago Hero Cycles*, pp. 46–55, 137–152.

importance, immediately emerge. Only when one knew the two individuals in question well can these differences be explained. Sam Blowsnake was facile of speech, sociable, superficial, self-important, possessed of very little religious feeling and with little interest in the past. He had, however, great literary gifts and a fluent style which was at its best when narrating personal events or novelettes, that is, *worak*, as opposed to *waikan*. He was fundamentally a non-conformist, and where tradition permitted, only there—for he was until he was fifty years of age, still rooted in the old culture—he introduced new stresses and nuances and at times even drastic remodellings. His brother was his complete antithesis. He was deeply religious, a complete conformist, insistent upon transmitting what he knew as faithfully, indeed, as meticulously as possible. Consciously he changed nothing. His version of *The Twins* is unquestionably closer in style of narration and in vocabulary to what can be termed the classical manner of telling this myth than is that of the younger Blowsnake.

The temperaments, the personalities and the literary gifts of the raconteurs are thus of tremendous significance in studying the myths of the Winnebago, in fact of all aboriginal peoples, and trying to determine what is fundamental, what accidental, what primary and what secondary.

IV

THE WINNEBAGO HARE CYCLE
AND ITS COGNATES

AMONG practically all the tribes where myths with Hare as a hero are found, he plays the double role of culture-hero and trickster. The exploits and incidents assigned among the Winnebago to both Trickster and Hare are, in these other tribes, credited to Hare alone. This two-fold function of benefactor and buffoon,[1] as we have already pointed out, is the outstanding characteristic of the overwhelming majority of trickster heroes wherever they are encountered in aboriginal America. Despite

[1] Cf. the famous introduction by F. Boas to J. Teit's *Traditions of the Thompson River Indians*, Boston, 1898.

tremendous differences, most of them agree in two respects: that Trickster is represented as the creator of the world and the establisher of culture, and that there is no fixed sequence in the order in which the episodes connected with him are told. Except where he is identified with Hare, and in a few other instances, he is depicted as a being who has always existed, and as an old man. When he is identified with Hare, he is, on the contrary, depicted as a being born of a virgin who dies in giving birth to him, and not creating the world originally, but recreating it after it has been destroyed by a flood brought about by the spirits who had been angered by the revenge Hare had taken on them for the death of his younger brother. For this part of the Hare cycle there is a fixed sequence which is adhered to fairly consistently. Immediately after this positive aspect of his activities, however, there follow his strictly trickster exploits, of which there is no fixed number and where no fixed order seems to exist.

The impression one gets in perusing these various trickster cycles is that one must distinguish carefully between his consciously willed creative activities and the benefactions that come to mankind incidentally and accidently through the Trickster's activities. This, of course, raises an old question, namely, whether Trickster was originally a deity. Are we dealing here with a disintegration of his creative activities or with a merging of two entirely distinct figures, one a deity, the other a hero, represented either as human or animal? Has a hero here been elevated to the rank of a god or was Trickster originally a deity with two sides to his nature, one constructive, one destructive, one spiritual, the other material? Or, again, does Trickster antedate the divine, the animal and the human?

A fairly good case could be made for all these interpretations. There is much to be said for the theory that primary archaic figures like Trickster always had two sides, divine culture-hero and divine buffoon. Yet we cannot rule out other interpretations entirely, particularly the possibility that a buffoon-hero has existed ever since man first became differentiated as a social being. Laughter and humour are, in fact, the indications that he is a human being as distinct from an animal. They are as primary as speech. However, to this whole question I shall return later, in section VIII.

Yet there is another question that must still be put. Why should a deity wish to bring culture to mankind? I think the answer must be that if he does so, this is not his primary purpose. It is incidental to his desire to express and develop himself. He cannot attain development in a void, and he consequently first attempts to bring some differentiation into this void. It is at this point that man intervenes. The latter cannot, quite correctly from his viewpoint, permit a deity to attain differentiation unless the possibility for man's differentiation is also provided. Thus man is more or less forcibly injected into the picture. He becomes merged with the gods and the gods with him, and the differentiation and education of the gods becomes as much the education of man as it does that of the gods. Since man begins as a completely instinctual being, non-social and undomesticated, dominated by sex and hunger, so also the gods must begin or, better, so the gods are forced to begin.

Let me illustrate what I have just stated by two examples, one from the Blackfoot[1] of Montana and northern Canada, where Trickster is described as having always existed, the other from the Menominee,[2] an agricultural Algonquian-speaking tribe of eastern Wisconsin. The first four incidents of the Blackfoot cycle deal with the creation of the earth, the origin of languages, how man first was given his present shape, the origin of death and the origin of the order of the appearance of life. Then follows the typical assortment of buffoon-like and Rabelaisian adventures in what looks like no fixed order at all. Yet at the end, Old Man— so the Blackfoot call their trickster—has become a more differentiated individual and has become conversant with nature and with man in all their aspects, good and evil.

How man is injected into the picture and how blurred the distinction between man and the gods can become, the following quotation from the Blackfoot myth will indicate.[3]

[1] Cf. C. Wissler and D. C. Duvall, *Mythology of the Blackfoot Indians*, Anthropological Papers, American Museum of Natural History, Vol. II, New York, 1909, pp. 5–39.

[2] A. Skinner and J. V. Saterlee, *Menominee Folklore*, Anthropological Papers, American Museum of Natural History, Vol. XIII, New York, 1915, pp. 217–304.

[3] Wissler and Duvall, pp. 19–20.

There was once a time when there were but two persons in the world, Old Man and Old Woman. One time, when they were travelling about, Old Man met Old Woman, who said, 'Now, let us come to an agreement of some kind; let us decide how the people shall live.' 'Well,' said Old Man, 'I am to have the first say in everything.' To this Old Woman agreed, provided she had the second say.

Then Old Man began, 'The women are to tan the hides. When they do this, they are to rub brains on them to make them soft; they are to scrape them well with scraping-tools, etc. But all this they are to do very quickly, for it will not be very hard work.' 'No, I will not agree to this,' said Old Woman. 'They must tan the hide in the way you say; but it must be made very hard work, and take a long time, so that the good workers may be found out.'

'Well,' said Old Man, 'let the people have eyes and mouths in their faces; but they shall be straight up and down.' 'No,' said Old Woman, 'we will not have them that way. We will have the eyes and mouth in the faces, as you say; but they shall all be set crosswise.'

'Well,' said Old Man, 'the people shall have ten fingers on each hand.' 'Oh, no!' said Old Woman, 'that will be too many. They will be in the way. There shall be four fingers and one thumb on each hand.'

'Well,' said Old Man, 'we shall beget children. The genitals shall be at our navels.' 'No,' said Old Woman, 'that will make child-bearing too easy; the people will not care for their children. The genitals shall be at the pubes.'

In the Blackfoot myth the welfare of man is of prime importance. Among the Menominee, on the other hand, where the trickster is Hare, where he has not existed from the beginning of things and where his birth is described in detail, man is mentioned only incidentally. The two main objects Hare acquires in his exploits, fire and tobacco, are for the use of his grandmother, Earth and himself. The companions of Hare are deities. Man and his needs are secondary. They are not forgotten, but a separate myth is devoted to them so that they do not disturb the Hare cycle, which is essentially the saga of a specific deity.

Yet after we have definitely made up our mind that Hare is a true deity we have only to look at the exploits interpolated into his saga proper—that is, his birth, the theft of fire and tobacco, the revenge he takes for the death of his brother, Wolf, the deluge and the re-creation of the earth—to realize that he is a typical trickster. So once again we are faced with our old problem, what is primary here, what secondary; or, indeed, are both primary? The answer would be comparatively simple if no trickster myths were found where the above contradictions do not exist. But this is not so. There are a number of tribes, all fairly closely related to the Winnebago, as well as the Winnebago themselves, where there are two tricksters, one a fully fledged one and one a partial one. We have two fairly detailed records of the cycles devoted to both, one from the Ponca[1] and one from the Winnebago.[2] Where he is a full trickster he does not, except secondarily and unconsciously, bestow benefaction upon mankind. Among the Ponca he is called Ishtinike, and he is in appearance like the Winnebago trickster Wakdjunkaga. The partial trickster is Hare and he acts basically like a true culture-hero.

For Ishtinike we have, among the Ponca, the following sequence of incidents:

1. Ishtinike hoodwinks turkeys and kills them.
2. Ishtinike is caught in the branch of a tree.
3. Ishtinike instructs anus to guard a roasted turtle.
4. Ishtinike eats elk's food and becomes an elk.
5. Ishtinike rides on buzzard's back and is finally dropped into a hollow tree.
6. Ishtinike pretends to weasel that he is a racoon.
7. Ishtinike transforms himself into a carcass and imprisons buzzard's head.
8. Ishtinike persuades woman to let him shoot at deer, but misses them.
9. Ishtinike becomes a warrior in another tribe and kills evil grizzly bear.

[1] J. O. Dorsey, *Cegiha Texts, Contributions to North American Ethnology*, Vol. VI, Washington, 1890.
[2] P. Radin, *Winnebago Hero Cycles*, op. cit., pp. 32–38, 93–114.

10. Coyote ties Ishtinike to a sleeping colt who wakes and kicks him. Afterward Ishtinike succeeds in pulling off Coyote's tail.

11. Ishtinike is ridiculed by Chipmunk for carrying his penis on his back. Chipmunk takes safety in hole and Ishtinike tries to force him out with penis. Parts of his penis are eaten. Ishtinike transforms parts into food plants.

12. Ishtinike wakes up to find his robe at end of penis erectus.

13. Ishtinike visits beaver, muskrat, kingfisher and flying squirrel and tries to reciprocate their hospitality, but is unsuccessful.

14. Ishtinike mistakes reflection of plum tree in water for tree itself and dives into water for plums.

15. Ishtinike kills young racoons entrusted to his care.

For the Hare cycle among the Ponca the sequence of incidents is the following:

1. Hare kills winter.

2. Hare kills the black bears, the abusers of men.

3. Hare kills the evil giant.

4. Hare is seized by an eagle, carried to its nest and kills the eaglets and their parents, and secures feathers to make arrows.

5. Hare is sucked in by the man-eating hill, but succeeds in killing it and making his way out.

6. Hare cohabits with Ishtinike (Trickster).

7. Hare kills the grizzly bear.

8. Hare is caught in the branch of a tree through Ishtinike's magic. The latter then steals his clothing and goes to Hare's home. Hare is released, pursues Ishtinike and kills him.

9. Hare is deprived of his fat.

10. Hare kills a giant.

11. Hare hoodwinks turkeys and kills them.

The trickster-like exploits in the Ponca cycle, as we see, are not numerous but they are by no means insignificant. Of interest, too, is the fact that some of these trickster-like adventures are predicated for both Ishtinike and Hare. In short, the plot is more or less like that of a typical culture-hero. There is not the slightest suggestion that Hare is divine. Of unusual importance is the antagonism of Hare to Ishtinike found here, and the fact that the latter is represented as being killed by him. We have come a long way from the Hare cycle as found among the Menominee and the Ojibwa.[1]

Turning now to the Winnebago we find a Hare cycle which, although it has much in common with that of the Ponca, shows significant differences. But let me first summarize its contents.

1. The immaculate conception of the hero, Hare, who is born in seven months and whose mother dies upon his birth. He is reared by his grandmother.

2. Hare encounters a human being who wounds him with an arrow.

3. He is sent by his grandmother to obtain part of the proper materials for making a bow and arrow.

4. He is sent to obtain the feathers for his arrow. He kills a thunderbird.

5. He is sent to obtain tobacco from the spirit-being who possesses it. He finally kills him.

6. He is sent to obtain the flint for the arrowpoints from the spirit who possesses it. He finally kills him.

7. He encounters the evil being named Sharp-elbow. He finally kills him.

8. He pays a visit to Bear. He finally kills it.

9. He and his grandmother carry the carcass of Bear home with them.

10. He pays a visit to the beings who have only heads. They are kind to him.

11. He pays a visit to the beings who have only heads. This time they try to kill him. He finally kills them.

12. He encounters a tall human being. He finally kills him.

13. He captures the sun in a trap.

14. He is engulfed by the water monster, but finally kills it.

15. He meets a bobtailed animal and finally kills it.

16. He causes his grandmother to have her menstrual flow. He cohabits with his grandmother. His eyes are gnawed by mice.

[1] Cf. W. Jones, *Ojibwa Texts*, Part I, New York, 1917.

17. He is threatened by an animal who turns out to be a long-toothed frog. He finally kills it.

18. He meets a man with a bandaged head, one who had been scalped, who sends him on a mission.

19. He dines with Beaver.

20. Beaver ferries him to his destination. He recovers the scalp of the man with the bandaged head and restores it to him.

21. He disobeys a specific injunction and cohabits with a (waterspirit) woman. He returns to his grandmother, relates his experiences and is whipped by her.

22. He recollects his proper mission. Prepares the food-animals for man.

23. He wishes immortality for man.

24. He institutes the Medicine Rite. . . .

There is little suggestion here of trickster-like behaviour. The same holds true for the Hare cycle of the close kin of the Winnebago, the Iowa and, as we have just seen, holds true, although to a lesser degree, for that of the Ponca. We must consequently conclude that among the Winnebago and Iowa the character of Hare has been purged in order to make him conform more perfectly to the picture of a true culture-hero. This transformation and renovation of his personality and activities presumably received its final expression when these two tribes, the Winnebago and the Iowa, developed the present form of the Medicine Rite, which could not have occurred before the beginning of the eighteenth century.[1] Hare, among the Ojibwa and Menominee or his equivalent, the *Wisaka* of the closely related Fox Indians, is always described as the founder of this rite. The purging of Hare, his evolution from a trickster to a typical culture-hero among these two tribes may, however, have begun much earlier. It was never more than partial. Only among the Winnebago did it become complete.

[1] This is on the assumption that the Medicine Rite in its present form originated among the Ojibwa in upper Michigan at the end of the seventeenth century. For this assumption there is overwhelming evidence as yet unpublished.

V

THE WINNEBAGO TRICKSTER FIGURE

THE Winnebago word for trickster is *wakdjunkaga*, which means *the tricky one*. The corresponding term for him in Ponca is *ishtinike*, in the kindred Osage, *itsike* and in Dakota-Sioux, *ikto-mi*. The meaning of the Ponca and Osage words is unknown, that of the Dakota is *spider*. Since all these three stems are clearly related etymologically, the question arises as to whether the Winnebago rendering, *the tricky one*, does not really mean simply *one-who-acts-like-Wakdjunkaga*, and is thus secondary. In no other Siouan language is the stem for *tricky* remotely like *wakdjunkaga*. It seems best, then, to regard the real etymology of *wakdjunkaga* as unknown.

The similarity of the exploits attributed to Wakdjunkaga and all other trickster-heroes in North America is quite astounding. The only possible inference to be drawn is that this myth-cycle is an old cultural possession of all the American Indians, which has remained, as far as the general plot is concerned, relatively unchanged. Just because of this fact the specific differences between the Winnebago myth-cycle and the others assume special importance and demand explanation. To do this adequately it will first be necessary to summarize the plot of the *Wakdjunkaga* myth-cycle in considerable detail.

The cycle begins with an incident found in no other version, namely Wakdjunkaga pictured as the chief of the tribe, giving a warbundle feast on four different days. He, although host and consequently obligated to stay to the very end, is described as leaving the ceremony in order to cohabit with a woman, an act which is absolutely forbidden for those participating in a warbundle feast. On the fourth day he stays to the end and invites all the participants in the feast to accompany him by boat. Hardly has he left the shore when he returns and destroys his boat as useless. At this piece of stupidity some of his companions leave him. He then starts on foot, but after a short time destroys both his warbundle and his arrowbundle and finds himself eventually deserted by everyone and alone; alone, that is, as far as human beings and society are concerned. With the world of nature he is still in close contact. He calls all objects, so our text tells us, younger brothers. He understands them; they understand him.

This is clearly an introduction and its purpose is manifest. Wakdjunkaga is to be desocialized, to be represented as breaking all his ties with man and society. Why our raconteur began the cycle in this particular fashion it is impossible to say, but it is best to assume that it is a literary device. Presumably he has decided that Wakdjunkaga is to be depicted as completely unconnected with the world of man and as gradually evolving from an amorphous, instinctual and unintegrated being into one with the lineaments of man and one foreshadowing man's psychical traits. He has, in short, like many another epic writer, begun *in medias res*. What he seems to be saying is: 'Here is Wakdjunkaga pretending to be thoroughly socialized and about to embark on a warparty. But let me tell you what he really is: an utter fool, a breaker of the most holy taboos, a destroyer of the most sacred objects!' And then he proceeds, in kaleidoscopic fashion, to reduce Wakdjunkaga to his primitive self.

The exploits that follow tell us precisely who Wakdjunkaga is. (See incidents 4–10 in text.) In the first he treacherously lures an old buffalo to destruction, kills him in most cruel fashion and butchers him. No ethical values exist for him. And how does he kill and butcher the buffalo? With only one hand, his right. The next incident shows why only one hand has been used. He is still living in his unconscious, mentally a child, and this is here symbolized by the struggle between his right and his left hands in which his left hand is badly cut up. He himself is hardly aware of why this has occurred. He can only ejaculate, 'Why have I done this?' In contradistinction to Wakdjunkaga, the world of nature is represented as conscious, and the birds, in a language he cannot understand, exclaim, 'Look, look! There is Wakdjunkaga. There he goes!'

In the next incident he is still Wakdjunkaga the undifferentiated and instinctual. He comes upon a being with four little children who must be fed in a certain manner and at a certain time lest they die. In short, the principle of order must be recognized. But he knows no such principle. The father warns him that if the children die because Wakdjunkaga has failed to follow his instructions, he will kill him. Yet Wakdjunkaga, because of his own hunger, disobeys the instructions given him and the children die. Immediately the father is upon him. Wakdjunkaga is pursued around the island world, that is the universe, and only by jumping into the ocean surrounding it does he escape death.

As he swims aimlessly in the water, not knowing where the shore is, if, indeed, one exists, completely without bearings, he asks fish after fish where he can find land. None of them knows. Finally he is told that he has been swimming along the shoreline all the time.

He has barely landed, that is, he has barely got his bearings, when he attempts to catch some fish. But all he can obtain is the water through which some fish have passed. Out of this he enthusiastically prepares a soup, and fills himself to his utmost capacity. As he lies there, practically incapacitated, his stomach shining from being distended, a dead fish drifts by. He seizes it, but he cannot eat any more and he buries it.

Here we find Wakdjunkaga completely unanchored. He is not only isolated from man and society but—temporarily at least—from the world of nature and from the universe as well. Small wonder, then, that he is described as thoroughly frightened and as saying to himself, 'That such a thing should happen to Wakdjunkaga, the warrior! Why I almost came to grief.' What the author intended here—the enraged father, the pursuit, the headlong flight and the submerging in the ocean—may well have been meant as a description of what can happen to anyone who leads the life instinctual.

However, there is also another point involved here. Being frightened is, in Winnebago symbolism, generally the indication of an awakening consciousness and sense of reality, indeed, the beginning of a conscience. And that seems to be borne out by the next incident (11 in text), where Wakdjunkaga is represented as imitating what he takes to be a man pointing at him but which turns out to be a tree stump with a protruding branch. The important point here is his reaction to his blunder and stupidity. 'Yes, indeed,' so he says, '*it is on this account that the people call me*

Wakdjunkaga, the foolish one! They are right.' He has one of the necessary traits of an individualized being now, a name. In Winnebago
society a child had no legal existence, no status, until he received
a name.

The episode which follows (12 in text) is known throughout
North America in a practically identical form. It describes how
Wakdjunkaga persuades some ducks to dance for him with eyes
closed and how he wrings their necks as they dance, though most
of them succeed in escaping. He roasts the few he has killed and,
exhausted from his encounter, goes to sleep after instructing his
anus to keep watch. His anus does its best to awaken him when
foxes appear, but to no avail, and Wakdjunkaga awakens to find
the ducks have been eaten. In anger he punishes his anus by
burning it, and when he can endure the pain no longer, he
exclaims, 'Ouch! This is too much! . . . *Is it not for such things
that I am called Wakdjunkaga? Indeed, they have talked me into doing
this, just as if I had been doing something wrong!'* Important for our
purpose is this exclamation, and also the one in incident 14,
where Wakdjunkaga discovers that he has been devouring parts
of his own intestines and commenting upon how delicious they
taste: *'Correctly indeed am I named Wakdjunkaga, the foolish one! By
being called thus I have actually been turned into a wakdjunkaga, a foolish
one!'*

With these incidents (12, 13, 14 in text) we have reached a
new stage in Wakdjunkaga's development. The emphasis is now
upon defining him more precisely, psychically and physically. He
is now to be shown emerging out of his complete isolation and
lack of all identity, and as becoming aware of himself and the
world around him. He has learned that both right and left hands
belong to him, that both are to be used and that his anus is part
of himself and cannot be treated as something independent of
him. He realizes, too, that he is being singled out, even if only
to be ridiculed, and he has begun to understand why he is called
Wakdjunkaga. But he does not as yet accept responsibility for his
actions. In fact, he holds other people, the world outside of himself, as compelling him to behave as he does.

It is only at this point that we are told anything specific about
Wakdjunkaga's appearance. Every Winnebago, of course, knew
what it was. Why then are we informed about it just here? The

answer seems to be that his original appearance is now to be altered. He is now to be given the intestines and anus of the size and shape which man is to have.

That this episode has not been placed here just through accident is proved by the fact that in the episode which immediately follows we have the first mention of his penis, of its size and of his manner of carrying it in a box on his back. And for the first time are we made aware of his sexuality. In all other specifically trickster myths lust is his primary characteristic; in these all his adventures reek with sex. If in the Winnebago Wakdjunkaga cycle it is not mentioned until now, this is because the author or authors who gave this cycle its present shape wished to give us not a series of Trickster's adventures as such but the evolution of a Trickster from an undefined being to one with the physiognomy of man, from a being psychically undeveloped and a prey to his instincts, to an individual who is at least conscious of what he does and who attempts to become socialized. Sex is treated primarily in its relation to Wakdjunkaga's evolution. Sexual escapades do not really seem to interest our raconteurs as such.

It is not strange then that the first sexual episode related of Wakdjunkaga should consist of his waking from his sleep to find himself without a blanket. He sees it floating above him, and only gradually recognizes that it is resting on his huge penis erectus. Here we are brought back again to the Wakdjunkaga whose right hand fights with his left, who burns his anus and eats his own intestines, who endows the parts of his body with independent existence and who does not realize their proper functions, where everything takes place of its own accord, without his volition. 'That is always happening to me,' he tells his penis.

It is not an accident that this episode is placed just here. It belongs here for it is to serve as an introduction to giving Wakdjunkaga an understanding of what sex is. Quite properly, we first have the symbol for masculine sexuality and an example of how it is thought of socially, namely as analogous to the banner raised by the chief when the tribal feast is given, and that then there follows an example (incident 16 in text) of how it is used concretely and properly.

Incident 16, the sending of the penis across the water so that

Wakdjunkaga can have intercourse with the chief's daughter, is as well known in North America as that of the hoodwinked ducks. In most of the trickster cycles it is immaterial where it is placed. Here, clearly, this is not true. It belongs here, for it is to be used to indicate how meaningless and undifferentiated Wakdjunkaga's sex drive still is inherently; indeed, to show how meaningless it is for all those involved. Penis, cohabitation are only symbols here; no sense of concrete reality is attached to them. That Wakdjunkaga has as yet developed no sense of true sex differentiation is made still clearer by the episode where he transforms himself into a woman (incident 20 in text).

Immediately following incident 16 we find the well-known theme of how he begs the turkey-buzzard to carry him on his back and fly with him. Whatever may be its larger psychological implications, this incident seems to play no role in the drama of Wakdjunkaga's development and must be regarded as an interlude. His rescue by women, after turkey-buzzard has treacherously dropped him into a hollow tree, is part of the secondary satire on man and society that permeates the whole cycle and about which we will have more to say in the next section.

We have now reached the crucial episode where Wakdjunkaga changes his sex and marries the chief's son. The overt reason given for his doing this is that he and his companions have been overtaken by winter and are starving and that the chief and his son have plenty. This episode like the preceding ones is well known; no trickster cycle omits it. The reason generally given is that Trickster does it to avenge some insult. The change of sex is a trick played on an oversexed individual in order to show to what lengths such a person will go, what sacred things he will give up and sacrifice to satisfy his desires. Such is its role in one of the most famous of all North American Indian trickster cycles, that of *Wisaka* of the Fox tribe.[1] But here in the Winnebago cycle it is not to avenge an insult but ostensibly to obtain food that the transformation of sex has occurred.

Taken in conjunction with the sex episodes which have preceded and the two incidents that follow, its meaning becomes clear. It is part of Wakdjunkaga's sex education. This must begin

[1] W. Jones, *Fox Texts*, Publications of the American Ethnological Society, Leyden, 1907, pp. 315 ff.

by sharply differentiating the two sexes. It is as if Wakdjunkaga were being told: this is the male; this, the penis; this is cohabitation; this is the female organ; this is pregnancy; this is how women bring children into the world. Yet how can Wakdjunkaga, with his generalized sexual organs, arranged in the wrong order and still living distinct from him in a receptacle on top of his body, how can he be expected to understand such matters? For that reason Wakdjunkaga's sex life, indeed, his whole physical life, is for him still something of a wild phantasmagoria. This phantasmagoria reaches its culmination point in incidents 20 and 21 of the text. Satire, Rabelaisian humour and grotesqueness are combined in these passages with amazing effect. Thrice, within very short intervals before the visit to the chief's son, the man-woman, Wakdjunkaga, is made pregnant; she, a woman, does her own courting; the man-woman becomes pregnant again. Whose are the children he brings forth? We are purposely left in ignorance in order to stress the fact that it makes no difference. Parenthood is immaterial, for they are born of a man-woman.

We have here reached a point where ordinary words and terms are indeed completely inadequate. Only symbols, only metaphors, can convey the meaning properly. As soon as the last child is born he begins to cry and nothing can stop him. A specialist at pacifying children, an old woman who has passed her climacteric, that is, one who is beyond sex, is called, but she is helpless. Finally the infant cries out, '*If I could but play with a piece of white cloud.*' To translate this into meaning then becomes the task of a special shaman. So it is with the child's other requests. They seem all unreasonable and unseasonable. What else can we expect in this phantasmagoria? Yet these requests are, at the same time, reasonable and have concrete non-symbolic significance. Not for the child, however, but for Wakdjunkaga, who is waiting for spring to come and for the time when he can obtain his food himself. Be it remembered: at no time is Wakdjunkaga represented as becoming a victim of this phantasmagoria. He always remains his old primordial self. He has as yet not learned very much and has forgotten even less.

The denouement arrives when Wakdjunkaga is chased around the fireplace by his mother-in-law, when his vulva drops from him and he is revealed as his true self. Ordinarily on such an occasion in the Wakdjunkaga cycle he is represented as laughing at the discomfiture of those on whom he has played a trick. But here he runs away. The reason is clear; the situation is fraught with too many difficulties. Too many taboos have been broken, the sensibilities of too many people have been outraged, too many individuals have been humiliated. It is serious enough for a chief's son to be indulging in what turns out to be homosexual practices, but far more serious is the situation in which the chief's wife, Wakdjunkaga's 'mother-in-law', finds herself. Among the Winnebago the mother-in-law taboo was very strict, yet here she is openly associating with one who could have married her daughter and become her son-in-law and thus a person with whom she is not allowed to speak and with whom no joking is possible. The right to joke with and to tease an individual implies a very special relationship. It can only take place between a very restricted number of blood-relatives and a less restricted number of relatives-by-marriage. Joking between a mother-in-law and son-in-law is simply unthinkable. Apparently it was even un-thinkable in this *Walpurgisnacht* atmosphere, for the narrator does not use the term *daughter-in-law* when he speaks of the chief's wife teasing Wakdjunkaga, but the term *hiciga*, brother's son's wife. The fact that Wakdjunkaga when functioning as the daughter-in-law could not possibly be *hiciga* a Winnebago audience, of course, would know, but, under the circumstances, any term was better than to call him daughter-in-law.

The shock of all these revelations to those participating in this comic-tragic drama is clear, and our raconteur has expressed this shock by bringing his narrative to a full stop. He apparently feels that one must get out of this insane atmosphere quickly. I think he has done this very astutely. He has Wakdjunkaga not only run away but suddenly come to some realization of what he was doing. Suddenly, and for the first time in the cycle, he is pictured as a normal man with a wife to whom he is legally married and a son for whom it is still necessary to provide. In short, he is suddenly represented as a good citizen, as a thoroughly socialized individual. And so he returns to his home, is received there with joy and stays with his family until his child is well able to take care of himself. The only indication that it is Wakdjunkaga with whom we are here dealing is found in the last three sentences of this episode. 'I will now go around and visit people for I am tired of staying here. I used to wander around the world in peace but here I am just giving myself a lot of trouble.' In these words we have his protest against domestication and society with all its obligations. Doubtless this also voices the protest of all Winnebago against the same things.

The biological education of Wakdjunkaga is now to be resumed. The next adventure is a utilization of a strictly Rabelaisian theme found throughout aboriginal America, the talking laxative bulb (incidents 23 and 24 in text). Although he now possesses intestines of normal human size he knows nothing about them. He comes upon a bulb which tells him that whoever chews it will defecate. Nature has never taunted him in this fashion before. So he takes the bulb and chews it to find that he does not defecate but only breaks wind. This expulsion of gas increases in intensity progressively. He sits on a log, but is propelled into the air with the log on top of him; he pulls up trees to which he clings, by their roots. In his helplessness he has the inhabitants of a village pile all their possessions upon him, their lodges, their dogs, and then they themselves climb upon him, for he tells them that a large warparty is about to attack them. And so the whole world of man is now on Wakdjunkaga's back. With a terrific expulsion of gas he scatters the people and all their possessions to the four quarters of the earth. And there, we are told, he stood laughing until his sides ached.

Apart from the grotesque humour and the obvious satire, is there anything else involved here? Yes. Broadly speaking, a Winnebago would say this is an illustration of what happens when one defies nature even in a minor fashion, that this is what happens when man climbs on Wakdjunkaga's back.

But this world to which he has fled to escape from society, the world where he could wander around in peace, has not finished its test with him. He now begins to defecate. The earth is covered with excrement. To escape it he takes refuge in a tree, but to no avail, and he falls into mountains of his own excrement. Blinded by the filth clinging to him he gropes helplessly for a path to water. The trees whom he asks for information mock and mislead him. Finally he reaches the water and can cleanse himself.

However, despite this reminder of ignorance, knowledge concerning himself and the outside world comes to him slowly. No sooner has he cleansed himself completely than he mistakes the reflection in the water of plums growing on a tree on the shore for the plums themselves.[1]

There now follows a series of incidents (27–46 in text) that have little bearing on the education of Wakdjunkaga. Apart from their manifest satiric implications they are more or less the typical adventures of all North American tricksters. They exemplify all the traits customarily attributed to him, the meaningless cruelty he inflicts upon others in order to obtain food, and how, at the last moment, he is always frustrated and cheated, cheated in fact, not only by others but by himself (see incidents 30, 31); how he comes to grief by trying to imitate others (incidents 32, 33, 41–44); and how occasionally he turns the tables on his tormentors (incidents 34, 45, 46). From a literary and psychological point of view our myth-cycle breaks down after incident 26, where Wakdjunkaga is knocked unconscious by diving after the reflection of plums in the water, although some of the threads are pulled together, albeit not too well, after incident 38.

What should have followed incident 26, I feel, is the episode where Wakdjunkaga, through the instrumentality of chipmunk, is taught where his genitals should be placed on his body and the proper order of penis and testicles. (See incidents 38 and 39 in text.)

The words of Wakdjunkaga in the dialogue between him and chipmunk are worth noting. They are meant to point out that Wakdjunkaga is at last to become aware concretely of his sex. 'Is it not your penis you are carrying on your back?' chipmunk shouts at him, and Wakdjunkaga answers, 'What an evil person it is who mentions that! He seems to have full knowledge of what I am carrying on my back.' Again chipmunk shouts at him, 'Your testicles together!' and Wakdjunkaga answers, 'Why, this being must have been watching me closely.' Throughout Wakdjunkaga acts bewildered and embarrassed. At first he behaves purely passively, although he follows the instruction. He becomes angry only when chipmunk finally shouts at him his last injunction—

[1] This incident is probably of European origin.

141

'Put the head of the penis on top, put it on top!' It is then, when his genitals are in their right place and correctly arranged, when he has really become aware of his sex and his masculinity, it is only then, that he pursues his tormentor. He attacks chipmunk with his penis, not, ostensibly, in order to cohabit with him but to punish and destroy him for making him aware of his genitals and of his sex. It is his final protest at becoming a mature male. Be it remembered that his penis is still of tremendous length. The farther he penetrates the hole in which chipmunk has sought refuge, the more of his penis the latter bites off until it finally has been reduced to human size. In such fashion does Wakdjunkaga become a male and attain sex consciousness.

A very important addendum now follows. In contrast to the manner in which he disposes of the sloughed-off portions of his intestines, namely, by eating them himself, the parts of the penis which chipmunk has bitten off are thrown into the water and transformed into food plants for man.

Wakdjunkaga's resistance to attaining sexual maturity has innumerable larger psychological and psychoanalytical implications the explanation of which, however, I must leave to others. What I would like to stress here are two questions: first, the fact that he cannot himself reduce his large and amorphous genitals to their normal human size, arrange them in their proper order or place them properly. This must be accomplished through some outside agency. Yet, on the other hand, he himself is represented as responsible for reducing the size of his intestines. Second, it might be asked, whether there is involved in the final act, where chipmunk in his hole bites off large parts of Wakdjunkaga's penis, some form of emasculation or some form of cohabitation. My own belief is that neither is involved, but that we are still dealing with Wakdjunkaga's biological evolution and that what is being implied here symbolically is his transition from a generalized natural and procreative force to a concrete heroic human being. This, I feel, is expressly stated in his exclamation, 'Of what a wonderful organ have I been deprived! But why should I say this? I can make useful objects of all these pieces of my penis for human beings!' Thus from being an unconscious benefactor he has now become a conscious benefactor not only of mankind but of nature as well.

Having attained biological maturity one would have imagined that the narrative would then indicate how he attains full psychical and social-ethical maturity. But the incidents that follow show this very inadequately and inconsistently, if at all. It was perhaps actually an impossible thing to do, considering Wakdjunkaga's traditional associations. One of the reasons for this failure, at least from a literary-psychological point of view, lay probably in the fact that one basic exploit or rather, series of exploits, connected with Wakdjunkaga and without which in the minds of the Winnebago the Wakdjunkaga cycle was unthinkable, had still to be included, namely his visits to various animals, the manner in which he was entertained by them and the manner in which he attempts, quite unsuccessfully, to reciprocate their hospitality. (See incidents 41–44.) But these episodes could only with the greatest of difficulty be used to illustrate any progressive development in Wakdjunkaga's character. An attempt, however, seems clearly to have been made, at least in one direction, namely, to show him as developing some sense of social and moral responsibility.

In the incident immediately following the transformation of the gnawed-off pieces of his penis we are told of Wakdjunkaga's meeting with coyote and his attempt to compete with him as a keen scenter. Its only significance in our cycle is to serve as an introduction to the theme of his visits to the muskrat, snipe, woodpecker and polecat (incidents 41–44), and to motivate his turning the tables on coyote (incident 46). What we have in the coyote episode is a very abbreviated form of a competition between Wakdjunkaga and coyote which plays a much greater role in trickster myths in other parts of North America.

The most that our raconteur can do with the episode of the visits to the various animals is to credit Wakdjunkaga with wishing to provide his family with food, to present him as a harmless, vainglorious blunderer and fool, and as one who succeeds in finally obtaining revenge on those who have humiliated him or desire to do so, like mink and coyote. (See incidents 40 and 46.) This is all part of his socialization. Thus, for example, after Polecat visits him and kills innumerable deer for his family we have the following idyllic scene. It is really best to quote it:

' "Well, wife, it is about time for us to go back to the village.

143

Perhaps our relatives are lonesome for us especially for the children." "I was thinking of that myself," replied his wife. . . . Then they packed their possessions and began to carry them away. . . . After a while they got near their home and all the people in the village came out to greet him and help him with the packs. The people of the village were delighted. "Kunu, first-born, is back," they shouted. The chief lived in the middle of the village and alongside of him they built a long lodge for Wakdjunkaga. There the young men would gather at night and he would entertain them for he was a good-natured fellow.' The prodigal son has made good and returned!

This reads almost like an account of the return of a successful warleader, or at least a great hunter. Yet something of his old un-regenerate self still adheres to him, as is seen in the delight he takes in humiliating mink and coyote. However, a Winnebago audience would have sympathized with this humiliation of mink and coyote. They would have agreed that Wakdjunkaga was a very good-natured person, a blundering fool, it is true, but more sinned against than sinning, one who really meant well but whose good intentions always went amiss. It is in this light that we must interpret the two episodes (incidents 47 and 48) which follow, Wakdjunkaga's removal of natural obstacles in the Mississippi River that would interfere with the free movement of human beings.

But before proceeding to the discussion of these, a few words about the implications of one of the points in the fourth of his visits, that to the polecat, seem in point. In that delightful and Rabelaisian episode polecat kills deer by shooting them with wind he expels from his anus. He 'loads' Wakdjunkaga with four such shots to take home with him. Wakdjunkaga is now faced with a new situation. In the case of his visits to muskrat, snipe and woodpecker (41–43), all he had to do to get himself into difficulties and inflict pain upon himself was to imitate them. But now, provided with the means for really accomplishing what his host, polecat, had done, how was he to fail, for fail he must? The problem is simply solved: he must waste these provisions. So, without any reason, he persuades himself that polecat has deceived him, and he shoots at four objects in succession blowing them to pieces—at a knoll, at a tree, at an enormous rock and at a rocky precipitous hill, the last the symbol of a sacred precinct. It is his last act of defiance against the world of nature with which he had, until recently, been on such intimate terms. It is Caliban protesting against the civilization which had been forced upon him.

It would be quite erroneous to think that the author-raconteurs of our cycle were trying in incidents 47 and 48 to exhibit to us a Wakdjunkaga who had now become a wholly beneficent being, a semi-deity in fact. What we have here is a purely secondary addition with no actual connection with what has preceded. It represents largely the influence of the most sacred of all Winnebago narratives, the *Origin Myth of the Medicine Rite*. There, after Earthmaker has created the universe and all its inhabitants, animal and human, he discovers that evil beings[1] are about to exterminate man. In order to help them he sends Wakdjunkaga, the first being comparable to man he has created, down to earth. This is what is meant when we are told that Wakdjunkaga suddenly remembered the purpose for which he had been sent to the earth. In the *Origin Myth of the Medicine Rite* Wakdjunkaga is described as failing completely. Not even Earthmaker apparently could properly 'rehabilitate' him. But on earth Wakdjunkaga could accomplish nothing. As the myth phrases it, 'Every variety of small evil animals began to play pranks on him and plague him and he finally sat himself down and admitted to himself that he was incapable of doing anything.'[2] Yet in spite of all his trickster antecedents he has here, for a moment, been elevated to the rank of a true culture-hero, although the specific role he is being given belongs properly to an entirely different hero, or rather heroes, the *Twins*.

As I have indicated above, I think that a large part of this transformation of the character of Wakdjunkaga is due to the role he plays or was intended to play in the founding of the Medicine Rite. However, to judge from the fact that there seems to have been a difference of opinion among the Winnebago two generations ago, and one which was definitely not of recent origin, as to

---

1 These are not represented as having been created by him.

2 Another version of the same myth states, 'He was like a small child crawling about. . . . All one saw of him was his anus. He accomplished no good and in fact injured Earthmaker's creation.'

how he was to be evaluated, it may very well be that people always interpreted him and his activities in two ways. But to this we will return in the following section when we deal with the Winnebago attitude toward Wakdjunkaga in the first decade of this century.

In the last scene (incident 49) we get still another picture of him. We see him as a deity, an aspect of his nature completely neglected in our cycle, and as the elemental trickster, an ageing trickster, indeed almost a demiurg, taking his last meal on earth. He is pictured sitting on top of a rock with his stone kettle, eating. He perpetuates this last meal for all time, leaving in the rock the imprint of his kettle, of his buttocks and his testicles. He then departs and, since he is the symbol for the procreating power as such and the symbol for man in his relation to the whole universe, he first dives into the ocean and ascends to that island-world over which he presides, that lying immediately under the world of Earthmaker. . . .

The above summary should give the reader some idea of the composite nature of the Winnebago trickster cycle and the degree to which the various episodes composing it have been welded together into a new whole. To obtain a better conception of the success the Winnebago achieved in this regard one must read the trickster cycles of other American Indian tribes. Then it will become clear to what an extent in the Winnebago Wakdjunkaga episodes, incidents, themes and motifs have been integrated, and then the consummate literary ability with which this has been done will stand out sharply. That this literary remodelling and reinterpretation is secondary there can be no question. It is apparently due to special circumstances in Winnebago history and to the existence of a special literary tradition there. To form some idea of what the Wakdjunkaga cycle was originally we must, however, divest our version of all those features which have made it an aboriginal literary masterpiece. This we shall attempt to do in the concluding section of this introduction when we deal with the North American Indian trickster-cycle in general.

VI

THE ATTITUDE OF THE WINNEBAGO TOWARD WAKDJUNKAGA

MUCH of the analysis given in section 5 is the analysis of an outsider, of a white man, and it goes without saying that such an analysis has its dangers and pitfalls, no matter how well such an outsider thinks he knows an aboriginal culture. It is always best to let members of the culture themselves speak, and I shall, there-fore, attempt to present now in a few words what were the ideas and evaluations of contemporary Winnebago—I am speaking of 1908–1918—in regard to Wakdjunkaga and how he was pictured in Winnebago literature. In those years when the new Peyote religion was spreading throughout the tribe and many Winnebago began to make evaluations and re-evaluations of their culture, Wakdjunkaga found both defenders and antagonists. Let me commence with the statement of an old conservative which he prefaced to a myth not included in the cycle being given here:

'The person we call Wakdjunkaga,' so he said, 'was created by Earthmaker, and he was a genial and good-natured person. Earth-maker created him in this manner. He was likewise a chief. He went on innumerable adventures. It is true that he committed many sins. Some people have, for that reason, insisted that he really was the devil.[1] Yet, actually, when you come to think of it, he never committed any sin at all. Through him it was ful-filled that the earth was to retain for ever its present shape, to him is due the fact that nothing today interferes with its proper functioning. True it is that because of him men die, that because of him men steal, that because of him men abuse women, that they lie and are lazy and unreliable. Yes, he is responsible for all this. Yet one thing he never did: he never went on the warpath, he never waged war.

'Wakdjunkaga roamed about this world and loved all things. He called them all brothers and yet they all abused him. Never could he get the better of anyone. Everyone played tricks on him.'

[1] He is referring to the followers of the Peyote rite.

What this particular Winnebago is undoubtedly trying to say is that Wakdjunkaga represented the reality of things, that he was a positive force, a builder, not a destroyer The reference to his not having gone on the warpath is very illuminating It indicates that, for this particular individual, Wakdjunkaga's failure to help mankind by destroying those who were plaguing it was not a reprehensible thing because it would have meant violence, meant waging war. If Wakdjunkaga was thus useless after he had prepared the earth for man that is quite intelligible. That men do not understand him, that they misinterpret and laugh at his activities, this too is intelligible. He does not belong in the world of men but to a much older world.

In contrast to this sympathetic attitude we have that of the members of the Peyote rite. They used Wakdjunkaga and his cycle to point a moral. It would be quite erroneous to imagine that this was an entirely new attitude; it existed long before the Peyote rite came into existence. The attitude of the Peyote people is best illustrated in the following homily:

'The older people often spoke to us of Wakdjunkaga. However, we never knew what they meant.[1] They told us how, on one occasion, he wrapped a racoon-skin blanket around himself and went to a place where there were many people dancing. There he danced until evening and then he stopped and turned around. There was no one to be seen anywhere, and then he realized that he had mistaken for people dancing the noise made by the wind blowing through the reeds.

'So do we Winnebago act. We dance and make a lot of noise but in the end we accomplish nothing.

'Once as Wakdjunkaga was going toward a creek he saw a man standing on the other side, dressed in a black suit and pointing his finger at him. He spoke to the man but the latter would not answer. Then he spoke again and again but without receiving any reply. Finally he got angry and said: "See here! I can do that too." So he put on a black coat and pointed his finger across the creek. Thus both of them stood all day. Toward evening, when he looked around again, he noticed that the man across the creek who had been pointing his finger at him was really a tree stump.

[1] That is, they did not understand the significance of Wakdjunkaga's actions. The following episode is not found in our version of the myth.

148

"O my! What have I been doing all this time? Why did I not look before I began? No wonder the people call me the Foolish-One!"

'Wakdjunkaga was walking around with a pack on his back. As he walked along someone called to him. "Say, we want to sing." "All right," said he. "I am carrying songs in my pack and if you wish to dance, build a large lodge for me with a small hole at the end for an entrance." When it was finished they all went in and Wakdjunkaga followed them. Those who had spoken to him were birds. He told them that, while they were dancing, they were not to open their eyes for if they did their eyes would become red. Whenever a fat bird passed Wakdjunkaga would choke it to death, and if the bird squeaked he would say, "That's it! That's it! Give a whoop!"

'After a while one of the birds got somewhat suspicious and opened its eyes just the least little bit. He saw that Wakdjunkaga was choking all the birds he caught to death, and he cried out, "Let all those who can run save themselves for he is killing us!" Then this bird flew out through the top of the house. Wakdjunkaga took the birds he had killed and roasted them. But he did not get a chance to eat them for they were taken away from him.

'So are we Winnebago. We like all that is forbidden. We say that we like the Medicine Rite; we say that it is good and yet we keep it secret and forbid people to witness it. We tell members of the society not to speak about it until the world comes to an end. They are, in consequence, afraid to speak of it. We, the Winnebago, are the birds and Wakdjunkaga is Satan.

'Once as Wakdjunkaga was going along the road someone spoke to him. He listened and he heard this person saying, "If anyone eats me, faeces will come out of him." Then Wakdjunkaga went up to the object that was talking and said, "What is your name?" "My name is Blows-himself-away." Wakdjunkaga would not believe it and so he ate this object. (It was a shrub.) After a while he blew himself away. He laughed. "O, pshaw! I suppose this is what it meant." As he went along it grew worse and worse, and it was really only after the greatest hardship that he succeeded in returning home.

'So are we Winnebago. We travel on this earth all our lives and then, when one of us tastes something that makes him unconscious,[1] we look upon this very thing with suspicion upon regaining consciousness . . .'

Here we have Wakdjunkaga as both the glorified image of man and as the tempter. The Winnebago term used for Satan here is Hereshguina. The latter is the great evil spirit who is believed to have existed from the beginning of time, who is as old as Earthmaker and always negating what Earthmaker creates. According to one etymology his name means 'he-of-whose-existence-one-is-doubtful'. That Wakdjunkaga should be equated with him by the members of the semi-Christian Peyote rite is not strange.

This insistence on Wakdjunkaga's purely negative side is a very old attitude. We find it among the Dakota-Sioux and the Ponca. But equally old is the interpretation of his character and of his positive activities to which I have referred before and which finds its best expression in a very old myth, *The Two Boys*.[2] In this myth he is represented as actively helping Hare in his endeavours to secure the powers that are eventually to help one of the great spirits to victory over his enemy. In this myth Wakdjunkaga is represented as addressing Earthmaker as follows:

'Father, it is well. That which we desired, this you have given us precisely as we wished it and without any hesitation. It is my friend Hare who is to see that our purpose is attained. He is the only one who can accomplish it. All the spirits in the lodge from which we have come listen and obey what he says, for his are good thoughts. It is he who helped the human beings before, and he will do this for them too.'

To this speech of Wakdjunkaga Earthmaker replies in the following fashion:

'Firstborn, you are the oldest of all those I have created. I created you good natured: I made you a sacred person. I sent you to the earth to remain there so that human beings would listen to you, honour you and obey you and that you might teach them by what means they could secure a happy life. This was the purpose for which you were created. What happened to you after you reached the earth that you brought upon yourself alone. It is because of your own actions and activities that you became the

[1] He is referring to the eating of the peyote.
[2] Cf. Special Publications of Bollingen Foundation, No. 3, Basel, 1954.

butt of everyone's jest, that everyone took advantage of you, even the smallest of insects. How is it then that now you are presenting as a model to be followed that very individual, Hare, who did do what I told him to? You, although you were given the greatest of powers, made light of my creation. It was not anything I told you to do. It is therefore your own fault if people call you the Foolish-One. I created you to do what your friend Hare actually did. I did not create you to injure my creation.'

This apparent bewilderment of the Winnebago supreme deity concerning the reasons for Wakdjunkaga's actions and this disavowal of responsibility for them, it will be important to keep in mind.

VII

THE WAKDJUNKAGA CYCLE AS A SATIRE

THAT those who gave the Wakdjunkaga cycle its present form intended, among other things, to make it a satire on man and on Winnebago society there is little question in my mind. On no other supposition could we possibly explain the inclusion of certain incidents and the very special amplification of others. Indeed, it is only when we take cognizance of this conscious overlay of humour and satire and recognize it as purposive that certain incidents can be properly understood. In order to elucidate the nature of this humour and satire on Winnebago society, it will be best to go through the whole plot and indicate what aspects of their culture are being satirized. The satire on human stupidity and foibles needs no pointing out.

If the double paradox is one of the highest forms of humour, I can think of few scenes where it is better and more skilfully used than in the opening scene of the cycle. The chief of the tribe, one who by definition cannot lead a warparty, is there represented as inviting people to attend a warbundle feast, and, although everyone knows he cannot go on the warpath, everyone must attend because the chief must be obeyed. The latter leaves in the middle of the ceremony and is found cohabiting with a woman, something which is absolutely taboo for one about to lead a warparty.

Finally he starts, but shortly after destroys the warbundle, the most sacred of all Winnebago possessions.

In no other trickster myth in North America do we find any such scene. What is its purpose? To show how evil Wakdjunkaga is? But the Winnebago Wakdjunkaga is not depicted as an evil being. Or are we to regard this as an incident belonging to an older version of the cycle where he was represented as the breaker of taboos and the destroyer of the holy of holies? For this, however, there seems to be little justification. What we really have here is something equivalent to certain semi-religious mediaeval performances where the participants feel that no harm can come to them and where they can pretend to themselves that they cannot be accused of sacrilege or of ridiculing the traditionally accepted order. After all, they can contend that it is about Wakdjunkaga they are speaking and about things that happened in a distant age that will never return. We have here, in short, an outlet for voicing a protest against the many, often onerous, obligations connected with the Winnebago social order and their religion and ritual. Primitive people have wisely devised many such outlets.

The next obvious piece of satire is to be found in incident 15, where Wakdjunkaga exclaims, 'Aha, aha! The chiefs have unfurled their banner! The people must be having a great feast!' The banner we know is the *penis erectus* with Wakdjunkaga's blanket on top of it. The satire here is directed at one of the most important of the Winnebago feasts, that given by the chief of the tribe once a year, at which he raises his emblem of authority, a long feathered crook. It is his obligation at this feast to deliver long harangues admonishing his people to live up to the ideals of Winnebago society.

Of a milder nature, but still unmistakable, is the parody on the ritualistic competition between the Thunderbird clan and the Bear clan in the fast-eating contest of the Warbundle Rite (incident 36). This satire has a double reference. According to the myth of the origin of the Thunderbird clan, a race originally took place between a member of this clan and one of the Bear clan to determine who was to be the chief of the tribe. In fact there is probably even another satire intended here, namely on the counting of war honours in battle. Only when all these facts

are remembered can we understand the full meaning of the
following passages:

'Let us run a race and let the one who wins be the chief. The
one who loses will then dish out the food' (said Wakdjunkaga to
mink). . . . 'The pot with the food in it is to be the goal, and
the one who first touches the food is to be declared the winner.'

It would take us too far afield to discuss at length why it is just
the chief of the tribe who is here and in other parts of the cycle
so repeatedly criticized. Perhaps it will be enough if I mention
that he was the symbol of order, the proponent of peace, one
whose function it was to interfere in all kinds of situations.
Moreover he, in a civilization where prestige was primarily
associated with warfare, could not go on the warpath.

One of the sharpest satires is that on puberty fasting (incidents
33 and 34). Individuals were always protesting against the rigors
connected with it and the restrictions imposed upon them, and
they must have thoroughly enjoyed the scene where Wakdjunkaga, his head helplessly caught in the elk skull, lies stretched
out on the ground near a stream, covered with his racoon-skin
blanket, 'quite a fear-inspiring object to look upon', as the myth
sarcastically and sacrilegiously says. The parody is perfect. A
woman, in the morning, going out to fetch some water comes
upon him and runs away. He calls her back and addresses her.
His words really must be given:

'Turn back; I will bless you. . . . Get an axe and bring it over
here. Then get all the offerings that are customary, of which your
relatives will tell you. If you strike the top of my head with the
axe, you will be able to use what you find therein as medicine and
obtain anything that you wish. I am an elk spirit. I am blessing
the village. . . . I am one of the great spirits living in these
waters.'

To understand the humour and satire here let me point out that
one can only obtain blessings from the spirits at night and by
properly preparing for it—blackening one's face and fasting.
Spirits do not appeal to a person to let them bless them.

What is interesting in this incident is that, at the end when
the elk skull has been split open and Wakdjunkaga revealed
laughing at everybody's discomfiture, the implied blasphemy in
the whole proceeding was more than the creators of the scene

wished to take upon themselves, and Wakdjunkaga says, ' "Inasmuch as you have made these offerings to me they will not be lost. For whatsoever be the purpose for which you use this head, that purpose will be accomplished." So the people made themselves various medicinal instruments and afterwards found that they were efficacious.'

So much for the important aspects of Winnebago culture satirized and ridiculed. To give examples of the less important aspects would require too much space. I will content myself with just one. In incident 27 where Wakdjunkaga induces the racoon mothers to entrust their children to him while they are looking for plums he says, 'If, toward evening, as the sun sets, you see the sky red, you will know that the plums are causing it.' This remark is a clear-cut parody of a scene from a well-known myth where the father tells his children that if, toward evening, they see the sky turn red this means that he has been slain. In fact this has become a metaphor for death from violence. Again, after Wakdjunkaga had killed and eaten the young racoons entrusted to his care, he cuts off the head of one of the children, puts a stick through its neck and places it at the door, as though the child were peeping out and laughing. This was a well-known Winnebago war custom. In short, what is being so savagely satirized are the war customs.

The above examples should suffice to prove that we are dealing in these passages with a deliberate satire. That such satire did not belong to the cycle originally, however, there can be little doubt. Yet this does not necessarily mean that it is not old. It is safe to assume that there always existed professional humorists and satirists in the tribe, and an audience that was delighted to listen to them.

VIII

THE WAKDJUNKAGA CYCLE AND ITS RELATION TO OTHER NORTH AMERICAN INDIAN TRICKSTER CYCLES

WE have now come to our last and, in many ways, our most difficult task, namely, to try to determine to what extent the Winnebago Wakdjunkaga cycle, in the form here presented, represents a special rendering of this narrative peculiar to the Winnebago. I put this question for two reasons: first, because nowhere else in North America is it told in this particular fashion, and, second, because there are indications in the Winnebago version that suggest very forcibly that there has been a remodelling of an older form. I am not referring here to the type of remodelling already dwelt upon—the satirical overlay or the psychological-ethical emphasis—but something that antedates these by many generations. To attack such a problem in the absence of historical data is difficult and perhaps foolhardy. Nevertheless it must be done. The only way in which this can be achieved with any hope of success is by comparing the Winnebago version with the trickster cycles of other parts of the continent.

The overwhelming majority of all so-called trickster myths in North America give an account of the creation of the earth, or at least the transforming of the world, and have a hero who is always wandering, who is always hungry, who is not guided by normal conceptions of good or evil, who is either playing tricks on people or having them played on him and who is highly sexed. Almost everywhere he has some divine traits. These vary from tribe to tribe. In some instances he is regarded as an actual deity, in others as intimately connected with deities, in still others he is at best a generalized animal or human being subject to death. One of the questions we will have to resolve is how to explain these fluctuations as to the nature of his identity.

It will be best to take up each one of these points separately and discuss them in terms of a limited number of tribes, these tribes to be selected in terms of the type of culture they possess and the richness and authenticity of the mythological material we happen to have concerning them. Because of these considerations my stress will be laid on the trickster cycles of the North-west Coast of Canada, the Algonquian-speaking tribes of the Western Plains of the United States, and of Wisconsin and Minnesota and the Siouan-speaking tribes in the area extending from Montana eastward to Nebraska and the Great Lakes.

On the North-west Coast[1] the trickster is Raven. The cycle connected with him consists of two parts, the first recording incidents dealing with the creation of the world and of natural phenomena, the second, those relating to Raven's insatiable hunger and how he, by force and trickery, obtains or tries to obtain all he wants. In the course of his adventures he suffers rebuff after rebuff, but in the end he is always successful. In the first part of the cycle the incidents are relatively well integrated, in the second no specific order need be followed. Not only does he obtain satisfaction for all his desires and impulses and appease his voracious appetite but in the course of his exploits, and never consciously willed, he creates many of the objects man needs, and fixes the customs they are to have. As we shall see, we have here a trait which we shall find throughout all North America.

Generally all the raven cycles begin in one of two ways. In the first the world is represented as originally covered by water, and Raven commences his activities after the water has subsided of itself or after he has caused it to subside. In the second the world is represented as being in complete darkness. In the first an account of the birth of Raven is given, and he is given a definite pedigree, in the second he apparently has always existed. Let me give two illustrations, one from the Haida,[2] the other from the Tlingit,[3] of how each type begins. The Haida account runs as follows:

'Over this island salt water extended, they say. Raven flew about. He looked for a place upon which to sit. After a while he

[1] F. Boas, *Tsimshian Mythology*, Bureau of American Ethnology, Vol. 31, Washington, D.C., 1916. Cf. particularly pp. 565–958.

[2] J. R. Swanton, *Haida Texts and Myths*, Bureau of American Ethnology, Bulletin 29, Washington, 1905, pp. 110–111.

[3] J. R. Swanton, *Tlingit Texts and Myths*, Bureau of American Ethnology, Bulletin 39, Washington, 1909, pp. 80–81. Cf. also pp. 104–108 of this book.

flew away to sit upon a flat rock which lay toward the south end of the island. All the supernatural creatures lay on it like Geno, with their necks laid across one another. The feebler supernatural beings were stretched out from it in this, that, and every direction, asleep. It was light then, and yet dark, they say.

'The Loon's place was in the house of Nankilstlas. One day he went out and called. Then he came running in and sat down in the place he always occupied. And an old man was lying down there, but never looking toward him. By and by he went out a second time, cried, came in, and sat down. He continued to act in this manner.

'One day the person whose back was turned to the fire asked: "Why do you call so often?" "Ah, chief, I am not calling on my own account. The supernatural ones tell me that they have no place in which to settle. That is why I am calling." And he said: "I will attend to it (literally, 'make')."

'After having flown about for a while Raven was attracted by the neighbouring clear sky. Then he flew up thither. And running his beak into it from beneath he drew himself up. A five-row town lay there, and in the front row the chief's daughter had just given birth to a child. In the evening they all slept. He then skinned the child from the foot and entered (the skin). He lay down in its place.

'On the morrow its grandfather asked for it, and it was given to him. He washed it, and he put his feet against the baby's feet and pulled up. He then put it back. On the next day he did the same thing and handed it back to its mother. He was now hungry. They had not begun to chew up feed to put into his mouth.

'One evening, after they had all gone to bed and were asleep, Raven raised his head and looked about upon everything inside the house. All slept in the same position. Then by wriggling continually he loosened himself from the cradle in which he was fastened and went out. In the corner of the house lived a Half-rock being, who watched him. After she had watched for a while he came in, holding something under his blanket, and, pushing aside the fire which was always kept burning before his mother, he dug a hole in the cleared place and emptied what he held into it. As soon as he had kneaded it with the ashes he ate it. It gave forth a popping sound. He laughed while he ate. She saw all that from the corner.

'Again, when it was evening and they were asleep, he went out. After he had been gone for a while he again brought in something under his blanket, put it into the ashes and stirred it up with them. He poked it out and laughed as he ate it. From the corner of the house the Half-rock one looked on. He got through, went back, and lay down in the cradle. On the next morning all the five villages talked about it. He heard them.

'The inhabitants of four of the five towns had each lost one eye. . . .'

Contrast this with the introduction to the *Raven Cycle* of the Tlingit:

'At the beginning of things there was no daylight and the world lay in blackness. They there lived in a house at the head of Nass river 'a being called Raven-at-the-head-of-Nass (Nas-caki-yel) . . . and in his house were all kinds of things including sun, moon, stars and daylight. . . . With him were two old men called Old-man-who-foresees-all-troubles-in-the-world (Adawul-canak) and He-who-knows-everything-that-happens (Tliewat-uwadjigi-can). . . . Under the earth was a third old person, Old-woman-underneath (Hayi-canake), placed under the world by Nas-caki-yel. Nas-caki-yel was unmarried and lived alone with these two old men, and yet he had a daughter, a thing no one is able to explain. Nor do people know what this daughter was. The two old persons took care of her like servants, and especially they always looked into the water before she drank to see that it was perfectly clean.

'First of all beings Nas-caki-yel created the Heron as a very tall and very wise man, and after him the Raven, who was also a very good and very wise man at that time.

'Raven came into being in this wise. His first mother had many children, but they all died young, and she cried over them continually. According to some this woman was Nas-caki-yel's sister, and it was Nas-caki-yel who was doing this because he did not wish her to have any male children. By and by Heron came to her and said, "What is it that you are crying about all the time?" She answered, "I am always losing my children. I cannot bring them up." Then he said, "Go down on the beach when the tide is lowest, get a small, smooth stone, and put it into the fire. When it is red hot, swallow it. Do not be afraid." She said, "All right." Then she followed Heron's directions and gave birth to Raven. Therefore Raven's name was really It-cAk, the name of a very hard rock, and he was hence called TAqlik-ic (Hammer-father). This is why Raven was so tough and could not easily be killed.

'Heron and Raven both became servants to Nas-caki-yel, but he thought more of Raven and made him head man over the world. Then Nas-caki-yel made some people.

'All of the beings Nas-caki-yel had created, however, existed in darkness, and this existence lasted for a long time, how long is unknown. But Raven felt very sorry for the few people in darkness and, at last, he said to himself, "If I were only the son of Nas-caki-yel I could do almost anything." So he studied what he should do and decided upon a plan. He made himself very small, turned himself into a hemlock needle and floated upon the water Nas-caki-yel's daughter was about to drink. Then she swallowed it and soon after became pregnant.

'Although all this was by the will of Nas-caki-yel and although he knew what was the matter with his daughter, yet he asked her how she had gotten into that condition. She said, "I drank water, and I felt that I had swallowed something in it." . . .

'Nas-caki-yel tried to make human beings out of a rock and out of a leaf at the same time, but the rock was slow while the leaf was very quick. Therefore human begins came from the leaf. Then he showed a leaf to the human beings and said, "You see this leaf. You are to be like it. When it falls off the branch and rots there is nothing left of it." That is why there is death in the world. If men had come from the rock there would be no death. Years ago people used to say they were getting old, "We are unfortunate in not having been made from a rock. Being made from a leaf, we must die." '

If we compare these two types of introduction it is difficult to escape the conviction that in the case of the Tlingit we are dealing with a secondary accretion, and that the Haida is much closer in form to the true beginning of the trickster myths. In the Tlingit myth there is a complete break between Trickster conceived of as a divine being and as a true transformer of the world and the Trickster whose actions have no purpose and who behaves like a fool. And this conviction is strengthened when we look at some of the trickster cycles of the other tribes where we find Trickster associated with the creation of the world. Thus among the Gros Ventre of northern Montana we find the following opening[1]:

'The people before the present people were wild. They did not know how to do anything. Nixant did not like the way they lived and died. He thought, "I will make a new world." He had the chief pipe. He went outdoors and hung the pipe on three sticks. He picked up four buffalo-chips. One he put under each of the sticks on which the pipe hung, and one he took for his own seat. He said, "I will sing three times and shout three times. After I have done these things, I will kick the earth, and water will come out of the cracks. There will be a heavy rain. There will be water over all the earth." Then he began to sing. After he sang three times, he shouted three times. Then he kicked the ground and it cracked. The water came out, and it rained for days, and over all the earth was water. By means of the buffalo-chips he and the pipe floated. Then it stopped raining. There was water everywhere. He floated wherever the wind took him. For days he drifted thus. Above him the Crow flew about. All the other birds and animals were drowned. The Crow became tired. It flew about crying, "My father, I am becoming tired. I want to rest." Three times it said this. After it had said so three times, Nixant said, "Alight on the pipe and rest." Repeatedly the Crow cried to him, and each time was allowed to alight on the pipe. Nixant became tired sitting in one position. He cried. He did not know what to do. After he had cried a long time, he began to unwrap the chief pipe. The pipe contained all animals. He selected those with a long

[1] A. L. Kroeber, *Gros Ventre Myths and Tales*, Anthropological Papers of the American Museum of Natural History, Vol. 1, New York, 1908, pp. 59–61.

breath to dive through the water. First he selected the Large Loon. The Loon was not alive, but Nixant had its body wrapped up in the pipe. Nixant sang, and then commanded it to dive and try to bring mud. The Loon dived. It was not half-way down when it lost its breath and immediately turned back. It came up almost drowned at the place where Nixant was. Then Nixant took the Small Loon's body and sang. Then the Small Loon dived. It nearly reached the mud at the bottom. Then it lost its breath and went up again, and, nearly dead, reached the place where Nixant was. Then he took the Turtle. He sang and it became alive, and he sent it and it dived. Meanwhile the Crow did not alight, but flew about crying for rest. Nixant did not listen to it. After a long time the Turtle came up. It was nearly dead. It had filled its feet and the cracks along its sides with mud. When it reached Nixant all the mud had been washed away, and it was nearly dead. Nixant said, "Did you succeed in reaching the mud?" The Turtle said, "Yes, I reached it. I had much of it in my feet and about my sides, but it all washed away from me before I came to you." Then Nixant looked at the inside of its feet and in the cracks of its sides. On the inside of its feet he found a little earth. He scraped this into his hand. Meanwhile the Crow had become very tired. Then Nixant, when he had scraped the earth into his hand, began to sing. After he had sung three times, he shouted three times. Then he said, "I will throw this little dust that I have in my hand into the water. Little by little let there be enough to make a strip of land large enough for me." . . . After he had made the land, there was no water anywhere. He went about with his pipe and with the Crow. They were all that there was to be seen in the world. Now Nixant was thirsty. He did not know what to do to get water. Then he thought, "I will cry." He cried. While he cried, he closed his eyes. He tried to think how he could get water. He shed tears. His tears dropped on the ground. They made a large spring in front of him. Then a stream ran from the spring. When he stopped crying, a large river was flowing. Thus he made rivers and streams. He became tired of being alone with the Crow and the pipe. He decided to make persons and animals. . . .'

The introduction to the Blackfoot Trickster myth we have already given. (See p. 127.) Among the Assiniboine[1] of the province of Alberta, Canada, the trickster cycle begins in the same way, and the same holds for the Crow of Montana.[2] 'Long ago,' so the Crow myth begins, 'there was no earth, only water. The only creatures in the world were the ducks and Old Man. He came down to meet the ducks and said to them, "My brothers, there is earth below us. It is not good for us to be alone." ' Thereupon Old Man makes them dive and one of them reappears with some mud in its webbed feet. Out of this Old Man creates the earth. Then, when he has made it, he exclaims, 'Now that we have made the earth there are others who wish to be alive.' Immediately a wolf is heard howling in the east. In this manner everything in the world was created.

In all these tribes we find the same break between Trickster conceived of as a divine being and as a buffoon. Nor is it only the outsider who feels this. Many Indians themselves felt it, and tried to explain it in various ways. Swanton found individuals among the Haida who insisted that the deity Nankilstlas, with whom Raven is identified, put on the skin of a raven when he wanted to act like a buffoon.[3] An educated Tlingit told Boas that the buffoon-like incidents were added to offset the serious parts of the myth.[4] Many other examples of the same kind of reaction could be found. For this reason, as well as the peculiar nature of the distribution of this opening of the cycle, it seems fairly certain that the original cycle did not begin in this manner, that this opening belongs to an entirely different cycle, either to that relating to the typical culture-hero and the transformer of the world, as illustrated by the Winnebago *Twin*, *Red Horn* and *Hare Cycles* (cf. pp. 119–121; 163–191), or to specific origin myths.

That, originally at least, Trickster was not a deity in the

---

[1] R. H. Lowie, *The Assiniboine*, Anthropological Papers of the American Museum of Natural History, Vol. IV, New York, 1910, pp. 100–101. Cf. also pp. 97–103 of this book.

[2] R. H. Lowie, *Myths and Traditions of the Crow Indians*, Anthropological Papers of the American Museum of Natural History, Vol. XXV, Part I, New York, 1918, p. 14.

[3] Op. cit., p. 146.

[4] F. Boas, op. cit., p. 582, note.

ordinary sense of the term seems evident. That attempts were constantly being made to elevate him to such a rank is, however, equally clear. The Tsimshian furnish us with an excellent example of just such a process.[1] There the myth opens with a description of the death of a much beloved son, for whom his parents mourn ceaselessly under the scaffold-bed upon which the body of the dead youth has been deposited. One morning the mother, paying her daily visit to where his corpse is lying, discovers instead of her son's body, a youth lying there, bright as a fire. Upon being asked if he is her son he answers in the affirmative. Soon the people of the village gather around, and to them the shining youth says, 'Heaven was much annoyed at your constant wailing so he sent me down to comfort your minds.' One thing, however, disturbed the parents about their newly recovered son. He ate practically nothing.

One day when the parents were out two slaves entered, threw some whale-fat into the fire and then ate it. The shining youth, seeing this, asks them, 'What makes you so hungry?' They reply, 'We are hungry because we have eaten scabs from our shin bones.' Thereupon he asks for some, but the slaves warn him not to eat it lest he become like themselves. However, he insists, is given and eats some and becomes hungry. So tremendous is his appetite that within a short time he has consumed all the provisions in his father's house, and then proceeds to consume those in the other houses of the village as well. The provisions of the whole tribe are soon exhausted and the father, in desperation, decides to send his son away because of the danger he has now become to the tribe and because of the humiliation he feels at his son's behaviour. Before despatching him he addresses him saying, 'My dear son, I am sending you away inland to the other side of the ocean.' Then he gives him a small round stone, a raven-blanket and a dried sea-lion bladder filled with all kinds of berries. Again he speaks to him, 'My son, when you fly across the ocean (with this raven-blanket around you) and you feel weary, drop this stone and you shall find rest on it. When you reach the mainland scatter the various kinds of fruit all over the land; and also scatter the salmon roe in all the rivers and brooks, and also the trout roe; so that you may not lack food as long as you live in the world.'

[1] F. Boas, op. cit., pp. 58–60.

Thus we see here, too, the attempt to give Trickster a divine pedigree is manifestly unsuccessful, just as it is in one of the Raven cycles recorded by Swanton,[1] where the father of Raven, definitely conceived of as a deity, instructs him from childhood so that when he grew up he could give him the strength to create a world. In another of the versions of the Raven cycle (see pp. 104–108), the attempt to give him a divine pedigree is much more successful. Broadly speaking, it can be said that only when Trickster has been definitely separated from the cycle connected with him, as among the Fox, the Ojibwa and the Winnebago, does he definitely become a deity or the son of one. In all these tribes, significantly enough, the episodes connected with him as a deity form an independent and well-integrated unit.

On the basis of all these facts only one conclusion is possible, namely, that Trickster's divinity is always secondary and that it is largely a construction of the priest-thinker, of a remodeller. This does not mean that it is not at times very ancient. Nor does it answer the important question of why, if he was not a deity, so many attempts have been made to equate him with one. I think the reason for these attempts is comparatively simple. He is admittedly the oldest of all figures in American Indian mythology, probably in all mythologies. It is not accidental that he is so frequently connected with what was regarded in all American Indian cosmologies as among the oldest of all natural phenomena, rock and sun. Thus he was a figure that could not be forgotten, one that had to be recognized by all aboriginal theological systematizers.

This recognition could be expressed in two ways, either to keep him on a par with the true deities or to treat him as one who had once been a deity and who had then been deprived of his divinity. The Winnebago and the Tlingit attempted the former although, as we have seen, they clearly found it difficult to do so. The majority of tribes do indeed postulate his divinity but then immediately question it in a number of ways, one of them being to represent him as being defeated by a real deity. A small, but important, number of tribes prefer to regard him as a deity who has been definitely displaced and reduced to the position of an evil-working semi-deity by a more powerful deity. One of the

[1] J. R. Swanton, *Tlingit Myths*, p. 3.

best examples of such a displacement is found among the Oglala Dakota. Here the systematizing and reorganizing activity of the priest-thinker can be seen at its highest.

According to Oglala theology Trickster, there called *Iktomi*, i.e. Spider, was the first-born son of the Rock and a being called the Winged One. In a myth[1] he himself states who he is: 'I am a god and the son of a god. My father, the Rock, is the oldest of the gods. It is he that named all things and made all languages that are spoken. I have done much good and should be treated as a god, but because my other parent, the Winged God, had no shape, my form is queer and all laughed at me. When I do good all laugh at me as if I were making sport, and since everyone laughs at me I will laugh at them.' In this myth he is represented as being punished by the supreme deity for having brought shame and ridicule upon other gods and is condemned to go to the world and remain there without friends, is condemned to the fate that all mankind will hate him. To this he is represented as responding with a long and loud laugh, and as telling the supreme deity that he had forgotten the birds and the other animals; that he would dwell with them and talk with each in its own language; and that on earth he would enjoy himself and make fools of mankind.

Assuredly no comment is needed here.

If then the episodes depicting Trickster as a divinity or as the primal creator can be eliminated as not belonging to the cycle connected with him originally, how did the cycle in its oldest form really begin? I think it is safe to assume that it began with an account of a nondescript person obsessed by hunger, by an uncontrollable urge to wander and by sexuality. Now this individual is often represented as an old man. Yet *old* must not be taken too literally here. It seems to imply ageless, existing from all time. Among the western tribes of North America, i.e. the North-west Coast of Canada and the Western Plains, his identity fluctuates but generally he is given an animal name. Since here, as in fact, everywhere, he can transform himself at will into any form, this animal form simply represents one of his aspects. There are, however, certain specific physical traits that he possesses among a

[1] J. R. Walker, *Oglala Sun Dance*, Anthropological Papers of the American Museum of Natural History, Vol. XVI, Part II, New York, 1917, pp. 166–167.

large number of tribes, the most important of which are his enormous penis and large intestines.

We now come to one of our most important questions, namely, what episodes can be safely postulated as having always been associated with him? To arrive at any satisfactory answer to this question we shall have to examine the cycle that so frequently exists side by side with that of Trickster, that of the culture-hero or Transformer, the cycle, that is, which corresponds to that of Hare, of Red Horn and of the Twins of the Winnebago. We have such a cycle in some parts of the North-west Coast and among many Siouan-speaking tribes, but it is conspicuously absent in most parts of the North-west Coast, throughout the Western Plains and Plateau areas of the United States and among all the Algonquian-speaking peoples of the Great Lakes.

As we have already pointed out (cf. p. 124ff.), and as a perusal of the complete cycle given on pp. 63–91 will make quite clear, the adventures of Hare—he is the typical culture-hero— are of two kinds. The first deals with his self-education, his progress from immaturity to maturity, from insecurity to security; the second, with his endeavours to make the earth habitable for man and with the establishment of man's customs. There is no question in this cycle, concerning his physical appearance or his belonging in a definite social environment. He has relatives. He has attachments. His task is to grow up and to see that human beings grow up with him. Most of the incidents in the cycle illustrate how this is accomplished. Wherever we find an independent culture-hero distinct from the Trickster cycle, this invariably holds true. We can safely regard most of the incidents in such a culture-hero cycle as having always belonged more or less together, and as having always had the purpose just mentioned.

Without being too dogmatic, it can be claimed that to the culture-hero cycle belong such well-known episodes as those narrating the securing of fire, of flint, of tobacco, of food in general and of the main cultivated plants; the regulation of the seasons and of the weather; the assignment of their proper and non-destructive functions to the forces of nature; the freeing of the world from monsters, ogres and giants; the origin of death; the gradual education of the hero's female guardian, generally pictured as inimical at first, and the gradual freeing of the hero from her tutelage. This freeing is symbolized by his being swallowed by a sea-monster, killing it and escaping from it and, finally, by his cohabiting with his guardian.

Wherever these incidents are found with these purposes implied, united with typical trickster episodes, and where the latter greatly predominate, we can be certain that they are intrusive. Such 'mixed' myth-cycles are very common and are widely distributed. Many American ethnologists regard them as representing the true trickster cycle. There seems little justification for this viewpoint, however. All the available evidence indicates that we are dealing here with typical trickster cycles into which have been incorporated incidents connected with an entirely different hero or, better supernatural being or beings, to whom the creation of the world and the establishment of customs are generally ascribed. In this mixed myth-type, Trickster's primary traits—his voracious appetite, his wandering and his unbridled sexuality—are always stressed. Apart from the North-west Coast of Canada, the emphasis is markedly on his unbridled sexuality.

To form some idea of the proportion of episodes relating to origins as compared to those of the purely trickster type, let me give some figures. On the North-west Coast there are seventeen of the former out of forty-five; among the Blackfoot, five out of twenty-six; among the Gros Ventre, three out of twenty-six; among the Assiniboine, five out of fifty-two; among the Menominee, three out of twenty-seven; among the Shoshone, five out of thirty-six; and among the Crow, five out of twenty-eight.[1]

If we eliminate from the mixed type of the trickster cycle all its intrusive elements, we arrive at a cycle approximating remarkably to that found among the Winnebago, leaving out, of course, the secondary additions, elaborations and reinterpretations which I have pointed out before. This leaves us with a plot that can be briefly summarized as follows:

In a world that has no beginning and no end, an ageless and Priapus-like protagonist is pictured strutting across the scene,

[1] For an excellent example of such a mixed type cf. R. H. Lowie, The Assiniboine, pp. 239–244. Cf. this book pp. 97–103.

wandering restlessly from place to place, attempting, successfully and unsuccessfully, to gratify his voracious hunger and his uninhibited sexuality. Though he seems to us, and not only to us but to aboriginal peoples as well, to have no purpose, at the end of his activities a new figure is revealed to us and a new psychical reorientation and environment have come into being. Nothing here has been created *de novo*. What is new has been attained either by the sloughing off and rearrangement of the old or, negatively, by the demonstration that certain types of behaviour inevitably bring about ridicule and humiliation and result in pain and suffering where they do not actually lead to death.

All the incidents connected with the transformation of the amorphous figure of Trickster as well as those that lead unconsciously to the creation of the new psychical orientation and environment, naturally belong to the original Trickster cycle. Since, however, this cycle has been revised, reorganized and reinterpreted for an untold period of time and since innumerable exploits have the same import as those just mentioned, many may have been attributed to Trickster that did not originally have any connection with him.

But what, we may well ask, is the content, what is the meaning of this original plot? About this there should be little doubt, I feel. It embodies the vague memories of an archaic and primordial past, where there as yet existed no clear-cut differentiation between the divine and the non-divine. For this period Trickster is the symbol. His hunger, his sex, his wandering, these appertain neither to the gods nor to man. They belong to another realm, materially and spiritually, and that is why neither the gods nor man known precisely what to do with them.

The symbol which Trickster embodies is not a static one. It contains within itself the promise of differentiation, the promise of god and man. For this reason every generation occupies itself with interpreting Trickster anew. No generation understands him fully but no generation can do without him. Each had to include him in all its theologies, in all its cosmogonies, despite the fact that it realized that he did not fit properly into any of them, for he represents not only the undifferentiated and distant past, but likewise the undifferentiated present within every individual. This constitutes his universal and persistent attraction. And so he became and remained everything to every man—god, animal, human being, hero, buffoon, he who was before good and evil, denier, affirmer, destroyer and creator. If we laugh at him, he grins at us. What happens to him happens to us.

Part Four

THE TRICKSTER
IN RELATION TO
GREEK MYTHOLOGY

By Karl Kerényi

1

FIRST IMPRESSIONS

THE publishers of this—as the reader will no doubt have gathered—somewhat unusual volume have requested me, in association with two authorities whose competence in this field of research is well known, to give my impressions of the text here made available to the general public for the first time.

Anyone who is concerned with mythology will naturally have to define his attitude towards narratives which are available only in translation. Even so, I would never have ventured to say anything in public about a Winnebago text unless I could express my views as I am now doing: not in the form of a commentary, but as an essay, and with all possible reserve in regard to nuances which only a Winnebago expert is sensitive enough to perceive.

Yet it may be that the publishers were right in thinking that the sensibility of one who finds himself in daily contact with the mythological material that lies closest to us—the Greek—might be able to offer something of more general interest. Certainly I can pass on my impressions and tentatively apply the viewpoints I have gained from a long and devoted study of mythology. Questioning first of all the utility of the viewpoint: does it shed light on this extraordinary material without reducing to abstract generalities the concrete human situations we there encounter?

It is obvious that any definition which seeks to reduce the essence of mythology to the magical power of the word is useless. Even if one took the evocative power of the narrator's word as such supposed magic—which would be to confuse magic with something else—one could not but notice that the narrator's words are themselves determined by the figure he wishes to evoke. This figure must be granted the logical priority: he comes before the expression in words. We must also grant him the greater consistency, an unchanging, indestructible core that not only antedates all the stories told about him, but has survived in spite of them. Let us call him the Trickster. A trickster he is and remains, even when the story-tellers would like to show him as a stupid buffoon and a *victim* of the world's trickery.

The logic inherent in a good story breaks down in face of the consistency and indestructibility of the core. According to the logic of the story, the hero would have to be the arch-fool, not the arch-trickster. This conclusion is drawn more than once (the story-teller was, after all, no fool and thought just as logically as we do), but in a very curious manner. We are told in episode fourteen: 'My, my! Correctly, indeed, am I named Foolish One, Trickster!' The retention of the Winnebago word for trickster—Wakdjunkaga—does not get rid of the contradiction, for we learn from Paul Radin that although this name is of unknown etymology it still means 'trickster' or 'cunning one'. As we shall have occasion to see, this connotation is well founded. The explanation given by the narrator himself contains the same contradiction: 'By calling me thus, they have at last turned me into a Foolish One, a Trickster.' Whichever way one looks at it, one cannot get rid of the contradiction except by abolishing the hero. But the hero is stronger than the stories told about him.

How are we to conceive that unrecorded, original situation in which a story was told about him for the first time? There is much trickery at large in the world, all sorts of sly and cunning tricks among human beings, animals and even plants, which could no more remain hidden from a story-teller whose inner life was as much bound up with the world as his outer one, than they could from an observer at a distance. Did he ask himself the specific question: 'Who played these tricks first, who introduced them into the scheme of things?' Was his story, like so many other mythologems, the answer to this question of origins? At any rate his story dealt neither with particular observations nor with slyness and cunning in general, but with a figure clearly envisaged by the eye of the myth-maker, pre-existent to any definite question: the arch-trickster himself, no matter whether

he appeared in human form, or as a cunning animal, the proto-
type of Reynard the Fox, whose equivalent for some tribes was
the coyote, for others the raven, but who in all his manifestations
was a primordial being of the same order as the gods and heroes
of mythology. Suddenly he must have sprung forth, the trickster
behind all tricksters, and have been there so compellingly that
all who heard tell of him recognized him at once as the figure
whom the story-teller had in mind.

This hypothesis seeks neither to isolate the 'first' story-teller
from his surroundings, the human world, nor to rob this world
of the possibility of becoming a theatre for manifestations of the
divine. In mythology, we hear the world telling its own story to
itself. The supposition that we are up against a phenomenon of a
kind which the science of mythology is not meant to 'explain',
just as the science of aesthetics is not meant to 'explain' the
phenomena of art, seems to me unavoidable. Rather, its task is to
help us understand this phenomenon in human terms. It is, of
course, not absolutely necessary to frame an origination hypothesis at all—which must moreover remain uncertain on one
point. At this early stage of research it must remain an open
question whether the original event, the hypothetical basis for a
group of mythological tales like those concerning the trickster,
was something unique, and man's readiness to accept them
universal, or whether it happened repeatedly and in many
different places.

In the present instance we have to do with a species of the genus
mythology, just as the picaresque novel without national or tem-
poral limitations, represented by Rabelais and others, and dating
from Petronius, is a species of the genus novel. 'Picaro' is the
Spanish word for a villain or rogue. What we are concerned with
here is picaresque mythology. It has always existed, only the
proper name for it was lacking, and a scientific survey capable of
grasping it in its essence. Its purpose was never magical or
didactic; it wished only to tell of its hero, who was its pre-
condition. Did it thereby exercise a special function apart from
entertainment—or rather, precisely through this manner of entertainment? We shall not be evading this question, either, if we
treat mythology in the proper way.

Even though they cannot be answered with certainty, the

175

questions as to where, when, and how the trickster myth originated should not divert our attention from the trickster himself, or from the manner of his telling. He himself determines this manner in its essential features, as well as that luxuriance of style which we shall be discussing presently. He could be defined as the timeless root of all the picaresque creations of world literature, ramifying through all times and countries, and not reducible to a merely literary entity; a being who is exalted above the petty limitations of mortal tricksters. I base this view on the mythology with which I am familiar, yet I cannot help seeing additional confirmation of it in the fact that the mythology of another American Indian tribe, the Wichita, credits the coyote with the faculty of telling endless roguish stories about himself, the animal equivalent of the trickster. From this it does not follow that the coyote is only a second-class figure in Wichita mythology, 'falsely invented' and somehow limited in his being. However the audience may have judged such stories, perhaps as the lying tales of an arch-deceiver, that does not deprive him of his existence. On the contrary, shameless untruthfulness is shown to be a property of the world, thereby revealing its timeless root.

This fact, however, still does not make the trickster of American Indian mythology as pregnant with meaning as a Greek god. As he appears in the Winnebago myth, he has nothing like the universality and plasticity of the Greek divinities. If, on the other hand, we follow the heroes of Greek mythology through all the stories told about them, we find the same indestructible consistency, though they lack the universal significance of the great gods. In the case of the trickster, the contradictory nature of certain stories suggests that his consistency is more important than his character. To judge by what Theophrastus says of character, the trickster could hardly be mentioned in the same breath with Heracles, the 'trickless' hero with the club. Yet the impression one gets from the Winnebago stories about the trickster, if one approaches him from the side of Greek mythology, is almost that one is encountering an easily outwitted, woman-chasing, gluttonous Heracles, rather than a double of the divine trickster of Greek mythology, Hermes!

II

STYLE

THIS impression goes hand in hand with another: that of the relatively late state of the stories. It is not so much a question of outward chronology, of the fact that the texts as we read them, and as recounted by one of the few remaining professional raconteurs, stem from our own century, although this absolute lateness is not without significance. Rilke's fear that God might get 'worn out'—and 'what is the good of a used up God?'—is as justified in the case of an archaic deity like the trickster as in that of the Supreme Deity, if not more so. By the twentieth century, any god is bound to be a bit worn out, even if his worshippers, their culture and religion have remained that long in an archaic state. The archaic itself gets used up and worn out in that time, and, in the case of peoples and races living at a quicker tempo, in a much, much shorter time.

And that is just what I mean by a relatively late state: a state in which the archaic no longer stands (in accordance with the basic meaning of the word) close to the beginning, the origin, the *arché*, but nearer the end, the breakdown or a transition, as during the transition from the archaic to the classical among the Greeks. Not all peoples have been capable of overcoming their archaicism. It is not a compulsory development which the whole of humanity passes through regularly. If it were, archaic conditions could never be found among peoples living in our own day—peoples who, be it noted, are not on that account made up of an 'inferior' or 'different' sort of human being—of Sort 1, shall we say, whereas we are Sort 3 or 4—but of human beings who have the same psycho-physical and mental structure as ourselves.

Wherever the archaic state was followed by a period of classicism, culminated in it and was then superseded, we find that the process was always a brilliant breakthrough to an 'exceptional' state of relatively short duration, which went on exerting an influence but did not itself survive. By no means all the Greek tribes achieved that breakthrough from archaicism to classicism. A late state of archaicism, such as we see in the Winnebago tales of the trickster, can also be found in the sphere of Greek culture. For instance the Doric farces of southern Italy, where the gods were represented by obese, phallus-bearing actors, the 'phlyakes', may be compared with the picaresque tales of Winnebago mythology—not in terms of outward chronology, but in terms of the inner chronology by which the archaic grows old. To judge by the scenes on the vases, these farces were no less picaresque than the adventures of the trickster himself; only they revealed more of the drama inherent in all mythological tales, heightening the miming of the story into stage play.

By our use of the terms 'archaic' and 'archaicism' we are applying a stylistic judgement not merely to the art works of a culture but to entire cultures as spiritual creations, perhaps in an even stricter sense than did Leo Frobenius, who was the first to introduce regard for style into ethnology and to apply it to all the phenomena of a given society. The stylistic judgement could be supplemented by listing the characteristics of the archaic style, though these would not be its real foundation. The fundamental thing is not the characteristics: they merely point to a mode of being, difficult to express in words, but expressed most clearly and most felicitously in art—not only in special works of art for festive occasions but also in artefacts for everyday use. This alone supports the stylistic judgement, giving it so broad a basis that it can cross the frontiers of historical art periods. Thus we learn from the Winnebago trickster stories what is 'archaic', or, to be more precise, what is meant by a late, 'worn out' archaicism that has outlived its use.

Though the phlyax farces themselves were older in style than the ancient Attic comedy, the southern Italian representations of them are, in their style of draughtsmanship, post-classical: mere surviving remnants of a late archaicism that had not quite lost touch with the achievements of archaic art at the time of its efflorescence, when scenes from mythology were immortalized on the Caeretan hydriae. Two examples of the blithe narrative art of those Ionian vase painters, whose masterpieces found their way to the Etruscan city of Caere, are reproduced in my *Gods of the Greeks* (Plates IIIa and VIIa). A third may be seen in the Louvre, showing the first theft committed by the infant trickster,

Hermes. Another archaic theme of Greek mythology is the fight of the two brothers, Apollo and Heracles, for the Delphic tripod, a theme likewise found in archaic works of art—'archaic' not merely because of its artistic treatment (the theme also appears in the classical period), but because of its content: the struggle between two divine brothers.

A scene that may have been taken from the same struggle was performed on the stage by the phlyakes, and was afterwards portrayed on a vase painting, probably by the painter Assteas of Paestum. Heracles, in the guise of a trickster, is shown trying to lure his brother, who has taken refuge on the roof of the temple, down to him with a basket of fruit or some other kind of delicacy. The club is all too visible in his other hand. As an excursion in the same style, and as a parallel to the Winnebago stories which show the trickster in an anything but heroic light, I would recommend the first half of Aristophanes' *Frogs*: an Attic example, so to speak, of a picaresque drama of the gods, the *picaro* being Dionysus himself. He cunningly chooses the costume of Heracles for his journey to the underworld, only to flee in terror from the spectacle of the Empusa and hide behind one of his own priests in the crowd. The consequences of his fright are disastrous:

Dionysus: 'Gosh, what a fright! I turned as pale as a corpse——'

Xanthias (pointing to his posterior): 'And *that there*, thanks to you, a ruddy brown!'

The second line (308) should probably be taken as indicating that the god's companion on his journey, the slave Xanthias, turns his back to the spectators and shows them the state he is in. Dionysus experiences these consequences not on his own person but on that of Xanthias, who was even more terrified than he—the consequences of cowardice, just as, in the Winnebago stories of the 'laxative bulb' (episodes 23 and 24), they were the consequences of stupidity. At the very least we can establish the same tendency: mythology passes over into scatology, though this has quite a different meaning here from what it has in the play by Sophron (the representative of a dramatic school originally related to the phlyax theatre) which I analysed in my *Apollo*. Whether it occurs in a scene from a comedy or in the lively prologue to a mythological tale—always, at bottom, a mythological

179

drama whose latent possibilities of development are realized on the stage—we have here a vivid example of a characteristic of style common to both: the predominance of drastic entertainment. Entertainment is never lacking in mythology, and the predilection for the drastic, for what is unseemly by human standards, is a peculiarity of archaic mythology. The emphasis on drastic entertainment is also characteristic of the late archaicism that breaks through in Aristophanes or in a phlyax play, and it provides the dominant note of the Winnebago trickster stories.

III

PARALLELS

THE distinctive feature of this style, the intensification of the drastic and absurd, comes to light when the narrators cause the trickster to appear as a predominantly stupid figure. In the latter-day folk tales of the Greeks this trait reminds one of Nasreddin Hodja, the typical cunning fool or stupid rogue, known and laughed at the world over, because it is impossible to tell where his cunning ends and his stupidity begins, and which of the two qualities is the primary one. Cunning and stupidity go essentially together, and this essential relationship is reflected more clearly in mythology before it sinks to the level of the popular anecdote and folk tale characterized by late archaicism, simplification, and *abaissement du niveau mental*. (The latter two qualifications do not, of course, apply to an archaic tribe like the Winnebago.) Among plants, animals and men, cunning is brought into the world by those who are stupid enough to get caught. But the mythological theme is cunning first and foremost; it makes stupidity appear as something secondary, including the stupidity of the cunning. Prometheus has affinities with the trickster because the cunning he practises on Zeus overreaches itself and turns into stupidity, personified by his own brother, Epimetheus.

Several of the American Indian trickster figures come even closer to Prometheus than the Wakdjunkaga of the Winnebago: the more so the more the trickster in them, instead of practising his tricks for his own ends, approximates to the figure of a beneficent creator and becomes what the ethnologists call a 'culture hero'. Prometheus, the benefactor of mankind, lacks self-interest and playfulness. Hermes has both, when he discovers fire and sacrifice before Prometheus did—without, however, bothering about mankind. In the playful cruelties which the little god practised on the tortoise and sacrificial cows at his first theft, and which conferred no benefit on mankind (at least for a long time to come), we see the sly face of the trickster grinning at us, whereas in the deeds of Prometheus we see the sly and the stupid at once: Prometheus *and* Epimetheus. Perhaps I may repeat what I said in my *Antike Religion*:

'Every invention of Prometheus brings new misery upon mankind. No sooner has he succeeded in offering sacrifice than Zeus deprives mankind of the fire. And when, after stealing the fire, Prometheus himself is snatched away from mortals to suffer punishment, Epimetheus is left behind as their representative: craftiness is replaced by stupidity. The profound affinity between these two figures is expressed in the fact that they are brothers. One might almost say that in them a single primitive being, sly and stupid at once, has been split into a duality: Prometheus the Forethinker, Epimetheus the belated Afterthinker. It is he who, in his thoughtlessness, brings mankind, as a gift from the gods, the final inexhaustible source of misery: Pandora.'

In my book on Prometheus (published in 1946) I wondered whether he and Epimetheus may not originally have formed a dual being, the primordial man who begot the human race with the primordial woman. I did not then suspect (Radin's *Winnebago Hero Cycles* did not appear until 1948) that the dualism of a sly-stupid primitive being could be expressed so drastically in a mythological tale that his left hand literally does not know what his right hand is doing. This episode (the fifth) brings out his laughable stupidity. But—isn't that just what he wanted: to raise a laugh, playing a cruel game with himself and making his arms quarrel bloodily? (Immediately before this he had killed a buffalo in exemplary fashion, a deed reminiscent of the prowess of little Hermes.) The whole of nature laughed at his antics and knew him for what he was. The birds called out: 'Look, look! There is Trickster!' He pretended not to know that the trickster had been recognized as the jester. 'Ah, you naughty little birds! I wonder what they are saying?' Thus he keeps up the pretence, with the birds as witnesses of the phlyax play he is performing.

Despite its late archaic absurdity, this episode breathes an air of the genuinely archaic, whose elements have not gone under in the flood of scatology and cheap slapstick. They still support the structure behind the comic façade of exaggeration, now worn somewhat thin. A peculiarity of the Winnebago trickster is that in contrast to the phlyakes, who had the phallus strapped on to them as an emblem of this kind of entertainment, he takes his phallus off and carries it around in a box. Episode fifteen describes the emancipation of this organ—nor, apart from the stylistic exaggeration, is there anything unnatural or infantile in that. 'A disobedient and self-willed thing it is, like an animal that will not listen to reason', says Plato in the *Timaeus* (91 b). In the next episode Trickster takes it out of the box (one must always bear in mind the comic effect) and sends it over the water on an amorous adventure. Meanwhile, his identity with this swimming part of himself—a veritable *pars pro toto*—does not cease; indeed, an expert can recognize it at once. Thus, the knowledgeable old woman who was called to the rescue gave this deputy an honorific title which shows Trickster's place in the original scheme of things: 'Why, this is First-born, Trickster. The chief's daughter is having intercourse with him and you are all just annoying her.'

This is not an unsuitable disguise for someone whose fundamental characteristic is precisely this identity: to speak of a 'sly phallus' or 'stupid phallus' would not be too absurd a description of the motivating force of the trickster's adventures, so far as this is not greed, which by nature hangs together with the sphere of the phallic. The phallus is Trickster's double and alter ego. Hermes too is often represented either by the phallus alone, set up as a 'Kyllenic image', or by the ithyphallic herm, the erect phallus and pillar bearing the god's head. No more than the Winnebago stories are these archaic representations of Hermes intended to exemplify the power of magic. The reduction of Hermes' thievishness to his trickery (N. O. Brown, *Hermes the Thief*, 1947) was the correct interpretation; the attempt (in the same book) to prove the trickster a magician and the herm an apotropaic boundary stone is confuted by a detailed study of the trickster texts. The trickster is neither a magician nor a guardian of frontiers; nor, conversely, can the magic wand of Hermes or his function of messenger be derived from his trickery, and there is no evidence that the profession of medicine-man even existed at that remote mythological period when the trickster held sway.

One possibility, then, that characterized the trickster was the fact that he could be represented by the phallus. For this he needed no special magical powers; it was consistent with his nature and character to be represented in that way. Hence a story in which this representation had a meaning and purpose is not out of place. Moreover, for the correct classification of textless monuments like menhirs and herms, it is of considerable value to have heard a story that is based on the same identification, even if it is in late American Indian style. The Greek accounts were kept secret. Only those who had been initiated into the Cabiric mysteries of Samothrace knew the sacred story of the ithyphallic herms, says Herodotus (II, 51). These mysteries celebrated an age-old event, they recapitulated or alluded to a tale that probably had to do with the masculine origin of life (as I called it in my *Hermes der Seelenführer*), and also with certain trickster-like manifestations, another aspect of which is described in the Homeric Hymn to Hermes.

Wakdjunkaga's box remains to puzzle us: it is as though he were carrying his own essential core about in it. A more sombre note is struck in the tale told by Clement of Alexandria about the Macedonian Cabiri cult: two Cabiri murdered their youngest brother and brought his phallus to Etruria in a casket (*Protrepticus*, II, 19). This was how the Dionysus cult spread among the Etruscans. According to the historian Nikolaos of Damascus (Jacoby, *Fragmente der griechischen Historiker*, 52), the city of Assessos in Asia Minor had a similar tradition: two young foreigners, with the Phrygian names of Tottes and Onnes, arrived with a mysterious casket, thereby saving the beleaguered city and founding the Cabiric mysteries there. Dionysus himself is never represented as a noticeably phallic deity; he is shown either clothed in a long robe, or in some other effeminate form. The carrying round of the phallus, its erection and unveiling, played some part in his cult. It was certainly not an element basically foreign to his nature; even though separated from him, it was something peculiarly his own.

This excursion into a different category and a different atmosphere, from comedy and the atmosphere of the phlyax plays into that of the mysteries, is not as arbitrary as it may seem, for the mysteries too could descend, just as suddenly, from the sublime to the ridiculous, in order to provide material for the droll tales of Petronius. The successor to the phlyax theatre in the Near East was the shadow play, whose hero was called in Turkish 'Karagös', Black Eye. Flaubert, in his *Voyage à Carthage* 1858, describes him as follows: 'Quant au Carragheuss, son pénis ressemblait plutôt à une poutre; ça finissait par n'être plus indécent. Il y en a plusieurs, Carragheuss; je crois le type en décadence. Il s'agit seulement de montrer le plus possible de phallus. Le plus grand avait un grelot qui, à chaque mouvement de reins, sonnait; cela faisait beaucoup de rire.'

Only by excessive simplification could this kind of material be reduced to the common denominator 'fertility cults and customs'. Even at its coarsest it requires the most delicate sense of discrimination for style, meaning and atmosphere. I can only hope that, if such finesse is justified on the classic soil of Greece and the Roman Empire, it will also be forthcoming for the province now opened out to us by Paul Radin.

IV

NATURE OF THE TRICKSTER

I MUST confess that I have not been able to discover, either in the Winnebago trickster stories or in any other archaic narrative or its dramatic representation, any such thing as the 'inner development' of the hero. Gods and primitive beings have no inner dimension, and neither have heroes, who inhabit the same sphere. The changes wrought by changing times and styles can be noticed, but what is so astonishing is the powers of resistance which enable the 'core' to survive these changes. My own observations confirm Emerson's definition of the hero: 'The hero is he who is immovably centred.' This holds true here. In the very first episode, where the trickster is not yet named and we only hear of a chief cohabiting with a woman in an unseemly way at an unsuitable time, he, Trickster, is already present, exhibiting his true nature as—so we might sum up, under a single active principle, the component elements 'phallic', 'voracious', 'sly', 'stupid'—*the spirit of disorder, the enemy of boundaries.*

Archaic social hierarchies are exceedingly strict. To be archaic does not mean to be chaotic. Quite the contrary: nothing demonstrates the meaning of the all-controlling social order more impressively than the religious recognition of that which evades this order, in a figure who is the exponent and personification of the life of the body: never wholly subdued, ruled by lust and hunger, for ever running into pain and injury, cunning and stupid in action. Disorder belongs to the totality of life, and the spirit of this disorder is the trickster. His function in an archaic society, or rather the function of his mythology, of the tales told about him, is to add disorder to order and so make a whole, to render possible, within the fixed bounds of what is permitted, an experience of what is not permitted.

Picaresque literature has consciously taken over this function. Rabelais, with his grand bawdy book, fights in the interests of humanism against the mediaeval forms of life. In Spain the picaresque novel constituted itself as a literary genus and remained the sole means of revolt against the rigidity of tradition. Goethe wrote *Reynard the Fox* during the French Revolution, and this trickster epic of his is a classic example of its kind. Thomas Mann's Felix Krull (*The Confessions of Felix Krull, Confidence Man*) also has his place here, the bourgeois trickster of the last surviving social order—as though the master novelist did not wish his tribute to this genre to remain unpaid.

Like every other trickster, Hermes, too, operates outside the fixed bounds of custom and law. I have described his field of operations as a 'no man's land, a sealed off, Hermetic region between the fixed bounds of property, where finding and thieving are still possible' (*Hermes der Seelenführer*, p. 33). And I added: 'Unscrupulousness alone is not Hermetic, it requires also sprightliness and skill. If the fool is lucky, his luck comes to him from the unsprightly Heracles, who was honoured in Italy as a god of luck.' Already this suggests a difference between Hermes and Wakdjunkaga: the latter is a combination of Hermes and Heracles even more than of Prometheus and Epimetheus. Not everything of Hermes, but certainly his unheroical traits, plus everything in Heracles that binds him to the joys and sorrows of life. A Herculean Hermes, so we might describe him, remembering at the same time that one of the Idaean dactyls, those primitive phallic beings whose name means 'finger', was also called Heracles. It is argued, of course, that this was another Heracles and not the son of Zeus and Alcmene, but the consistency of his basically phallic nature comes out no less in the adventures of the club-bearer.

It was not easy for comparative religion to accommodate this powerful life-spirit, this Herculean Hermes in his American Indian manifestations, after he had lost his function, which he could only have in a vigorous and archaic social order. Even the Indians themselves found it difficult. There were several ways of disposing of him. The first, and more arbitrary, was to reduce his original function to harmless entertainment by stressing his ridiculous traits. A second was to assimilate him to the culture heroes. In the Winnebago tales, aimed predominantly at entertainment, there are few indications of this, the most significant being the thirty-ninth, which shows him at work in a decidedly phallic sphere. The third way was his transformation into a devil, either under Christian influence, by equating him with Satan, or by treating him as one who had once been a deity and had then forfeited his higher divine rank to a more powerful and genuine deity. All these ways have been amply documented for us by Radin, the last-named view being upheld not by Radin himself but by the systematizers of religion who lose themselves all too easily in abstractions and are bound to be embarrassed by a figure like the trickster.

Following the publications of W. B. Kristensen and Josselin de Jong,[1] who first introduced the controversial problem of a 'divine deceiver' into the history of religion, an attempt to prove this theory was made by R. Pettazzoni (*Paideuma*, 1950). From among all the trickster's modes of manifestation he singled out

[1] 'De goddelijke bedrieger', 1928, and 'De oorsprong van den goddelijken bedrieger', 1929. Both in *Mededeel. Akad. Wetensch. Afd. Letterk.*

one of the animal forms for special mention—that of the coyote or prairie wolf, arguing that in a life which depended mainly on hunting, this animal, as the 'Ruler' or 'King of Beasts', might easily have been taken for a 'rudimentary Supreme Being', who was then ousted by another Supreme Being, the creator-god, and became his antagonist. Therefore the tales he told—in Wichita mythology he does, in fact, appear as a 'story-teller' in the pejorative sense—were nothing but a pack of lies. It is not asked whether, in the eyes of the Indians, the coyote ever deserved the dignified title of 'Ruler and King of Beasts', nor whether he might not be better suited by nature to carry the characteristic traits of the trickster, as the fox did in Europe. The wealth of concrete detail offered by the present book, which can hardly be reduced to the tenuous notion of a 'rudimentary Supreme Being', could have refuted such an over-simple construction. It is not true that mythological beings, when they fail to fit the concept of gods made to our own theological measure, must necessarily be dethroned antagonists—in other words, 'devils'. They are neither devilish nor are they moral, and yet they are divine in the manner of Wakdjunkaga. They remain so even in the most ridiculous situations: Dionysus in the *Frogs* of Aristophanes is an example of the fact that laughter and belief in the divinity of the laughed-at are not mutually exclusive. When the laughter gains the upper hand, it is a sign that the god is getting 'worn out', not of disbelief.

Of the animal forms assumed by the trickster, one in particular nevertheless deserves our notice. We learn from Radin that the name for the trickster, among the Oglala Dakota tribe, means 'Spider'. This is a clear indication that the trickster figure does not have its roots exclusively in man: its most impressive natural image is the spider. The decisive factor here is not the spider's physical appearance but its trickery. In a book of African folk tales (Rattray, *Akan-Ashanti Folk-Tales*, 1930) about spiders it is to be noticed that the native illustrators drew the hero sometimes as an animal and sometimes as a man. Were they forgetting his animal form, as Rabelais occasionally forgot the giant stature of his chief characters? It should not be forgotten, anyway, that the animal form in mythology is only the phenomenal form, with the real form—glimpsed by the eye of the myth-maker—

187

shining through. Here it glimpsed the sly, lumbering daemon of the body.

V

HIS DIFFERENCE FROM HERMES

BETWEEN the spider, the trickster of the animal world, and Hermes, the trickster among the gods, stands the trickster of the Winnebago. His nature, inimical to all boundaries, is open in every direction. He enters into the beasts, and because his own sexuality knows no bounds, he does not even observe the boundaries of sex. His inordinate phallicism cannot limit itself to one sex alone: in the twentieth episode he cunningly contrives to become a bride and mother—for the sake of the wedding feast and also, no doubt, for the fun of it. Classical audiences, too, enjoyed the fun of seeing men dressed up as brides, as in the *Casina* of Plautus, or the Atellan farces of Pomponius, not to speak of similar disguises in Aristophanes. Dancers pretending to be women, yet simultaneously emphasizing their masculinity, appeared on the Hellenistic popular stage, after having been at home in the cult of Artemis Cordaca. Dionysus himself became the exponent of Wakdjunkaga's self-chosen passivity. Dionysian ecstasy had the same function as the trickster myth: it abolished the boundaries, not least the boundaries of sex. Trickster's metamorphosis into a mother reaches down into the comic depths of the Dionysian realm, and its ultimate basis is to be found in the mystery of Priapus: he, too, was not exclusively masculine. It was said that he was none other than the hermaphrodite, and certainly not without reason as regards his bodily form. (Cf. my *Gods of the Greeks*, p. 175; concerning Dionysus, p. 259.)

Yet, paradoxically, such limitlessness implies its own limitation. In emphasizing this, let us not use the criterion of the Greek pantheon only, which accepted Dionysus but not the daemons of the dance, the denizens of that lower realm, the sileni and satyrs. Nor would it accept Priapus, whereas Hermes belonged to Olympus despite his office of intermediary between the higher and the lower. Not even by Winnebago standards did Wakdjunkaga become a deity equal in rank to one of the Olympians. His restriction to the lower sphere is expressed by the fact that his wanderings on earth must come to an end before the era when orderly life was established. In the last episode he departs from the earth after eating a final meal, leaving characteristic traces of his corporeality behind him, and goes up to heaven. It is possible that there is a Christian model for this, yet much the same thing might have happened to a Greek hero, Heracles for instance. Ever since then he has ruled over another world, and there he is banished except when the story-tellers call him back and re-enact his adventures. As we have said, he possesses no magic wand. Yet in the hand of Hermes this wand has nothing to do with the works of earthly magicians; it is the staff of the psychopomp, of the messenger and mediator, of the hoverer-between-worlds who dwells in a world of his own: a symbol of those *divine* qualities which transcend mere trickery.

This is not the place to repeat all that I have said about this god in my *Hermes der Seelenführer*, or to cite the relevant passages from W. F. Otto's *Homeric Gods*. But the repetition of the crucial points which may help to delimit the trickster hero, as known to the Winnebago, from the trickster god who contains him, is unavoidable. We spoke earlier of a spirit of disorder, of an enemy of boundaries, a mighty life-spirit. Hermes, too, disregards boundaries, yet he is not a spirit of disorder. And though it would not be wrong to call him a life-spirit, it would not be enough. We could call him, with Otto, the 'spirit of a [life-style] which recurs under the most diverse conditions and which embraces loss as well as gain, mischief as well as kindliness. Though much of this must seem questionable from a moral point of view, nevertheless it is a configuration which belongs to the fundamental aspects of living reality, and hence, according to Greek feeling, demands reverence, if not for all its individual expressions, at least for the totality of its meaning and being.' (*The Homeric Gods.*)

The trickster hero may perhaps be the source of a literature, naïve and picaresque at first, then extremely refined and consciously artistic. The trickster god, on the other hand, is the

transpersonal source of a particular life-style and way of experienc-
ing the world. There is, firstly, the known experience of the
world, based on the assumption that man stands there alone and
self-dependent, endowed with a consciousness which is receptive
only to sense impressions that can be evaluated scientifically. For
that type of experience, however, which expresses itself not
scientifically but mythologically, there is no such assumption.
Rather, it is open to the possibility of a suprasensual guide and
psychopomp, capable of affording impressions of another kind:
impressions grounded in sense experience, which do not contradict the observations and findings of science, and which yet
transcend the scientific view of the world. With Hermes as our
guide through life, the world is viewed under a special aspect.
This aspect is utterly real and remains within the realm of
natural experience.

The sum of the ways as the Hermetic arena; chance and
mischance the Hermetic substance; its transformation, through
'finding and thieving', into Hermetic art (not unmixed with
artifice), into riches, love, poetry, and all the ways of escape from
the narrow confines of law, custom, circumstance, fate: all these
are not *just* psychic realities. They are the world around us, and,
at the same time, a world revealed to us by Hermes.

The reality of this Hermes world at least proves the existence
of a standpoint from which it may be glimpsed; indeed, it
testifies to some active force which, seen from that point, is no
empty vision, but something that forcibly brings the variegated
forms of Hermetic art and artifice into reality. The source from
which we gain this experience of the world, once we have reached
that standpoint, is—whether we name him or not—Hermes. It
must possess the full Hermetic span, ranging from the phallic to
the psychopompic.

Only at this point do we cross the boundary of experiences
resting on sense impressions, but not the boundary of those which
have undoubted psychic reality. These likewise belong to the
Hermes world. Yet playing tricks with death in the ghostly
regions of the psyche, where spirits and poltergeists reign, is a
very different thing from conducting the souls of the dead to
rest. To be a god means to be the creator of a world, and a world
means order. This decisive verdict can be pronounced upon

Hermes. Even his loyal Winnebagos have never believed that Wakdjunkaga, the creator of a literature, could be the creator of a world. Hermes opens the ways, Wakdjunkaga the eternal phlyax stage that outlives the fall of empires and the flux of vanishing cultures.

Part Five

ON THE PSYCHOLOGY
OF THE
TRICKSTER FIGURE

By C. G. Jung

ON THE PSYCHOLOGY OF THE
TRICKSTER FIGURE

I‍T is no light task for me to write about the figure of the trickster in American-Indian mythology within the confined space of a commentary. When I first came across Adolf Bandelier's classic on this subject, *The Delight Makers*,[1] many years ago, I was struck by the European analogy of the carnival in the mediaeval Church, with its reversal of the hierarchic order, which is still continued in the carnivals held by student societies today. Something of this contradictoriness also inheres in the mediaeval description of the devil as 'simia dei' (the ape of God), and in his characterization in folklore as the 'simpleton' who is 'fooled' or 'cheated'. A curious combination of typical trickster motifs can be found in the alchemical figure of Mercurius; for instance, his fondness for sly jokes and malicious pranks, his powers as a shape-shifter, his dual nature, half animal, half divine, his exposure to all kinds of tortures, and—last but not least—his approximation to the figure of a saviour. These qualities make Mercurius seem like a daemonic being resurrected from primitive times, older even than the Greek Hermes. His rogueries relate him in some measure to various figures met with in folklore and universally known in fairy tales: Tom Thumb, Stupid Hans, or the buffoon-like Hanswurst, who is an altogether negative hero and yet manages to achieve through his stupidity what others fail to accomplish with their best efforts. In Grimm's fairy tale the 'Spirit Mercurius' lets himself be outwitted by a peasant lad, and then has to buy his freedom with the precious gift of healing.

Since all mythical figures correspond to inner psychic experiences and originally sprang from them, it is not surprising to find certain phenomena in the field of parapsychology which remind us of the trickster. These are the phenomena connected with

---

[1] 1st edition, New York, 1890.

poltergeists, and they occur at all times and places in the ambience of pre-adolescent children. The malicious tricks played by the poltergeist are as well known as the low level of his intelligence and the fatuity of his 'communications'. Ability to change his shape seems also to be one of his characteristics, as there are not a few reports of his appearance in animal form. Since he has on occasion described himself as a soul in hell, the motif of subjective suffering would seem not to be lacking either. His universality is co-extensive, so to speak, with that of shamanism, to which, as we know, the whole phenomenology of spiritualism belongs. There is something of the trickster in the character of the shaman and medicine-man, for he, too, often plays malicious jokes on people, only to fall victim in his turn to the vengeance of those whom he has injured. For this reason his profession sometimes puts him in peril of his life. Besides that, the shamanastic techniques in themselves often cause the medicine-man a good deal of discomfort, if not actual pain. At all events the 'making of a medicine-man' involves, in many parts of the world, so much agony of body and soul that permanent psychic injuries may result. His 'approximation to the saviour' is an obvious consequence of this, in confirmation of the mythological truth that the wounded wounder is the agent of healing, and that the sufferer takes away suffering.

These mythological features extend even to the highest regions of man's spiritual development. If we consider, for example, the daemonic features exhibited by Yahweh in the Old Testament, we shall find in them not a few reminders of the unpredictable behaviour of the trickster, of his pointless orgies of destruction and his self-appointed sufferings, together with the same gradual development into a saviour and his simultaneous humanization. It is just this transformation of the meaningless into the meaningful that reveals the trickster's compensatory relation to the 'saint', which in the early Middle Ages led to some strange ecclesiastical customs based on memories of the ancient saturnalia. Mostly they were celebrated on the days immediately following the birth of Christ—that is, in the New Year—with singing and dancing. The dances were the originally harmless *tripudia* of the priests, the lower clergy, children, and subdeacons, and they took place in the church. An *episcopus puerorum* (children's bishop) was elected and dressed in pontifical robes. Amid uproarious rejoicings he paid an official visit to the palace of the archbishop and distributed the episcopal blessing from one of the windows. The same thing happened at the *tripudium hypodiaconorum*, and at the dances for other priestly grades. By the end of the twelfth century the subdeacons' dance had already degenerated into a *festum stultorum* (fools' feast). A report from the year 1198 says that at the Feast of Circumcision in Notre-Dame, Paris, 'so many abominations and shameful deeds' were committed that the holy place was desecrated 'not only by smutty jokes, but even by the shedding of blood'. In vain did Pope Innocent III inveigh against the 'jests and madness that make the clergy a mockery', and the 'shameless frenzy of their playacting'. Nearly three hundred years later (12th March, 1444) a letter from the Theological Faculty of Paris to all the French bishops was still fulminating against these festivals, at which 'even the priests and clerics elected an archbishop or a bishop or pope, and named him the Fools' Pope' (*fatuorum papam*). 'In the very midst of divine service masqueraders with grotesque faces, disguised as women, lions and mummers, performed their dances, sang indecent songs in the choir, ate their greasy food from a corner of the altar near the priest celebrating mass, got out their games of dice, burned a stinking incense made of old shoe leather, and ran and hopped about all over the church'.[2]

It is not surprising that this veritable witches' sabbath was uncommonly popular, and that it required considerable time and effort to free the Church from this pagan heritage.[3]

In certain localities even the priests seem to have adhered to the 'libertas decembrica', as the Fools' Holiday was called, in spite

---

[2] Du Cange, *Gloss. Med. et Inf. Lat.*, 1733, s.v. Kalendae, p. 1666. Here there is a note to the effect that the French title 'sou-diacres' means literally 'saturi diaconi' or 'diacres saouls' (drunken deacons).

[3] These customs seem to be directly modelled on the pagan feast known as 'Cervula' or 'Cervulus'. It took place in the kalends of January and was a kind of New Year's festival, at which people exchanged 'strenae' (étrennes, gifts), dressed up as animals or old women, and danced through the streets singing, to the applause of the populace. According to Du Cange (ibid., s.v. cervulus), sacrilegious songs were sung. This happened even in the immediate vicinity of St. Peter's in Rome.

(or perhaps because?) of the fact that the older level of consciousness could let itself rip on this happy occasion with all the wild-
ness, wantonness, and irresponsibility of paganism.[4] These ceremonies, which still reveal the spirit of the trickster in his original
form, seem to have died out by the beginning of the sixteenth
century. At any rate, the various conciliar decrees issued from
1581 to 1585 forbade only the *festum puerorum* and the election of
an *episcopus puerorum*.

Finally, we must also mention in this connection the *festum
asinarium*, which, so far as I know, was celebrated mainly in
France. Although considered a harmless festival in memory of
Mary's flight into Egypt, it was celebrated in a somewhat curious
manner which might easily have given rise to misunderstandings.
In Beauvais the ass procession went right into the church.[5] At the
conclusion of each part (Introitus, Kyrie, Gloria, etc.) of the high
mass that followed, the whole congregation *brayed*, that is, they
all went 'Y-a' like a donkey ('hac modulatione hinham conclude-
bantur'). A codex dating apparently from the eleventh century
says: 'At the end of the mass, instead of the words "Ite missa
est", the priest shall bray three times (*ter hinhamabit*), and instead
of the words "Deo gratias", the congregation shall answer "Y-a"
(*hinham*) three times.'

Du Cange cites a hymn from this festival:

> Orientis partibus
> Adventavit Asinus
> Pulcher et fortissimus
> Sarcinis aptissimus.

Each verse was followed by the French refrain:

> Hez, Sire Asnes, car chantez
> Belle bouche rechignez

[4] Part of the *festum fatuorum* in many places was the still unexplained ball
game played by the priests and captained by the bishop or archbishop, 'ut etiam
sese ad lusum pilae demittent' (that they also may indulge in the game of
pelota). *Pila* or *pelota* is the ball which the players throw to one another. See
Du Cange, ibid., s.v. Kalendae et pelota.

[5] 'Puella, quae cum asino a parte Evangelii prope altare collocabatur' (the
girl who stationed herself at the side of the altar where the gospel is read).
Du Cange, ibid., s.v. festum asinorum.

> Vous aurez due foin assez
> et de l'avoine à plantez.

The hymn had nine verses, the last of which was:

> Amen, dicas, Asine (hic genuflectebatur)
> Jam satur de gramine
> Amen, amen, itera
> Aspernare vetera.[6]

Du Cange says that the more ridiculous this rite seemed, the greater the enthusiasm with which it was celebrated. In other places the ass was decked with a golden canopy whose corners were held 'by distinguished canons'; the others present had to 'don suitably festive garments, as at Christmas'. Since there were certain tendencies to bring the ass into symbolic relationship with Christ, and since, from ancient times, the god of the Jews was vulgarly conceived to be an ass—a prejudice which extended to Christ himself,[7] as is shown by the mock crucifixion scribbled on the wall of the Imperial Cadet School on the Palatine—the danger of theriomorphism lay uncomfortably close. Even the bishops could do nothing to stamp out this custom, until finally it had to be suppressed by the 'auctoritas supremi Senatus'. The suspicion of blasphemy becomes quite open in Nietzsche's 'Ass Festival', which is a deliberately blasphemous parody of the mass.[8]

These mediaeval customs demonstrate the role of the trickster to perfection, and, when they vanished from the precincts of the Church, they appeared again on the profane level of Italian theatricals, as those comic types who, often adorned with enormous ithyphallic emblems, entertained the far from prudish public with ribaldries in true Rabelaisian style. Callot's engravings preserved these classical figures for posterity—the Pulcinellas, Cucorognas, Chico Sgarras, and the like.[9]

---

[6] Caetera instead of vetera?

[7] Cf. also Tertullian, *Apologeticus adversus gentes*, XVI.

[8] *Thus Spake Zarathustra*, Part IV, ch. LXXVIII.

[9] I am thinking here of the series called 'Balli di Sfessania'. The name is probably a reference to the Etrurian town of Fescennia, which was famous for its lewd songs. Hence 'Fescennina licentia' in Horace, Fescinninus being the equivalent of φαλλικός.

In picaresque tales, in carnivals and revels, in sacred and magical rites, in man's religious fears and exaltations, this phantom of the trickster haunts the mythology of all ages, sometimes in quite unmistakable form, sometimes in strangely modulated guise.[10] He is obviously a 'psychologem', an archetypal psychic structure of extreme antiquity. In his clearest manifestations he is a faithful copy of an absolutely undifferentiated human consciousness, corresponding to a psyche that has hardly left the animal level. That this is how the trickster figure originated can hardly be contested if we look at it from the causal and historical angle. In psychology as in biology we cannot afford to overlook or underestimate this question of origins, although the answer usually tells us nothing about the functional meaning. For this reason biology should never forget the question of purpose, for only by answering that can we get at the meaning of a phenomenon. Even in pathology, where we are concerned with lesions which have no meaning in themselves, the exclusively causal approach proves to be inadequate, since there are a number of pathological phenomena which only give up their meaning when we inquire into their purpose. And where we are concerned with the normal phenomena of life, this question of purpose takes undisputed precedence.

When, therefore, a primitive or barbarous consciousness forms a picture of itself on a much earlier level of development and continues to do so for hundreds or even thousands of years, undeterred by the contamination of its archaic qualities with differentiated, highly developed mental products, then the causal explanation is that the older the archaic qualities are, the more conservative and pertinacious is their behaviour. One simply cannot shake off the memory image of things as they were, and drags it along like a senseless appendage.

This explanation, which is facile enough to satisfy the rationalistic requirements of our age, would certainly not meet with the approval of the Winnebagos, the nearest possessors of the trickster cycle. For them the myth is not in any sense a remnant—it is far too amusing for that, and an object of undivided enjoyment. For

[10] Cf. the article 'Daily Paper Pantheon' by A. McGlashen in *The Lancet*, 1953, p. 238, pointing out that the figures in comic strips have remarkable archetypal analogies.

them it still 'functions', provided that they have not been spoiled by civilization. For them there is no earthly reason to theorize about the meaning and purpose of myths, just as the Christmas tree seems no problem at all to the naïve European. For the thoughtful observer, however, both trickster and Christmas tree afford reason enough for reflection. Naturally it depends very much on the mentality of the observer what he thinks about these things. Considering the crude primitivity of the trickster cycle, it would not be surprising if one saw in this myth simply the reflection of an earlier, rudimentary stage of consciousness, which is what the trickster obviously seems to be.[11]

The only question that would need answering is whether such personified reflections exist at all in empirical psychology. As a matter of fact they do, and these experiences of split or double personality actually form the core of the earliest psychopathological investigations. The peculiar thing about these dissociations is that the split-off personality is not just a random one, but stands in a complementary or compensatory relationship to the ego personality. It is a personification of traits of character which are sometimes worse and sometimes better than those the ego personality possesses. A collective personification like the trickster is the product of a totality of individuals and is welcomed by the individual as something known to him, which would not be the case if it were just an individual outgrowth.

Now if the myth were nothing but an historical remnant one would have to ask why it has not long since vanished into the great rubbish heap of the past, and why it continues to make its influence felt on the highest level of civilization, even where, on account of his stupidity and grotesque scurrility, the trickster no longer plays the role of a 'delight-maker'. In many cultures his figure seems like an old river-bed in which the water still flows. One can see this best of all from the fact that the trickster motif does not crop up only in its original form but appears just as

[11] Earlier stages of consciousness seem to leave perceptible traces behind them. For instance, the chakras of the Tantric system correspond by and large to the regions where consciousness was earlier localized, *anahata* corresponding to the breast region, *manipura* to the abdominal region, *svadhistana* to the bladder region, and *visuddha* to the larynx and the speech consciousness of modern man. Cf. Arthur Avalon, *The Serpent Power*.

naïvely and authentically in the unsuspecting modern man—whenever, in fact, he feels himself at the mercy of annoying 'accidents' which thwart his will and his actions with apparently malicious intent. He then speaks of 'hoodoos' and 'ginxes' or of the 'mischieviousness of the object'. Here the trickster is represented by countertendencies in the unconscious, and in certain cases by a sort of second personality, of a puerile and inferior character, not unlike the personalities who announce themselves at spiritualistic séances and cause all those ineffably childish phenomena so typical of poltergeists. I have, I think, found a suitable designation for this character component when I called it the *shadow*.[12] On the civilized level it is treated as a personal 'gaffe', 'slip', 'faux pas', etc., which are then chalked up as defects of the conscious personality. We are no longer aware that in carnival customs and the like there are remnants of a collective shadow figure which prove that the personal shadow is in part descended from a numinous collective figure. This collective figure gradually breaks up under the impact of civilization, leaving traces in folklore which are difficult to recognize. But the main part of him gets personalized and is made an object of personal responsibility.

Radin's trickster cycle preserves the shadow in its pristine mythological form, and thus points back to a very much earlier stage of consciousness which existed before the birth of the myth, when the Indian was still groping about in a similar mental darkness. Only when his consciousness reached a higher level could he detach the earlier state from himself and objectify it, that is, say anything about it. So long as his consciousness was itself trickster-like, such a confrontation could obviously not take place. It was possible only when the attainment of a newer and higher level of consciousness enabled him to look back on a lower and inferior state. It was only to be expected that a good deal of mockery and contempt should mingle with this retrospect, thus casting an even thicker pall over man's memories of the past, which were pretty unedifying anyway. This phenomenon must have repeated itself innumerable times in the history of his mental development. The sovereign contempt with which our modern age looks back on the

---

[12] The same idea can be found in the Church Father Irenaeus, who calls it the 'umbra'. *Advers. Haer.* I, ii, 1.

taste and intelligence of earlier centuries is a classic example of this, and there is an unmistakable allusion to the same phenomenon in the New Testament, where we are told in Acts 17:30 that God looked down from above (ὑπεριδών, despiciens) on the χρόνοι τῆς ἀγνοίας, the times of ignorance (or unconsciousness).

This attitude contrasts strangely with the still commoner and more striking idealization of the past, which is praised not merely as the 'good old days' but as the Golden Age—and not just by uneducated and superstitious people, but by all those millions of theosophical enthusiasts who resolutely believe in the former existence and lofty civilization of Atlantis.

Anyone who belongs to a sphere of culture that seeks the perfect state somewhere in the past must feel very queerly indeed when confronted by the figure of the trickster. He is a forerunner of the saviour, and, like him, God, man, and animal at once. He is both subhuman and superhuman, a bestial and divine being, whose chief and most alarming characteristic is his unconsciousness. Because of it he is deserted by his (evidently human) companions, which seems to indicate that he has fallen below their level of consciousness. He is so unconscious of himself that his body is not a unity, and his two hands fight each other. He takes his anus off and entrusts it with a special task. Even his sex is optional despite its phallic qualities: he can turn himself into a woman and bear children. From his penis he makes all kinds of useful plants. This is a reference to his original nature as a Creator, for the world is made from the body of a god.

On the other hand he is in many respects stupider than the animals, and gets into one ridiculous scrape after another. Although he is not really evil he does the most atrocious things from sheer unconsciousness and unrelatedness. His imprisonment in animal unconsciousness is suggested by the episode where he gets his head caught inside the skull of an elk, and the next episode shows how he overcomes this condition by imprisoning the head of a hawk inside his own rectum. True, he sinks back into the former condition immediately afterwards, by falling under the ice, and is outwitted time after time by the animals, but in the end he succeeds in tricking the cunning coyote, and this brings back to him his saviour nature. The trickster is a primitive

'cosmic' being of *divine-animal* nature, on the one hand superior
to man because of his superhuman qualities, and on the other
hand inferior to him because of his unreason and unconsciousness.
He is no match for the animals either, because of his extraordinary clumsiness and lack of instinct. These defects are the
marks of his *human* nature, which is not so well adapted to the
environment as the animal's but, instead, has prospects of a much
higher development of consciousness based on a considerable
eagerness to learn, as is duly emphasized in the myth.

What the repeated telling of the myth signifies is the therapeutic anamnesis of contents which, for reasons still to be dis-
cussed, should never be forgotten for long. If they were nothing
but the remains of an inferior state it would be understandable if
man turned his attention away from them, feeling that their re-
appearance was a nuisance. This is evidently by no means the case,
since the trickster has been a source of amusement right down to
civilized times, where he can still be recognized in the carnival
figures of Pulcinella and the clown. Here we have an important
reason for his still continuing to function. But it is not the only
one, and certainly not the reason why this reflection of an extremely primitive state of consciousness solidified into a mythological personage. Mere vestiges of an early state that is dying out
usually lose their energy at an increasing rate, otherwise they
would never disappear. The last thing we would expect is that
they would have the strength to solidify into a mythological figure
with its own cycle of legends—unless, of course, they received
energy from outside, in this case from a higher level of consciousness or from resources in the unconscious which are not yet
exhausted. To take a legitimate parallel from the psychology of
the individual, namely the appearance of an impressive shadow
figure antagonistically confronting a personal consciousness: this
figure does not appear merely because it still exists in the individual, but because it rests on a dynamism whose existence can only
be explained in terms of his actual situation, for instance because
the shadow is so disagreeable to his ego consciousness that it has
to be repressed into the unconscious. This explanation does not
quite meet the case here, because the trickster obviously represents a vanishing level of consciousness which increasingly lacks
the power to take shape and assert itself. Furthermore, repression

would prevent it from vanishing, because repressed contents are the very ones that have the best chance of survival, as we know from experience that nothing is corrected in the unconscious. Lastly, the story of the trickster is not in the least disagreeable to the Winnebago consciousness or incompatible with it, but, on the contrary, pleasurable and therefore not conducive to repression. It looks, therefore, as if the myth were actively sustained and fostered by consciousness. This may well be so, since that is the best and most successful method of keeping the shadow figure conscious and subjecting it to conscious criticism. Although this criticism has at first more the character of a positive evaluation, we may expect that with the progressive development of consciousness the cruder aspects of the myth will gradually fall away, even if the danger of its rapid disappearance under the stress of white civilization did not exist. We have often seen how certain customs, originally cruel or obscene, became mere vestiges in the course of time.[13]

This process of neutralization, as the history of the trickster motif shows, lasts a very long time, so that one can still find traces of it even at a high level of civilization. Its longevity could also be explained by the strength and vitality of the state of consciousness described in the myth, and by the secret attraction and fascination this has for the conscious mind. Although purely causal hypotheses in the biological sphere are not as a rule very satisfactory, due weight must nevertheless be given to the fact that in the case of the trickster a higher level of consciousness has covered up a lower one, and that the latter was already in retreat. His recollection, however, is mainly due to the interest which the conscious mind brings to bear on him, the inevitable concomitant being, as we have seen, the gradual civilizing, i.e. assimilation, of a primitive daemonic figure who was originally autonomous and even capable of causing possession.

To supplement the causal approach by a final one therefore enables us to arrive at more meaningful interpretations not only in medical psychology, where we are concerned with individual

---

[13] For instance, the ducking of the 'Ueli' (from Udalricus=Ulrich, yokel, oaf, fool) in Basel during the second half of January was, if I remember correctly, forbidden by the police in the 1860's, after one of the victims died of pneumonia.

fantasies originating in the unconscious, but also in the case of collective fantasies, that is myths and fairy tales.

As Radin points out, the civilizing process begins within the framework of the trickster cycle itself, and this is a clear indication that the original state has been overcome. At any rate the marks of deepest unconsciousness fall away from him; instead of acting in a brutal, savage, stupid and senseless fashion the trickster's behaviour towards the end of the cycle becomes quite useful and sensible. The devaluation of his earlier unconsciousness is apparent even in the myth, and one wonders what has happened to his evil qualities. The naïve reader may imagine that when the dark aspects disappear they are no longer there in reality. But that is not the case at all, as experience shows. What actually happens is that the conscious mind is then able to free itself from the fascination of evil and is no longer obliged to live it compulsively. The darkness and the evil have not gone up in smoke, they have merely withdrawn into the unconscious owing to loss of energy, where they remain unconscious so long as all is well with the conscious. But if the conscious should find itself in a critical or doubtful situation, then it soon becomes apparent that the shadow has not dissolved into nothing but is only waiting for a favourable opportunity to reappear as a projection upon one's neighbour. If this trick is successful, then immediately there is created between them that world of primordial darkness where everything that is characteristic of the trickster can happen—even on the highest plane of civilization. The best examples of these 'monkey tricks', as popular speech aptly and truthfully sums up this state of affairs in which everything goes wrong and nothing intelligent happens except by mistake at the last moment, are naturally to be found in politics.

The so-called civilized man has forgotten the trickster. He remembers him only figuratively and metaphorically, when, irritated by his own ineptitude, he speaks of fate playing tricks on him or of things being bewitched. He never suspects that his own hidden and apparently harmless shadow has qualities whose dangerousness exceeds his wildest dreams. As soon as people get together in masses and submerge the individual, the shadow is mobilized, and, as history shows, may even be personified and incarnated.

The disastrous idea that everything comes to the human soul from outside and that it is born a tabula rasa is responsible for the erroneous belief that under normal circumstances the individual is in perfect order. He then looks to the State for salvation, and makes society pay for his inefficiency. He thinks the meaning of existence would be discovered if food and clothing were delivered to him gratis on his own doorstep, or if everybody possessed an automobile. Such are the puerilities that rise up in place of an unconscious shadow and keep it unconscious. As a result of these prejudices the individual feels totally dependent on his environment and loses all capacity for introspection. In this way his code of ethics is replaced by a knowledge of what is permitted or forbidden or ordered. How, under these circumstances, can one expect a soldier to subject an order received from a superior to ethical scrutiny? It still hasn't occurred to him that he might be capable of spontaneous ethical impulses, and of performing them—even when no one is looking!

From this point of view we can see why the myth of the trickster was preserved and developed: like many other myths, it was supposed to have a therapeutic effect. It holds the earlier low intellectual and moral level before the eyes of the more highly developed individual, so that he shall not forget how things looked yesterday. We like to imagine that something which we do not understand does not help us in any way. But that is not always so. Seldom does a man understand with his head alone, least of all when he is a primitive. Because of its numinosity the myth has a direct effect on the unconscious, no matter whether it is understood or not. The fact that its repeated telling has not long since become obsolete can, I believe, be explained by its usefulness. The explanation is rather difficult because two contrary tendencies are at work: the desire on the one hand to get out of the earlier condition and on the other hand not to forget it.[14] Apparently Radin has also felt this difficulty, for he says: 'Viewed psychologically, it might be contended that the history of civilization is largely the account of the attempts of man to forget his transformation

---

[14] Not to forget something means keeping it in consciousness. If the enemy disappears from my field of vision, then he may possibly be behind me—and even more dangerous.

from an animal into a human being.'[15] A few pages further on
he says (with reference to the Golden Age): 'So stubborn a refusal
to forget is not an accident.'[16] And it is also no accident that
we are forced to contradict ourselves as soon as we try to formulate
man's paradoxical attitude to myth. Even the most enlightened
of us will set up a Christmas tree for his children without having
the least idea what this custom means, and is invariably disposed to
nip any attempt at interpretation in the bud. It is really astonishing to see how many so-called superstitions are rampant nowadays
in town and country alike, but if one took hold of the individual
and asked him, loudly and clearly, 'Do you believe in ghosts? in
witches? in spells and magic?' he would deny it indignantly. It
is a hundred to one he has never heard of these things and thinks it
all rubbish. But in secret he is all for it, just like a jungle dweller.
The public knows very little of these things anyway, and is convinced that superstition has long been stamped out in our enlightened society and that it is part of our general education to
pretend never to have heard of such things: it is just 'not done' to
believe in them.

But nothing is ever lost, not even the blood pact with the devil.
Outwardly it is forgotten, but inwardly not at all. We act like the
natives on the southern slopes of Mt. Elgon, one of whom accompanied me part of the way into the bush. At a fork in the path we
came upon a brand new 'ghost trap', beautifully got up like a
little hut, near the cave where he lived with his family. I asked
him if he had made it. He denied it with all the signs of extreme
agitation, and told us that only children would make such a 'jou-
jou'. Whereupon he gave the hut a kick and the whole thing fell
to pieces.

This is exactly the reaction we can observe today in Europe.
Outwardly people are more or less civilized but inwardly they are
still primitives. Something in man is profoundly disinclined to
give up his beginnings, and something else believes it has long since
got beyond all that. This contradiction was once brought home to
me in the most drastic manner when watching a 'Strudel' (a sort of
local witch doctor) taking the spell off a stable. The stable was
situated immediately beside the Gotthard line, and several

[15] P. Radin: *The World of Primitive Man*, New York, 1953, p. 3.
[16] Op. cit. p. 5

international expresses sped past during the ceremony. Their occupants would hardly have suspected that a primitive ritual was being performed a few yards away.

The conflict between the two dimensions of consciousness is simply an expression of the polaristic structure of the psyche, which like any other energic system is dependent on the tension of opposites. That is also why there are no general psychological propositions which could not just as well be reversed; indeed, their reversibility proves their validity. We should never forget that in any psychological discussion we are not saying anything *about* the psyche, but that the psyche is always speaking about *itself*. It is no use thinking we can ever get beyond the psyche by means of the 'mind', even though the mind asserts that it is not dependent on the psyche. How could it prove that? We can say, if we like, that one statement comes from the psyche, is psychic and nothing but psychic, and that another comes from the mind, is 'spiritual' and therefore superior to the psychic one. Both are mere assertions based on the postulates of belief.

The fact is, that this old trichotomous hierarchy of psychic contents (hylic, psychic, and pneumatic) represents the polaristic structure of the psyche, which is the only immediate object of experience. The unity of the psyche's nature lies in the middle, just as the living unity of the waterfall appears in the dynamic connection of above and below. So, too, the living effect of the myth is experienced when a higher consciousness, rejoicing in its freedom and independence, is confronted by the autonomy of a mythological figure and yet cannot flee from its fascination, but must pay tribute to the overwhelming impression. The figure works, because secretly it participates in the observer's psyche and appears as its reflection, though it is not recognized as such. It is split off from his consciousness and consequently behaves like an autonomous personality. The trickster is a collective shadow figure, an epitome of all the inferior traits of character in individuals. And since the individual shadow is never absent as a component of personality, the collective figure can construct itself out of it continually. Not always, of course, as a mythological figure, but, in consequence of the increasing repression and neglect of the original mythologems, as a corresponding projection on other social groups and nations.

If we take the trickster as a parallel of the individual shadow, then the question arises whether that trend towards meaning, which we saw in the trickster myth, can also be observed in the subjective and personal shadow. Since this shadow frequently appears in the phenomenology of dreams as a well-defined figure, we can answer this question positively: the shadow, although by definition a negative figure, sometimes has certain clearly discernible traits and associations which point to a quite different background. It is as though he were hiding meaningful contents under an unprepossessing exterior. Experience confirms this; and what is more important, the things that are hidden usually consist of increasingly numinous figures. The first thing we find standing behind the shadow is the anima,[17] who is endowed with considerable powers of fascination and possession. She often appears in rather too youthful form, and hides in her turn the powerful archetype of the wise old man (sage, magician, king, etc.). The series could be extended, but it would be pointless to do so, as psychologically one only understands what one has experienced oneself. The concepts of complex psychology are, in essence, not intellectual formulations but names for certain regions of experience, and though they can be described they remain dead and irrepresentable to anyone who has not experienced them. Thus, I have noticed that people usually have not much difficulty in picturing to themselves what is meant by the shadow, even if they would have preferred instead a bit of Latin or Greek jargon that sounds more 'scientific'. But it costs them enormous difficulties to understand what the anima is. They accept her easily enough when she appears in novels or as a film star, but she is not understood at all when it comes to seeing the role she plays in their own lives, because she sums up everything that a man can never get the better of and never finishes coping with. Therefore it remains in a state of perpetual emotion which ought not to be touched.

[17] By the metaphor 'standing behind the shadow' I want to give a concrete illustration of the fact that in proportion as the shadow is recognized and integrated, the problem of the anima, i.e. of relationship, is constellated. It is understandable that the encounter with the shadow should have an enduring effect on the relations of the ego to the inside and outside world, since the integration of the shadow brings about an alteration of personality. Cf. *Aion*, 1951, pp. 22ff.

The degree of unconsciousness one meets with in this connection is, to put it mildly, astounding. Hence it is practically impossible to get a man who is afraid of his own femininity to understand what is meant by the anima.

Actually, it is not surprising that this should be so, since even the most rudimentary insight into the shadow sometimes causes the greatest difficulties for the modern European. But since the shadow is the figure nearest his consciousness and the least explosive one, it is also the first component of personality to come up in an analysis of the unconscious. A minatory and ridiculous figure, he stands at the very beginning of the way of individuation, posing the deceptively easy riddle of the Sphinx or grimly demanding answer to a 'quaestio crocodilina'.[18]

If, at the end of the trickster myth, the saviour is hinted at, this comforting premonition or hope means that some calamity or other has happened and been consciously understood. Only out of disaster can the longing for the saviour arise—in other words, the recognition and unavoidable integration of the shadow create such a harrowing situation that nobody but a saviour can undo the tangled web of fate. In the case of the individual, the problem constellated by the shadow is answered on the plane of the anima, that is, through relatedness. In the history of the collective as in the history of the individual, everything depends on the development of consciousness. This gradually brings liberation from imprisonment in ἀγνοία, unconsciousness,[19] and is therefore a bringer of light as well as of healing.

As in its collective, mythological form, so also the individual shadow contains within it the seed of an enantiodromia, of a conversion into its opposite.

---

[18] A crocodile stole a child from its mother. On being asked to give it back to her, the crocodile replied that he would grant her wish if she could give a true answer to his question: 'Shall I give the child back?' If she answers 'Yes', it is not true, and she won't get the child back. If she answers 'No', it is again not true, so in either case the mother loses the child.

[19] Erich Neumann, *The Origins and History of Consciousness*, New York and London, 1954, *passim*.